PRAISE for *The Big Life*

"A heartwarming story of growing up under anything but usual circumstances. Fans of Jeanette Walls' The Glass Castle will find a familiar and equally fascinating perspective on surviving parental dysfunction, loss, abandonment, continually changing environments, and riding out the highs and lows of 'the big life.' The book is an excellent read for anyone struggling with navigating life's uncertainties. The passages on adaptability, determination, and faith make this true-to-life story wonderfully empowering!"

Elizabeth Lee
Co-author of "A Call to Leadership"
from *Success Strategies from Women in STEM*

"What an incredible journey it is to read Diana Lynn's *The Big Life*! And to think this story is true! Following the story of her family's life from Illinois to California and back, the author takes you along for the wild ride. With whimsical touches like family holidays spent in an idyllic setting, this book transports you back in time. Then, with the flip of a page, we are knee-deep in the mob? Espionage? Only time will tell. A wonderful story of family bonds, faith, and determination that keeps you guessing all the way to the end."

Karen Frier
REALTOR®

"*The Big Life* takes you on an adventure of a girl whose life is unexpectedly jolted out of normalcy and comfort into that of insecurity, confusion, and intrigue. As she navigates all the twists and turns of her life, you'll be in for another kind of adventure: that of the heart. Your bags will be packed along with hers as you are transported with her, and the final destination is only the beginning! This is an inspirational and moving true tale!"

Penny J. Rizzo
Retired teacher

"*The Big Life* is a fascinating biography of the childhood and young adult life of an amazing woman who overcame a life of frequent, often disruptive, changes in her family life without knowing why. While the story is intriguing and often mysterious, its message to readers is how the love and support of those around you, brothers, relatives, and friends, can help fill the void left by dysfunctional parents. With their support, Diana was able to find love, self-worth and a partner, Luke, who, with her, created the family life she never knew. It is an uplifting story of the ability to cope, dream of something better, and then realize that dream. You will enjoy the read!"

John Hillenmeyer
Retired healthcare executive

"As Diana's younger cousin, reading her book opened my eyes to so many things I didn't understand at the time. I couldn't wait for the next chapter! Her story provides hope and encouragement to those currently growing up with their own difficult family challenges."

Marie

"This is a heartwarming story that every woman can identify something from her own life. There is mystery, fear, love, joy, and the sustaining power of faith."

Anne Sullivan

"The author of this book has one of the 'biggest hearts' you will ever encounter, and if she could survive her mixed-up childhood, so can you!"

Gale Phillips

"Oh my goodness, this compelling memoir regarding the heartbreaking childhood of a sister and brother forced to live a life of insecurity, fear, and lies is a read you will remember long after you turn the last page. The promised wonderful 'Big Life' was anything but."

Kimberly Cunningham

"If you liked *The Glass Castle*, you will love this story and will not be able to put it down."

RCP Focus Group

"My very dear friend Diana is a superb and humorous storyteller. She shares her resilient story overcoming odds, drama, and mystery in her young life. Her key message is embedded throughout as she eloquently carries her reader though her journey. Guaranteed you will walk away uplifted and filled with hope for your own circumstances."

Maria Penzes

"The story of youth, resilience, and faith should inspire each of us to live our lives with a renewed sense of purpose. Diana leads us, through the lens of a child, to what we already know but are often too afraid to believe in."

Nicolas Gaines
Aspiring writer

"You will be captivated by the tales of a child's unknown moves so often it will make you want to read more. A true story of the adjustments and the leading of God in her life."

Shirley Hawkins

THE *Big Life*

THE *Big Life*

GROWING *UP* ON THE RUN

DIANA LYNN

Your Choices, LLC

The Big Life: Growing up on the Run

Your Choices, LLC
4300 W. Lake Mary Blvd
Ste 1010 #207
Lake Mary, FL
32746-2012
yourchoicesllc@yahoo.com

Published 2020.

Printed in the United States of America

ISBN
paperback: 978-1-7351320-0-6
hardback: 978-1-7351320-2-0
ebook: 978-1-7351320-1-3

Dedication

Aunt Lulu

*I am who I am today, because of who Aunt Lulu has
always been for me.
I will be forever grateful to her and love her more than
I can put into words.
It is to her that I dedicate my story.*

CONTENTS

PART 1
Chicago, 1946–1957
How It All Began

PART 2
California–Chicago Area, 1957–1958
Bad Things Can Happen to Good Kids

PART 3
San Diego, 1958–1960
Catch Us If You Can

PART 4
St. Louis, 1960–1962
Hallelujah Highschool

PART 5
Chicago, 1962–1964
It's My Life

PART 6
Chicago, 1964–1966
The Great Escape

A Note from Diana

This is my true story.

It is a tale of resilience, faithfulness, hope, and choices.

For privacy purposes, a few names of places and people have been altered; however, all the characters have been a part of my real life. To the best of my memories, every event happened as it is written.

My brother's and my childhood was filled with a curious happiness in spite of our parents and the unstable, sometimes perilous, life they created for us. Together we survived by focusing on the road ahead, often impeded by detours and obstacles, but we never looked backward.

I share my story so that the seeds of hope may begin to bud in those of you who need a few flowers in your garden of life. I've discovered that hope doesn't ever abandon us, we abandon it.

My passionate wish is that all who read my story will realize that every one of us always has choices. You can choose to remain a victim, allowing your past to define your future or choose to be victorious and learn from those experiences —building yourself a better life. After all, your future is really the life you create by the choices you make daily.

LIFE is what happens to us twenty-four hours a day, every second we are on this planet. Each new dawn brings a fresh opportunity to write your unique story. The ultimate goal is to survive and thrive—making peace with our past so we don't let it screw up our present!

There are those people who are interested in stories about God and those who are not. I tell my story with love for both.

— Diana

PART 1
Chicago, 1946–1957
How It All Began

Chapter 1
Northfield, IL, Early Morning,
Monday, November 4, 1957

Good Morning Diana!
❧

"Diana, wake up! You need to get up, now!"
While tightly wrapped in my soft pink comforter like a baby swaddled, hugging my most beloved stuffed animal Fifi, I hear my mother's voice. I am startled as I wake from my deep, dreamy sleep. It's so warm and cozy here in my bed. I hug Fifi closer as I burrow further into my self-made cocoon. It is cold here in the house. I don't want to get up. Maybe if I stay right here in the safety of my room, I won't have to pretend my life is now so different. Mom isn't that strange woman who sits in her blue and yellow pajamas at the kitchen table, crying, while she drinks from the bottle with the brown smelly liquid called bourbon, smoking a yucky Salem cigarette. Her long nails used to always be shiny red with polish but now her nails are all chipped and broken. She doesn't wash or comb her pretty chestnut hair anymore and she's stopped putting on makeup. Some days she stays curled up in her bed; I can't even remember the last time she took a bath or shower. It's like she doesn't care about anything or anyone. She has stopped cooking or making any food for me or my older brother, Sonny. We are okay though because we like Skippy peanut butter and Welch's grape jelly sandwiches. Yummy Campbell's Chicken Noodle and Tomato soups are our favorites, too.

3

The Big Life

In late August, my family moved to this Chicago suburb and fancy house in a town called Northfield. I have a huge bedroom with my own private bathroom and king-size bed. Everything matches and is in my favorite color, pink. Our next-door neighbor is nice and must be famous because he is on his own TV news show every night. He has a big swimming pool and told Sonny and me that we can swim in it anytime we want. Before we moved in, I dreamed about how neat it would be to live here, but it is nothing like my dreams.

Since the move, lots of strange, weird things have been happening. Like my dad secretly leaving one day without even kissing me goodbye. He never told me that he was going away or when he would be coming back. I don't think he'll be here for my eleventh birthday, which is only twelve days away. He's never missed my birthday before. It makes me feel sad because I miss my dad. It's creepily eerie here without him. We often have strange people come to our house. They buy a lot of our favorite things. In the last two weeks, we haven't turned the lights on at night. Mom says we don't want anyone to know we still live here. She never tells me why and I am way too afraid to ask questions. We used to hug, laugh, do fun stuff, and talk all the time. She would tell me how happy I made her, and now she barely talks to me. I think she is mad at us. Well, since Sonny doesn't ask many questions or bug her for answers, she's probably only mad at me. Even so, I can't think of anything I have done to make her this angry and sad. Sonny and I are trying so hard not to argue or cause any problems. Sometimes I wonder if she and Dad even care about us anymore. I am so glad that I have my big brother.

There are other things going on around here too. My grandparents, Aunt Lulu, and Uncle Steve are staying with us. They are always whispering, a lot of whispering; they stop when I come in the room. I hear things that I know I'm not supposed to hear—terribly scary things. I even heard them say the reason we don't go to school anymore is because Mom is afraid someone bad might take us. I am not exactly sure what that means. I think it might mean kidnap Sonny and me. Mom always told me that I was too nosey for my own good. Maybe she was right because these things I hear are terrifying me. I hate it and have scary spooky nightmares about it. I don't tell Sonny because

I don't want him to get scared, too. I don't tell anyone because then they'll know I was spying on them. I'll get into big trouble.

I hear my bedroom door open. Mom's soft footsteps make a swishy sound on the pink carpet. I struggle to pry my sleepy eyes open. It's so dark, it has to be the middle of the night. I turn to look out the frost patterned window. I think, *I'm right! It is pitch black outside! I can't see anything, so why do I have to get up? We never get up this early; school starts at nine, but we don't go to school anymore, so why is Mom waking me up?*

I feel her sit lightly on the edge of my bed. She turns on my bedside lamp. The bright light makes me squint as I look up into her hazel eyes. They look different but still beautiful. She reaches out and softly caresses my cheek. Mom smells good this morning. Maybe not exactly like my old mom, but better than yesterday. Hugging me close to her, I inhale her perfumed scent. Mmm, it's Shalimar, her favorite. She kisses my forehead and softly whispers, "Always remember how much I love you." For a sweet moment, I feel my loving mom is back when suddenly my warm pink comforter is pulled away. My cozy safe cocoon is instantly shed. I am cold, inside and out. Her face changes as she announces, "I have a surprise for you and your brother ...and we must hurry or you will miss your plane to California..."

Chapter 2
November 4, 1957 5:08am

Oh No, Now What?

❦

S tunned, I lay for a few seconds worrying, biting on my nails, and wondering if Mom has gone crazy. Sonny and I are going to California today?

Mom slips quickly out of my room before I even have a chance to process all my thoughts or ask questions. My ten-and-a-half-year-old mind is spinning like the big red tilt-a-whirl ride at Riverview Park. In a matter of seconds, tons of questions start whizzing through my brain. *Why are we going to California? Is Daddy going to meet us there? How long will we be there? What about my clothes, my Ginny dolls, all my Nancy Drew books? My birthday party? And, oh yeah, what about school?*

I throw all my questions at her. She doesn't answer, but I know she hears me because I can still see her shadow moving down the hallway. A few minutes later, she calmly tells me over the intercom, "Diana, get up and get dressed. Breakfast is almost ready." Jumping out of bed, I sprint down the long hallway to my big brother's room and throw open his door. He's gotta know something more than me because he's fourteen and has just started high school. I need to know if he knows stuff that I don't, like, are we really going to California this cold, grey, foggy morning? Why?

I race into his room. Sonny is just getting out of his disheveled bed. His thick, dark hair is sticking out in all directions. Moving slowly, he looks like he is still half asleep. I am now in wide-awake, outright panic mode and bombard him with all my questions at once. He turns to face me and calmly answers, "I don't know, just go get ready."

What a dumb answer! I should have figured he'd go along, following directions, no questions asked. In the past, I often overheard my mother talk about how he was so easy to get along with but I had a strong mind and will of my own. I agree—Sonny is easygoing and nice and I am always loaded with questions, ideas, and sometimes, I do like my way better. That's okay with me. I like me just as I am. Right now, his lack of reaction is making me crazy as I shout, "You're stupid and a complete idiot!" Stomping out, I head back to my room to get dressed for California.

We hastily gulp down oatmeal and toast in silence, each deep in our thoughts (or nightmares). I'm not hungry and think I might throw up. My stomach hurts a lot. Around seven o'clock, Sonny and I are herded to the garage by my mother. It is a cold, damp, dark morning—the perfect match for how I feel. Grandpa stands in the doorway to the garage, looking terribly sad. He gathers me tenderly in his arms, hugging me so tight to his heart that I can hear it beating. Whispering softly, his breath tickling my ear, he says, "Don't worry, sweetheart. Everything will be okay." He tenderly tells me I am a good girl and he loves me very, very much. I wish he could hold me forever and never let me go.

We are told to hurry up as Sonny and I crawl into the backseat of the 1957 blue and white Oldsmobile, both of us making sure we stay on our self-proclaimed sides of the car. My grandmother performs her ritual of blessing each one of us with the sign of the Cross before we can leave the garage. Once we are on the road, my mother quietly explains, "You kids are going to live with Uncle Gil and Aunt Sue in California." I know my uncle is her older brother and an Air Force officer. He lives by an Air Force base near Sacramento, but why?

Suddenly, it hits me. Mom isn't going with us and she isn't going to be with me on my eleventh birthday either. I have no idea where Dad is or when I will see him again. A sick empty feeling sweeps over me. My breakfast threatens to make a second appearance.

Curled up and sinking deeper into my corner of the backseat, I can't look at Sonny. I don't want anyone to see me cry or the horrible shame I am feeling. I truly thought my mother loved me, but she is sending me away to live with strangers. She knows her older brother, but I have only seen him three times in my whole life! I want to scream, cry, and promise her that I will try even harder to be good. Silently, I beg her not to send us away. Yet, deep down in my insides, I know it is too late. I know it is something I have or haven't done that pushed her too far. Had I forgotten to make my bed too many days? And there were the times when I tried on clean clothes to wear to school, then decided I didn't want to wear that skirt or blouse, so I would put the clean clothes in the dirty clothes hamper because I was too lazy to hang them back in my closet. She'd caught me a few times and told me she was disappointed in me. She further explained what I did was just like lying and I had to acknowledge it at Saturday's confession.

Could it be she may not want me anymore because I was too nosey, argued with Sonny too much, or read my Nancy Drew mystery book with a flashlight under the covers when I was supposed to be sleeping? Well, at least now I figured out why we were being sent away. I was the reason she sat at the kitchen table in her yellow and blue pajamas all day, drinking from the brown bottle. She didn't love me anymore and needed to get me out of her hair. Worse, Sonny was being punished and sent away because of me. I fully accepted the blame and the shame, but I didn't know what I could to do about it. I knew this plan of hers was set in stone and there wasn't anything I could do to change it. I silently prayed. Maybe Jesus could command my mother to change her plan and make her love and want me again.

The gloomy drive to Midway Airport went too fast. Suddenly I realized Mom had unloaded our suitcase and was waiting for Sonny and me on the curb. We followed Mom and Grandma through the airport to the United Airline counter where the smiling lady in the blue suit checked us in. We were right on time and told to go ahead to the gate and get in the "red carpet" service line. The "red carpet" service was supposed to be extra special, or so they said. I imagine they thought that would make us excited and not focus on the fact we were being sent away. I tried hard to be brave and not cry. I wished to be so good that she'd miss me and want me back. I was still the little girl who desperately wanted and needed to stay with her mother. In this last moment, I reached out and grabbed on to my beloved mom. Looking in to her eyes, I pleadingly promised, "I won't be a bother to you anymore. I am begging you, please don't send us away." For a second, I think she might give in, but then abruptly she gave each of us a quick hug and handed us over to the stewardess who helped us board the "special" red carpet flight to San Francisco. I hoped and prayed my guardian angel was getting on this plane, too.

As I climbed the big silver stairs to the plane, I hesitated at the top and turned to look at my beloved mother. I gave her a final wave. Little did I know the wave was not just goodbye to her, but goodbye to my childhood.

Chapter 3
Mid-morning, November 4, 1957

Fasten Your Seatbelt!

Stepping through the doorway into the plane, I knew my life had changed and nothing would ever be the same. My heart broke while I prayed for help to hold back the threatening tears. I felt unloved and abandoned but didn't want anyone to see my sadness. I hung on to Sonny as we followed the stewardess down the aisle to our seats.

He quietly asked, "Do you want to sit in the window seat?"

I shrugged, looked down, and replied, "I don't care." Right at this moment, I really didn't care ... about anything.

True to his protective and sweet nature (most of the time), he told me, "Sit in the window seat so you can see how little everything looks from the sky."

All I could manage was a quiet "thank you." What I truly wished to do was hibernate in my seat and finally free the tears I'd been yearning to shed. I reminded myself that I only needed to keep it together for a few more seconds.

I climbed into my seat and turned to face the window; at last, I allowed the tears to fall. Strangely, the brimming tears I had bravely held back no longer threatened to spill down my cheeks. My extreme distress over leaving my mother, including the fears of my uncertain future, were comforted by a soothing calmness coming from deep inside me. I heard—or rather, felt—a vaguely familiar inner voice.

11

This soft loving voice told me I am loved and never alone. I had heard this same voice once before when I was seven. I always hoped it was Jesus speaking to me. This proved to me that what Sister Clare told me in second grade was true: Jesus *did* give each of us our own guardian angel. He had just reminded me that mine was on this plane.

While I was deep in my thoughts, the captain left the gate, revved up the big noisy engines, and taxied down the runway, full speed ahead. Despite my sad situation, this was kind of exciting. A new adventure, and I was usually always up for new adventures. Quickly, we were airborne and climbing. The foggy gray clouds were left behind as we soared higher and higher. Fortunately, my spirits were lifting too. I began to wonder how far we were from Heaven.

Sadly, my excitement of the plane gliding across the crystal blue sky quickly wore off. All my unanswered questions had jumbled in my brain. I didn't understand why no one would give me any answers, not even Grandpa or Aunt Lulu. Things must be bad because they never kept secrets from me—at least, I didn't think they had. I wasn't too sure of anything anymore.

It's almost as if my whole life before we moved back to Chicago was an imagined, sweet dream. I thought we all loved each other more than anything. We were the perfect, happy family. The best family in the whole wide world. As of that morning, except for Sonny, I was alone, wondering if our once-happy family was forever gone, or if we ever were a loving happy family at all.

Sonny's and my new life was unknown. I'd never felt so sad, frightened, or alone. A part of me wondered if Little Orphan Annie or Cinderella had felt this way.

Sonny and Me waiting in San Francisco for flight to Sacramento

Chapter 4
Chicago, IL, 1946–1950

My Fairytale World

I am one of the original Baby Boomers. I was born in Chicago, right after WWII ended and my dad returned from serving in the Navy. I was blessed with a loving and happy family: two beautiful parents and one big brother, Sonny, who was three years older than me. I was their second child, a girl. My parents told us that they had always wanted two healthy children, a boy first and then a girl. God had blessed them with their perfect family of four.

For the first three years of my life, most of my maternal extended family lived within walking distance of our Sunnyside Avenue apartment. Being surrounded by our nurturing grandparents and other loving family members enabled us to develop close relationships at an early age. Parents and grandparents enveloped us in an environment of love of God, respect, trust, and security. We'd see each other every day.

I was fortunate to have an amazing aunt/godmother who became my lifetime mentor, friend, and the stabilizing cornerstone through my childhood's tough times. Even now, Aunt Lulu is the most special and cherished influence that I've had throughout my entire life. I feel so blessed to still have her with me today.

Sadly, I never knew my paternal grandparents. Dad and his younger brother were orphaned by the time Dad was thirteen. His maternal grandfather owned a large brownstone in Lincoln Park

13

where the entire family lived in the six separate apartments. His father died of bad oyster food poisoning when Dad was three and their mother passed away nine years later due to gall bladder surgery complications. The two boys were raised by their mother's parents, sisters, and brothers.

We never spent much time with Dad's side of the family. His brother had three children and I always loved getting together with these cousins. All of Dad's family were extremely loving and sweet to Sonny and me.

Being Catholic was a major life component for each side of our family. My parents were both raised in strict traditional Catholic households. Dad spent twelve years in parochial school, continuing to a local Catholic college. This tradition continued as my brother and I were also exposed to early Catholic school education and values. We were taught right from the beginning to love and trust God in all things.

One of my earliest memories begins around the age of two-and-a-half. My godmother, Aunt Lulu, was getting married. She courageously chose me to be her flower girl. I would walk down the aisle with my brother, the ring bearer, who was almost six. My grandmother, an accomplished seamstress, made my special floor-length ruffled dress with matching big bonnet along with long gloves that stopped right before my fingertips. All the bridesmaids had the same color blue dresses. I loved my long blue flower girl dress, but not the big bonnet with the big itchy bow that often became untied, perhaps helped along by my two-and-a-half-year-old fingers.

The night before the wedding, I remember Aunt Lulu coming over with a special present for me. A little girls' faux pearl necklace and bracelet to wear with my dress. I think that's the first present that I remember receiving. I felt so special and could hardly wait for the next day.

In the church vestibule, my mom held my hand as the music started and the ladies went down the aisle, one by one. Next, it was my mom's turn, then Sonny and me. As we walked down the aisle, I flashed my best smile while holding my brother's hand with my right hand and my coveted basket of flowers in my left hand, just as I had practiced the night before. We were almost at the altar when, out of nowhere, my dad plucked me up, and carried me to the pew to sit with him. Until that moment, I had naturally assumed I would stand with my mom and the beautiful bride at the altar. I was not happy with the new turn of events and made sure the whole church knew it by screaming and crying as my aunt made her way down the aisle on my proud grandfather's arm. Dad eventually quieted me down. My best memory of the day was me dancing and singing to anyone who would listen at the reception. That was the auspicious debut and finale of my singing career. However, due to a talent which I must have inherited from my Great Aunt V, a Follies dancer in the 1920s, my dancing was a smashing hit.

On my third birthday, my surprise at breakfast was a kiddie table with two chairs all set with my birthday princess breakfast of a raspberry jelly donut adorned with three candles and a special cup filled with chocolate milk. One plate for me and another plate for my imaginary friend, Meeka. Meeka was my first "best girlfriend." I think she only lasted about two weeks. I don't know why or where Meeka went, but Mom indulged me with my made-up friend because she thought imagination was a sign of creativity and intelligence.

I have many happy memories of my early childhood, with two exceptions. We moved from the apartment to our first house: a two-story, brick home in a nice Chicago suburb not far from my grandparents. For the first time, Sonny and I had our own bedrooms. I can still envision my room, decorated in pink *Three Little Kittens* story wallpaper. Every night, I asked Mom to read me *The Three Little Kittens* book before bedtime.

It was in this room that I graduated from my crib to a big girl bed. It was also in this room that I became aware of the scary darkness of the night ... and a nightmare of a dark shadowy presence standing over the side of my bed watching me intently. Whether it was a bad reoccurring dream or something else, I honestly don't know. The feeling of a haunting dark presence hovering over me in the darkness of night frightened me well into adulthood. However, I found as I got older, praying gave me a calmness that allowed me to go back to a more pleasant and peaceful sleep.

In this same house, I received my first and only spanking. It was totally Sonny's fault. The event occurred early one Sunday morning as my parents slept in after a serious late night of partying. Apparently, the previous day, Dad had painted the basement and six-year-old Sonny had been busy watching. He must have thought it looked like fun because he tiptoed into my room early Sunday morning, quietly coaxing, "Come with me, we are going to make a big surprise for Mommy and Daddy while they are sleeping." Trusting Sonny completely, I dutifully followed him down to the basement where he promised to teach me how to paint. Somehow, he managed to get the paint can open and find two paintbrushes. With brushes in hand and a bucket of green paint at our feet, we energetically and artistically proceeded to paint the basement walls, floor, and anything and everything else our little brush-held hands could reach.

At some point, we got bored or maybe hungry and decided it was time to go upstairs, get our parents, and show them our handiwork. Unfortunately for our parents, we still were young enough to wear pajamas with attached cloth feet, which were now paint-soaked cloth feet that left a trail of four perfect green footprints up the wooden basement stairs, through the cozy kitchen, the newly carpeted dining room, staircase, upstairs hallway, and finally, their bedroom. We burst into their room and jumped onto their bed to tell them of our great surprise. Their sleep-deprived, over-served hungover faces said it all. The fun of the morning ended there. I don't ever remember both my parents sleeping in again for several years.

Mom, Me, Aunt Lulu Grandma & Sonny, Summer 1947

Aunt Lulu and Me, Spring 1948

Sonny & Me Loving Aunt Lulu's Wedding, 1949

Chapter 5
Chicago, IL, 1946–1954

Grandma and Grandpa
❧

As an extremely devout Catholic, my maternal grandmother played a serious role model for me in many ways. She was always preparing food, remaking donated hand-me-down clothes to take to the Little Sisters of the Poor, or sewing vestments for the priests in poor parishes. I adored the times I got to tag along with her on her Missions of Love, listening closely while she explained, "Diana, God wants us to love and help others, even if we don't know them or maybe they don't look or talk like us." She would patiently answer my questions while we rode the trolley car to where we caught the bus that took us to the EL train, which delivered us to poor, ethnic neighborhoods imbedded deep within the city.

On other occasions, she would treat Sonny and me to special day trips like the wonderful Chicago museums, State Street shopping with lunch at Marshall Fields Walnut Room, or take us to see a movie at a fancy downtown theatre. For an added treat, we would make an afternoon snack stop at the Woolworth Dime store where we could twirl on the red counter stools while munching on hot, salty French fries and sipping our favorite chocolate malted milkshakes.

Grandma was a good grandmother, but not the warm hugging type. She was strict and her punishments were harsh and scary. I had panic attacks when she ordered me to sit on the attic stairway in total darkness with the door closed to *think* about what I had done wrong. Once or twice, she mentioned that a witch maybe lived up in the attic. I could never *think* because I was traumatized by the dark ... and then there was the *witch*! I am sure she never realized my genuine fear of the dark or the lifelong, lasting impact this punishment had on me. But I assure you, I tried extra hard never to cross her in any way, nor did I ever volunteer to spend a week visiting her during any school vacation.

On the flip side, my maternal grandfather will forever be one of my most cherished relatives. His favorite pastime was listening to his classical and opera records playing on his vintage Victrola phonograph as he conducted the entire musical score seated in his favorite comfy, blue armchair in front of the cozy, living room fireplace. Often, Grandpa was charged with the dubious honor of watching me while the rest of the family devotedly attended Sunday Mass. I was a little too antsy and way too chatty during Mass, so Mom left me behind. Secretly, staying home alone with my beloved Grandpa was a treat and always my favorite part of Sunday. Grandpa's way of babysitting was having me stand in front of him while he sat in his chair listening and conducting his music. I mimicked his hand and arm movements as we directed the symphony together. As a bonus, I entertained Grandpa by embellishing the art of conducting with my impressionistic dance routines, constantly interrupting him, "Hey Grandpa, look! You're not watching! Do you like this dance or the other one?"

I don't think Grandpa was ever a real fan of my impromptu dramatic dances. However, he magically managed to instill a love of classical music including a touch of basic music theory without me ever realizing it, along with a lifetime of treasured memories.

This loving, gentle man loved filmmaking and his family was his favorite subject. In his finished attic rooms, he created a unique space for himself, complete with a big (or what seemed huge to me) movie screen and a projector, always ready to go. He'd splice together his collage of homemade sixteen-millimeter movies to share with everyone on holidays. This special grandpa saved old 1930s children's black-and-white movies for Sonny and me to watch when we visited. We never grew tired of our favorite movie, *Chimp the Chimpanzee*. I can still envision Chimp dressed up in his fireman hat saving someone or something from the fire. Often, after dinner, he would slip Sonny and me each a dime for the corner Tastee Freeze, with our promise we'd eat all our ice cream before we came home so Grandma wouldn't know.

Grandpa's enchanting attic hosted a big wooden library table where he worked tirelessly on his extensive rare stamp collection. When we visited, he placed two chairs at this special table for Sonny's and my own not-so-rare stamp collections. He patiently taught us how to attach the stamps to the little books and gently caution us on the fragility of these tiny delicate pieces of colored paper with scalloped edges.

So many cherished memories of my early childhood years were created in those marvelous magical attic rooms. Hours and hours of playing games, dressing up in tattered forgotten costumes found in dusty old trunks, even finding toys that Mom and her siblings played with years ago, could not compare with Grandpa's big wooden Philco tube radio, which broadcasted the local police radio calls. Listening to these calls entertained us for hours. Sonny and I pretended to be police detectives, just like on the famous black-and-white TV show, *Dragnet*. The two of us parked ourselves on the floor in front of the huge radio creating our own dramas as we practiced interrogating the probable suspects (in our case, each other): "Were you there when the robbery occurred, sir? Ma'am, could you tell us how many robbers were involved? Did they ever call each other by name? Did you see anyone's face? Just state the facts ma'am, nothing but the facts!"

This was a great adventure until it began to get dark, then I'd panic because I knew too soon I would have to sleep on the dreaded scary, scratchy couch in the front room, alone, under the big window next to the front door and front porch. What if the robbers and kidnappers were waiting, just outside, watching *me* through the window? I'd lie awake most of the night petrified by the shadows created by the moon and street lights. If I shut my eyes, my imagination made my fears worse. I knew I couldn't run to or call for Grandma, Mom, or Dad. They'd tell me, "Quit acting like a baby; there is nothing to be afraid of." I would have called for Grandpa, but he slept upstairs with Sonny and wouldn't hear me.

Chapter 6
Wisconsin, 1951–1954

Lavatory or Laboratory?
❧

We moved to southern Wisconsin when I was four. Dad had quickly become a successful car dealer and Mom was a traditional stay-at-home mom.

Some of my crazy yet endearing recollections involve her routine attempts to make my naturally poker-straight blonde hair unnaturally curly. I suffered through Tonette and Party Curl Kiddie Perms every few months. I particularly liked the Party Curl perm because it had cutout dolls to entertain me during the drippy, smelly, solution-dabbing torture. Sadly, my new hairdo never came out looking like the darling girl's hairdo pictured on the box. In fact, I remember my dad coming home from work after an especially successful curling event where my new curly frizzed hairdo resembled that of an electrocuted French Poodle. He immediately inquired rather loudly of my mother, "What the hell did you do to her hair?"

Of course, that made me cry because during the Party Curl perm torture, my mother kept telling me, "Quit fussing and think about how pretty your hair will look when we're finished. Daddy's going to love it!"

On subsequent nights of "Beauty Shop Day" dinners, Dad would smile at me, shake his head, and wisely say nothing.

It was around this time, I could go outside unsupervised and play with other neighborhood children. We were all around four or five and learning how to make friends and share nicely with everyone. One day, there was some "name calling" and that evening at dinner, with great dramatic flair, I retold the name-calling tale.

Of course, Mom and Dad reminded me, "Diana, it is not nice to call someone a not nice name. You must always be kind and considerate to everyone and treat them like you want them to treat you."

My young mind instantly thought, *I've heard Dad call people lots of bad names, especially when he's driving. I don't think he'd want others to call him those names.* This also backfired on Mom because that's when I realized she called me another name. A name I didn't like: *Irma*. This was the special name that my mother used when she talked about me in secret code to her friends. I'm not exactly sure how I figured this out, but I knew this was not a "nice" thing. Mom referred to me as Irma when she didn't want me to know that I was the main character in her less-than-complimentary commentary.

Mom's best friend, Aunt Babs, was visiting from Chicago when I overheard them discussing Irma. Feeling insulted, I marched into the kitchen and sternly informed them, "My name is not *Irma*. It is *Diana*. I know you were talking about me and it is not nice. I do not like it and it hurts my feelings. You are being not nice or kind." Once the cover name Irma was blown, I don't remember hearing Mom ever refer to me as Irma again.

My fifth birthday fell after the public-school kindergarten admission cutoff date, so I never attended kindergarten. I simply started first grade at the Catholic school the following September. Lots of preparations took place before my first day of school, including another Party Curl perm. This time Mom paid closer attention to how long the curling solution should stay on and my hair looked much better.

At last, the big day arrived. It was both exciting and scary for me. Exciting because I could finally wear one of my brand-new school dresses and my new red leather school shoes. FYI, I chose the red plaid dress with a big red and white collar, because it matched my red shoes. Most importantly, I was "big" enough to go to school, but nervous because I didn't like that my mom was going to leave me there alone.

That morning, Mom walked me to my class, helped me find my seat, then quickly kissed me goodbye and left. Bravely, I held my tears back and quietly sat at my desk, for a few seconds, anyway. Then, my Miss Chatty persona took over and I busied myself talking to all the other kids and sort of forgot about my mom. I was almost starting to think this was fun when Sister quieted us with the ringing of her little brass bell and explained a nice nurse was going to come in and have a look at us. Well, the nice nurse—dressed in full nurses' garb including a white hat, blue cape, white dress, white stockings, and white shoes— entered the classroom and began checking our tongues, hands, and hair. Once the nurse was satisfied that we all had acceptable tongues, hands, and hair, Sister announced we were going to take a break and go to the lavatory.

I froze, having absolutely no idea what a lavatory was. To my ears, it sounded like "laboratory." I thought, *the nice nurse just left and now we are all being sent to the* laboratory? *I am not going, even if all the other kids go to the laboratory.* I politely informed Sister of my decision.

Sister replied, "Diana, you must go along."

I whimpered, "I need to see my big brother who is in the fourth grade."

Sister patiently humored me and walked me to his class. She knocked on his classroom door, requesting, "Sister Nora, would you please send Sonny out here? I need to speak to him." At the time I didn't know that my short little nun, Sister Pius, was also the school principal. Sonny, however, was quite aware of her position.

Sonny came out into the hall and glared at me. Through clenched teeth, he whispered, "My class is in the middle of making book covers and it is a really hard job. You interrupted me and embarrassed me in front of Sister Nora, *the giant nun,* and my whole class. Now everyone thinks I am in trouble and that I have a crybaby for a sister."

I latched on to his arm while informing him, "They want to take me to the *laboratory* and I know Mommy wouldn't want me to go."

To his credit, he took mercy on me and explained, "They said 'lavatory,' not 'laboratory.' A lavatory is just a fancy way of saying 'the bathroom.' The girls have one and the boys have one too."

With that info, I relented, trusting Sister Mary Pius by obediently following her to the girls' lavatory. It didn't take long for me to adore

27

this loving, kind, patient, fifty-six-inch high nun. I also realized learning was fun and easy.

Now, just to be perfectly transparent, I must confess I did have moments where the "good Jesus lessons" taught by Sister Pius differed slightly from my actions. One such incident, the day before the end of my first-grade year, began innocently enough. Sonny was recovering from the chicken pox and I was instructed to collect his school things after school. As soon as we said our closing prayer for the day, I walked as fast as I could (no running in the halls allowed) to the giant Sister Nora's fourth grade class. She handed me Sonny's school folder and a whole Hershey's milk chocolate bar to take home to him. I carefully carried his papers and the Hershey bar as I walked, all by myself, home. Somewhere along the way, I convinced myself, *Poor Sonny was probably way too sick to eat this candy bar and it would be so mean of me to bring it to him when he couldn't have it. Maybe I should just eat it right now on the way home.* So, I did. I ate every single delicious square. It tasted so good. Licking my fingers of gooey melted chocolate, the godly teachings of Sister Pius started kicking into my conscience. *Maybe I just stole Sonny's candy bar. After all, it wasn't given to me to eat. Sister told me to take it to him.* Suddenly, the guilt set in and eating that candy bar didn't seem like such a good idea after all. Once home, I dutifully gave Sonny his school stuff, but never mentioned to anyone about the horrible deed I had committed on my way home. I was sure God was going to punish me big time.

The following morning, Sonny felt well enough to go back to school, but more importantly, it was the last day of school for the year. A special day of fun games and treats. I had been anxiously awaiting my first end-of-school "fun" day for weeks. It was finally here. However, I wasn't going. I'd caught my brother's itchy chicken pox and fever. I felt awful. First, because I was sick, and secondly, I knew this was my punishment for eating Sonny's candy. So, while Sonny had a fun day, I was feverish, itching, and miserable, lying on the living room couch, watching Queen Elizabeth's boring coronation on our black-and-white TV. From that day on, I have never been a fan of Hershey's milk chocolate candy bars.

Chapter 7
Wisconsin, 1951–1957

One Adventure, Two Adventures, Three Adventures, More!

During the winters of my fourth, fifth, and sixth years of life, Sonny and I were taken on three two-week family vacations that included my grandparents. I will never forget these car trips with them or our assigned seats. Dad and Mom in the front, Grandma and Grandpa in the back, with Sonny and I taking turns between sitting in the middle seats in the front or back.

Grandma made Dad wait to start the car until she performed the sign of the cross over each of us. Once on the highway, she had me sneak a peek over his shoulder and whisper what the numbers on the speedometer read. Upon hearing the first number was a seven or an eight, she'd silently pray with her mouth moving faster than a pair of windup chattering teeth. More than once after Grandma made the sign of the cross over us, I spied her giving Dad the stink eye as she blessed him. Grandma loved to travel, but I'm certain she wasn't crazy about our driver's driving habits or as I surmised in later years, the driver himself.

On these winter trips, we traveled to warm and exotic places, such as the Florida Keys, Mexico, Southern California, and San Francisco. My parents felt travels were an invaluable learning experience and fortunately, the nuns agreed and prepared school work to take with us.

I was five when, during our trip to Mexico, we visited Taxco, the Mexican silver capital. As we strolled through the silver market, a small peasant girl, who looked around eight years old, dressed in filthy rags and holding a crying infant wrapped in a torn dirty shawl, tugged on my mom's arm. She spoke in Spanish, but we knew she was offering her tiny infant sister to us in return for a few pesos. I felt so sorry for this poor girl; she looked so sad. I desperately begged, "Please, please Mom, can we take this little baby home with us?" but of course, we couldn't.

The scariest thing that happened on this south-of-the-border trip occurred just past midnight, high in the Mexican mountains. Mysteriously, our nighttime hotel reservations were cancelled and upon arriving at the inn, we were informed they had no rooms for us. The adults decided to continue driving to our next destination, the Taninul Resort. This involved driving through the mountains at night. The dangerous, dark, winding roads were extremely narrow. Around midnight, we came around a sharp blind curve to find a big truck loaded with bananas on fire—a huge blazing fire. The rusty, beat-up truck blocked most of the two narrow lanes. Several scary-looking men with long machetes were milling around on the road by the truck. Dad abruptly stopped to avoid hitting them. My grandparents, who were in the backseat with Sonny and me, told us to hide on the floor under their legs and not to look up or speak. I heard the men outside banging on our car and windows, speaking in a language I didn't understand. The only word I recognized was "Americanos."

Even I could feel the tension in the car as the four adults quickly discussed their options. "Should we stay, wait for the fire to burn out, and hope we will be left alone or take our chances going around the blazing truck as fast as we can?" The issue with option two was that the inflamed banana truck was in the middle of the narrow road with no guardrails on the edge of the cliff. In a quick second, Dad floored the car and drove right on to the edge. As we careened around the flaming truck with our tires skidding on the dirt, there was dead silence except for Grandma's pleading whispers to God. Once safely past the truck with all four tires back on the actual road, Dad explained if we had stayed and waited for the fire to burn itself out, he was fearful we would be robbed or worse. He confessed he was afraid for our lives.

Other than Dad jumping fully dressed in his white linen suit to save me from "drowning" in the resort pool the next day, Sonny getting sunstroke while deep sea fishing off the coast of Acapulco, and Mom losing her bathing suit top in the Pacific Ocean, the rest of the trip was uneventful.

(I'd like to set the record straight, I was not "drowning." I had put my arms up over my head, kicked my feet and was quickly rising to the surface, but Dad was overzealous with his life-guarding skills, "saving" me before my head had a chance to clear the water.)

Being seven was my favorite year of my childhood. It began with my special sugar-charged birthday breakfast and a dreamy new pink party dress featuring a rhinestone studded collar, plus a pair of black Mary Jane suede shoes with bows on the toes. Dad brought me to school loaded with enough candy treats for my entire class. When I arrived home for lunch, a florist showed up with a mini pink rose corsage. Dad had sent it for me to wear at school and for my big birthday party with friends later in the afternoon. Mom went all out, planning party games, buying neat prizes, making homemade mini hamburgers, and having a beautifully decorated petite cake for each guest. The dining room was decked out in pink and a fire in the fireplace added a festive glow on the cold, dreary November afternoon. It remains one of my most memorable birthdays.

That year, Sister Clare was my second-grade teacher. She stood young, tall, and beautiful. I learned she was a bride of Jesus. She told us how much she loved Him and He loved her. This was the year I, too, fell in love with Jesus. I idolized Sister Clare and wanted to grow up and become a nun, just like her.

Our main church was not on the same campus as the church school. In the winter, we drove a few of the nuns back to their convent after Sunday Mass. We always took Sister Clare in our car and I always sat on her lap for the short ride between church and convent. I hated when I had to jump off her lap and say goodbye. She made me feel holier and a little closer to Jesus just by looking at her. Monday morning school couldn't come fast enough for me. I wished to be good and work hard at school so she would be proud of me. I wanted to learn about Jesus because in my mind, she was like His *wife*.

The crowning glory of the year was preparing for and making my First Holy Communion in May. I could hardly wait for the day. Of course, there was the special prayer book, rosary, the white communion dress, and the veil—oh yeah, the veil. I would look like a mini bride, myself. I woke my parents up at least four times during the night to be sure we didn't oversleep and miss my Communion Mass. In all honesty, I was probably more jazzed about wearing the veil and the white dress than anything else about the day. I mean, I truly felt holy walking down the aisle to the communion rail and then receiving the Communion Host, but I was maybe a little bit more thrilled about the veil and the dress.

Three days later, I felt the Holy Spirit making me aware of the abundant love God had for me. While walking back from receiving Communion, feeling close to Jesus, I thought I heard a voice tell me, *"I will always love you and protect you. You will never be alone."* Startled, yet strangely calm, I felt a warm, loving kind of wash fill me inside, then a goose bump like shiver, but not exactly goosebumps because I wasn't cold. This lasted only seconds and was over before I reached my seat on the pew. I knelt and prayed, promising Jesus that I would forever love Him first, treat others as I would like others to treat me, and always try to do my best. I knew deep in my heart and soul that Jesus, the Holy Spirit, and my personal guardian angel would always be with me, loving me, protecting me, and guiding me through anything. All I needed to do was to obey, pray, and trust them.

For the first eight years, my life was filled with loving relatives, a special brother, and a mom and dad who loved each other and us a lot. I imagined everyone had a wonderful family, amazing travels, fun experiences, a beautiful home, and pretty much whatever they wanted. We were so happy and I assumed everyone lived like we did: happy, loved, and secure, now and forever.

Things began to change a few weeks before I turned eight. We moved to a small resort town in Wisconsin. My dad had opened another car dealership. I remember my mom crying and being upset about leaving her friends, the town we lived in, and the dream house they had built the year before. Obviously, Dad's new dealership meant relocating, so we did.

I was too young to grasp the what's and why's of the move or the dynamics between my parents. All I knew was I liked my new school, St. Anthony's. I made lots of friends and it was only a block from our house to church and school. Best yet, I could walk the four blocks into town with just Sonny. I was also promised that when summer came, I could walk, roller-skate, or ride my bike to the library downtown by myself.

The more successful my dad became, the more he wasn't at home. He traveled mostly to Chicago, I think. He'd go a few days here and there, and eventually more days there than here. Maybe Mom wasn't too happy with Dad being gone so often or exactly what he was up to while he was away. I was a clueless, happy, eight-year-old girl at the time. Once I did overhear (I was *not* snooping) Mom tell her friend from Chicago, "I hate it here and I'll never forgive him for making me give up my life and house to move here. He didn't discuss any of this with me; just came home and announced it! I had no say and no choice." That was a surprise to me because I thought she liked it here. She was deeply involved with lots of new friends, the church, and our new town. Mom was constantly going somewhere and often wasn't home when we returned after school. When Aunt Lulu and her family moved near us, life was perfect as far as I was concerned. I never recognized my mom had changed. I thought she seemed like the same Mom ...almost. Perhaps, I should have realized something was wrong sooner. There were signs, but I was still too young to understand.

The Christmas after we moved was the first Christmas we didn't spend all our vacation with our grandparents. Dad had business in Florida and decided the four of us would go and turn it into an after-Christmas vacation. Sonny and I could each choose one present because the trip was our big gift. Early on the morning of December 26, we piled into Dad's Cadillac, excited to leave cold weather behind and head to the sunny Florida beaches. We had a studio apartment at a Ft. Lauderdale hotel right on the ocean. Sonny and I loved spending the warm, carefree days making sandcastles, playing in the ocean, and swimming in the pool.

One morning, Dad told us, "Grab your swimming suits. We are going to Miami Beach. You can swim in the big hotel pool while Mom and I have our poolside meeting. You can't bother us, but we'll be able to see you." Sonny and I were excited to kind of be on our own. After all, I was eight and Sonny was eleven, and being on our own at a hotel sounded like a fun adventure.

The huge swimming pool had a three-story high dive. Sonny got a gleam in his eye as he baited me, "Hey Diana, I dare you to climb to the top the high dive and jump in!"

I retorted, "Okay, but you go first."

This high dive was as far from Mom and Dad as it could be while staying within the pool area. We climbed the set of stairs, I let Sonny go first. At the top, he took two steps out on the board, stopped, looked down, then turned around and came back by me, announcing, "I don't think Mom and Dad would want us to do this, so let's go back down."

I knew he had chickened out, so I answered, "Double dare you, I'm going!" With that, I walked to the end of the diving board, held my nose, bounced up, and jumped. The feeling of leaping from so high and knowing the water would catch me was thrilling and I wanted to do it again.

As I climbed out of the pool, I felt the vice-like grip of Dad's hand yank me out. He was livid. "What in the hell do you think you're doing?"

I answered him rather cheekily, "Jumping from the highest high dive. I guess you saw me."

With that, I was walked to a pool lounge, then he snarled, "You! Sit here and do not move until I come back and get you. Do you understand?"

Keeping my head down, I nodded, trying to look chastened, but I purposely kept my head down so he couldn't notice me grinning. I was so proud of my jump and how I finally beat Sonny at his own dare game that it was worth the punishment. However, I didn't understand why Dad was so angry. It wasn't like he'd told me to stay off the diving board.

Once we returned to our hotel, I heard Mom and Dad arguing in the bedroom. I couldn't hear exactly what they said, but I heard enough to know it was about our recent move, not spending more of Christmas with my grandparents, and something about the poolside meeting. They fought a lot during the rest of our vacation, often sending us down to the beach alone.

Since Sonny and I were so naive, we continued blissfully living life, unaware of the erosion happening to our family's foundation.

Meanwhile, I kept busy with schoolwork, helping the Sisters after school, solo trips to the store and library downtown, art lessons, dance lessons, ice skating, and Girl Scouts. The summer passed quickly with horseback riding lessons, summer day camp, swimming lessons, and lots of time spent cruising around our resort town's lake in Dad's big wooden Chris Craft speedboat. Some of my fondest memories of those summer nights are staying up late with my nose buried in another exciting book of Nancy Drew mysteries or Trixie Belden escapades, all read by flashlight under my covers.

Sonny, the easygoing, quiet, doesn't-ruffle-anyone's-feathers-except-mine kind of guy, took private flying lessons, made tons of model airplanes, learned to hunt, and owned a BB gun. (He once shot a BB into my neck. He claimed it was an accident.) He also would "help" my dad rearrange—which meant drive—cars around the used car lot. School and church activities filled in the gaps.

Admittedly, there wasn't much not to like about my brother. He was brave, loyal, fun, smart, considerate, honest, caring, and easy to get along with. Ever since I could remember, I'd always heard or overheard from my parents, grandparents, and others how kind and good Sonny was, especially to me. I knew what they said was true. I also knew they referred to me as stubborn, busy, bossy, smart, had a mind of my own, and told it like I saw it. As in: I was not as easy going as Sonny. If anyone had asked me, I would have agreed with both descriptions. I was the child that saw and heard everything, and never-missed-a-trick kind of kid. I had a strong sense of what I felt was right or wrong, which was probably challenging and irritating for my parents every day. Frankly, I liked being me. I wasn't trying to be a pain in the neck; I was merely observant and interested in anyone and everything around me. Sonny, on the other hand, was quiet and more accepting. He was the dream child who went along cheerfully, but when he did occasionally mess up, he did it in a spectacularly grand way.

For instance, at six, he was the instigator of the infamous painting the basement escapade. In fourth grade, he skipped school one afternoon when my mom wasn't going to be home and practiced his Cub Scout fire-making skills on the front porch. He was so successful that he set the porch on fire and was severely punished. Ironically, two years later, this same talent won him the Boy Scout fire-making badge. At ten, he was practicing his driving skills by backing in and out of the garage, but accidentally messed up by crashing through the rear brick garage wall. The age-old axiom of "practice makes perfect" was true. He was an excellent driver by age twelve.

The crowning glory occurred while Dad was driving over the speed limit down a country road on our way to deliver a brand-new Lincoln Continental to the new owner. Sonny and I were in the backseat, where I had duly separated our space by drawing the invisible, down-the-middle boundary line. Sonny's side was behind Dad and mine was behind Mom. It was a dreary Sunday after church and we were extremely bored with the bleak, grey, barren scenery. The only things interesting were the doors on this Lincoln. The front seat doors opened like a normal car door, but the backseat doors opened out in the opposite direction, reminding me of the two French doors in our living room. Sonny, who loved figuring out how things worked, accidentally hit the door handle, and the wind, caused by Dad's eighty MPH speed, caught the open door and ripped it backward, off the car's door hinges. We heard it hit and bump down the road behind us. Fortunately, Sonny wasn't holding on to the door or he would have blown right out of the car too.

Dad shrieked a bunch of bad words and pulled off the road as quickly as he could. There are no words to describe his rage. He was so furious with Sonny that I was scared for him. He whipped off his belt as I told Sonny to come to my side of the car. I was afraid Dad would kill him if he could reach him. Instead, my dad knew better than to deal with my brother in that moment. Luckily, no other cars came along as Dad walked back down the middle of the road to the bent, dented, and scraped Lincoln rear door, then with great effort dragged it back to the car. He proceeded to devise some way to use his belt around the center post and secure the door. Driving at a snail's pace, the belt held good enough to get us to a gas station for help.

I can't tell you what happened after that. I don't recall how we got home or what the punishment was or if there was one. I also don't remember Sonny doing anything that would get him in big trouble ever again.

Despite the fact we were rival siblings, we got along incredibly well. Secretly, down deep, I mean *way* down, I knew we truly loved and enjoyed each other's company. I considered him to be my best friend. Of course, I never admitted such a thing out loud, but this close relationship we shared would become each other's life raft soon.

As the months passed, Dad was home less and less. Often, on these nights, under the guise of "let's go out to eat," Mom took us to the big hotel in the downtown of this small town. We had dinner first, then she went into the bar for mingling with friends, sipping Manhattans and smoking a lot of smelly cigarettes. I thought it was great because my best friend's parents managed the hotel. I would play with my friend until it was time to go home. We worked on our homework in the coffeeshop and ordered anything we wanted to eat or drink. In fact, my favorite thing was a sleepover with my friend because we had our own hotel room—including the room keys—for the night and stayed up talking way past our normal bedtime. Sometimes, but not too often ... well okay, maybe only one time, I wished Sonny could stay at the hotel and get his own hotel room and room key too.

Sonny was always a good big brother. He truly did watch out for me. Even when I told him, "I wish I was an only child," I think he knew I didn't mean it. (Deep, deep, deeper than deep down, that is.)

As time progressed, the more Dad wasn't home, the more our mother "mingled", "suppered", and "sipped" at the downtown small-town hotel. On many of these evenings, when Sonny was around twelve, we had to drive Mom home. First, we helped her out to the car and into the backseat so she could lay down and take a nap. Sonny jumped in the driver's seat, I'd jump in the shotgun seat, and he'd drive us home, after taking several detours, of course. We had so much fun and thought we were so cool. Sonny and I both considered him to be an excellent driver and frankly, he did drive well. Fortunately he was just tall enough to see over the steering wheel. Since we lived about four blocks from the hotel, we drove around the block a few extra times to enjoy and extend our driving opportunity. During the summer, we put the top down on the car and took the long way home. Mostly, we slowly cruised through the local cemetery, hoping to stay out of sight and not get caught. Once home, we left the car parked in the driveway with Mom still napping in the rear seat. Sonny and I would put ourselves to bed. In the morning, Mom greeted us with breakfast on the table and nothing about the night before was ever mentioned.

Other evenings, Mom had a friend or friends over for martinis and Manhattans, including a local clergyman. He showed up on Wednesday nights right before we went to bed. In the morning, Mom always cautioned me, "Do not tell anyone he was here because then everyone else will want him to come to their house and he can't possibly go to everyone's home." In reflection, there were other unsettling clues during this time, but as I was only an innocent girl of nine or ten, everything flew over my head.

Mom, Dad, Sonny & Me, Key West 1951

Sonny, Dad & Me on Mexico Trip, February 1952

Chapter 8
Wisconsin, Spring 1956–May 1957

Storm Clouds on the Horizon

❧

Around this time, I noticed subtle changes and home life quickly unraveled. Our once-loving parents began to argue, a lot. When Dad left, Mom had her drinking pals over or went out herself. One night, Dad came back earlier than expected and Mom wasn't home. He was furious and waited up for her. I was awakened by lots of arguing, crying, and other loud frightening noises. I didn't get up to look. I decided pretending to sleep was my best option. Later that night, Mom came into my room, climbed into my bed crying, trying to snuggle up to me. With slurred words she told me, "I hate your father. He's so mean to me." Of course, she smelled of bourbon and cigarettes.

That first night she came to my room crying, I promptly got up and stood in front of my dad with my hands on my hips, hissing, "I hate you!" Today, I so regret that action. I can still recall the hurt and sadness on his face. A drunken, crying mother sharing my bed quickly became a common nighttime pattern. I got good at pretending to be sleeping. As I lay, barely breathing, I prayed this was a bad dream that would go away.

May, the month of honoring Mary, the mother of Jesus, with a crown of flowers was also the month that my favorite flower, lilacs, bloomed. I loved to cut blossoms off our backyard lilac bushes then set jelly glasses filled with lilacs next to each of my Virgin Mary statues that I carefully placed around my bedroom. This year, I reverently placed a glass of lilacs and a Mary statue on my nightstand. I figured that when I heard Mom coming up the stairs on her way to my bed, I would grab Mary and a small branch of fragrant lilacs. By holding a Mary next to my heart and the lilacs under my nose, maybe I wouldn't smell the bourbon or cigarettes. I also hoped St. Mary might be able to hear my prayers better.

When Dad was home, things were different. He was strict, but mostly fair—life felt more normal with him home. For example, Mom had gone shopping in Milwaukee. Since she wasn't home at lunch, Sonny and I made baloney sandwiches with tons of mayonnaise on Wonder bread then treated ourselves to an unprecedented bowl of ice cream. He loved vanilla and I adored chocolate. We only had vanilla, so I decided to make mine chocolate via the new can of Hershey's chocolate syrup in the cupboard. I used the bottle cap opener with the sharp point to open it.

My brother commanded, "You can't open it."

I retorted, "You are *not* my boss ...blah, blah, blah." Ignoring him, I went ahead and opened the can while he kept harassing me, so I threw the pointy opener at him. He ducked and the opener broke the window behind him. We were in shock when we heard the glass shatter. (Who knew I had such great aim or Sonny had such great ducking instincts?)

It was just our luck that Dad was in town, so we called him about our little mishap. He calmly responded, "I'm too busy to come home to punish you right now, so I am calling Monsignor at school and informing him of your behavior. I'll deal with you two tonight."

Yikes. I am sure you can picture the two of us scared out of our minds, slowly doing the march of the condemned back to school, while imagining every humiliating and mortifying punishment about to come down from the stern Monsignor. We knew we would also have to go to confession on Saturday then deal with our godly penance.

Each time the classroom door opened that afternoon, I was positive I was being summoned to Monsignor's office. Five minutes before the end of class, the door opened; my name was called. I almost threw up. Anxiously waiting outside Monsignor's office on the bench of shame, I prayed, *"Please Jesus, forgive me for my temper tantrum. I promise I will never throw anything like that at Sonny again."* Finally, Monsignor came into the hall, ushered me in to his office, and pointed to the chair across from his desk. I was shaking, fully believing that he was going to suspend me or worse, kick me out of school. Instead, he reached for a small white box on his desk and handed it to me. As he watched me open the box containing the coveted St. Anthony school charm bracelet, he explained Sister Carlene made him aware that I truly deserved the honor of placing the crown of flowers on the big Virgin Mary statue during the special St. Mary mass. However, Sister chose Sheila because she felt she was less fortunate than me. Sister relayed to Monsignor that when she told me I was the worthiest but she had chosen Sheila, I was happy for Sheila and gracious about Sister's decision to not choose me. (I wasn't upset, but I must admit I was pretty darn disappointed.)

Monsignor leaned over his desk, smiling, while stating, "It is my honor to present this bracelet to you for being an outstanding student and a true example of Jesus' kindness, charity, and humility."

Umm, really? It quickly became obvious to me that Dad had not called the Monsignor. Now I felt worse than I did before. I asked myself, *"Am I being dishonest by not telling Monsignor about the unkind deed I just did at lunchtime?"* Okay, I did feel guilty, but I chose to keep my latest sin to myself. I gratefully accepted the bracelet, deciding to confess my crime to a different priest at next Saturday's confession.

As for Dad's punishment? I'm guessing he figured making us sweat it out all afternoon by thinking we would be called into Monsignor's office at any moment was punishment enough. The new window was in place prior to our arrival home from school. I'm betting he never told Mom.

Home stopped being a happy place despite Dad staying in town more and Mom ratcheting back her partying. The nasty heated arguments about her drinking woke me up most nights. Awake, I often sensed an eerie presence like something evil watching me from the side of my bed. I'd be so scared, I squeeze my eyes shut really tight, and hold my breath while lying helpless just waiting for this monster to grab me. I wanted to scream out for Dad or Mom but I knew they couldn't hear me over their loud fighting—or worse, they'd chastise me, "Don't be a baby. You're too old to be afraid of the dark. It's just your imagination." But I knew it was real, so I prayed to Jesus, which calmed me and eventually I'd fall back asleep. I never told anyone about my paralyzing night terrors, as there already were more than enough problems going around.

Chapter 9
Chicago, IL, June–August 1957

You Can't Fool the Kids

꿍

In the summer of 1957, my parents announced, "We are moving back to Chicago. We've bought a really special house." My brother, a freshman, was starting at Loyola Academy. I was going into the sixth grade at a new Catholic school. Our parents insisted we would make lots of new friends and love it.

That summer, we were in Chicago, a lot, meeting with Dad's new business partner. If anyone asked me, I would have told them we spent way too much time with Mr. Evil, aka Mr. Art. There was something about him and the way his sneaky, shifty eyes looked that creeped me out. He was pure evil (I felt it in my gut), and reminded me of that mysterious dark presence from my night terrors. This man, who appeared to be friends with all types of famous influential people, was on a personal mission to have my parents meet each one of them. It was just our luck that they dragged Sonny and me along with them making sure that Sonny and I were appropriately and expensively attired. Prior to each outing, we were sternly reminded, "Be on your best behavior. Remember, you are to be seen, not heard. Even if you get tired and bored, you better sit up straight, napkins on laps, elbows off the table. Chew with your mouths closed and be quiet unless spoken to. Oh, yeah. Smile, look into the person's eyes when you are introduced, and shake their hand." Did they think we were stupid?

45

The Big Life

We heard this same speech every time. I guess they figured we both already knew "please", "thank you", and "It was nice to meet you."

The red-carpet royal "goody" package included staying at the best downtown hotels, dining in fancy downtown restaurants, seeing current plays, and even visiting several area country clubs. Another bribe treated us to several Chicago Cubs games with VIP seats ending with meeting the Cubbies and Milwaukee Braves players. These "perks" were wasted on me because I viewed it all as a bribe to get us to like moving to Chicago. It didn't work on Sonny and me, but our parents seemed to be falling right into Mr. Evil's trap.

Probably, the most memorable and worst event of the summer was the day spent on Lake Michigan on this detestable man's fancy yacht. For some unknown reason, Sonny was put in charge of the liquor to be brought onboard. In the chaos of everyone boarding, my poor brother forgot about the liquor sitting on the dock. About twenty minutes out from shore, my dad realized the liquor was missing and was he ever angry. Unfortunately, Sonny was the recipient of Dad's wrath. I've never understood why a thirteen-year-old boy was made responsible for the adults' liquor to be loaded on the boat.

According to Sonny, who was ordered to drive the boat while Dad and Mr. Evil met, this was the ill-fated day, out in the middle of Lake Michigan, that turned the tide (no pun intended) on our supposedly naive father's decision to partner with this shady, deceitful imposter. They sealed the deal, obviously without the booze, on this nightmare partnership. Beginning to end, this whole day was a bad omen. It marked the kick-off for the first day of our "shoot for the moon, you're gonna love the big life" era that permanently devastated our family, changing our world and each of our lives forever.

Finally, on a weekend in August, we were taken to see our new "big life" house. Our parents built it up and sold it hard to us. The house was big and beautiful, but for me the only positive was living closer to my grandparents and my aunt. I couldn't shake the ominous feeling that plagued me about this new house. Dad insisted, "This new business will take us 'to the moon.' I know we are all going to love our new home and living our new big life." For me, I never understood exactly why we had to move to live "the big life", because what exactly was "the big life"? I had no desire to go to the moon; I was quite happy here on Earth.

It occurred to me that this big deal "to the moon big life" had squashed my earthly big deal little life's horse dream. Now, because of this move, I knew, for sure, I wasn't getting the horse that I'd been riding and secretly hoping and praying to get for my upcoming eleventh birthday. I wondered, *Will my brother have to give up his flying lessons? It's his most favorite thing in the whole wide world. Wasn't life already good? By the way, has anyone else noticed this summer we didn't go to Mass at all? Why?*

Chapter 10
Chicago, IL, September–November 4, 1957

Poof! Where's Dad?
❦

We finally moved in to our new big house around the first of September, 1957. I was nervous about not knowing anybody or anything regarding the new school or my teacher. At my old school, I liked walking to and from school with my friends and staying after to help Sister. Now, Mom drove and picked me up every day. I don't think she enjoyed being my private school bus.

Shock was my first reaction as I walked into my crowded new classroom: a duo class of sixty-seven fifth and sixth graders and one overwhelmed nun. I don't know how long it took her to learn all the names of her students. I don't think she ever knew mine and I don't think I learned anything at all.

Within that first week of school, Dad disappeared like Houdini in his magic show act. No goodbyes or kisses, just abracadabra, *poof*, Dad was gone. No clues where or why Dad was missing. Immediately, Mom escalated her Manhattan "sipping" to a whole new level. However, she struck the fear of God in us with her stern instructions, "Under no circumstances are you allowed to go to any friend's house and don't invite anyone to ours. You can't tell a soul, including anyone at school, that Dad is gone. From now on, you wait inside school until you see my car."

If we arrived home after dark, Mom turned off the car's headlights as we drove down our street into our garage. "Don't turn on any lights," she warned. In the dark, I would streak past our front door's three long windows, praying no one would see that anyone was home. For two or three weeks, the three of us hid in this strange, dark, huge ("you're gonna love it") house. I felt like a captive actress in a gruesome late-night horror movie—except this wasn't a movie, it was my real life.

Suddenly, Mom announced, "You two aren't going to school anymore. Think of this as a surprise vacation. You can forget about any of your school work too." *What? She's got to be drunk, because we always take our school work with us on vacations.* I had a bad feeling about this. Maybe Mom had lost her mind.

We hid out at my grandparents' summer lake cottage. It was a small primitive cottage that my grandfather built for getaway weekends from the city. I pretended we were pioneers while gathering twigs from the woods for the old wood burning kitchen cook stove. Mom had to light the wood before she could even make oatmeal. We never needed many twigs because most of our meals consisted of peanut butter and jelly sandwiches, each specially handcrafted by Sonny and me. Mom cooked an occasional can of soup, but mostly was lost in her bourbon and forgot to feed us.

This ghastly situation was the real deal, the nightmare I couldn't wake up from. In the rush of leaving our house, I forgot my stuffed dog, Fifi, and my Nancy Drew books. Now, bored and frightened, especially at night, I missed cuddling up with Fifi and hiding under the covers to read by my flashlight. With all the summer residents gone, the isolation and the pitch-black darkness of the night terrified me. Then I would remember my own guardian angel was here with me, to help me and protect me, no matter what. Of course, I had Sonny, who I hoped had his own guardian angel with him.

Mother, however, did not forget her best friends, bourbon and a carton of Salems. She spent her days and nights worshipping the bottle and smoking like a chimney, escaping into her own world. In my world, I felt invisible, ignored, unloved, and unwanted by this sad, broken down, strange drunken woman who my mom had now become. Each time she made another drink, I felt like she was stabbing me in my heart.

Sonny and I stayed quiet, while we cautiously watched this sad crying "stranger" who looked a lot like our old real mother. While we played our games, we created a system that gave each other a status report on Mom, via the "look." Sonny was a master at eyeballing his "look" report to me. He made me giggle with his imitation of Groucho Marx's eyebrow wiggles. I tried hard to give him even better "looks" back, but at the end of the day, I had to concede he gave the best "looks." The looks report game sounds silly now, but it helped us cope and try to forget how abandoned and frightened we were in these terror-filled desperate times. We hid out at the cottage till Halloween time. The summer cabin had no heat and the weather had turned cold.

Upon returning to the "you're gonna love it" big house, I discovered my grandparents and Aunt Lulu's family living there. I assumed they were kind of there for Sonny and me, but knew they were mostly there for my strange-acting mother. She never left the kitchen table except to find her secret stash of smelly bourbon or another carton of cigarettes. Since Dad vanished, she hardly ever talked, and wouldn't eat or make us any food. She quit washing our clothes or cleaning up. I couldn't remember when she last showered or put on makeup. Mom only left the house if she absolutely had to, but mostly stayed in bed. As I passed by her room, I often saw her lying completely still in the middle of her king size bed, curled up on her side like a baby. The long, silky, champagne-colored drapes were completely closed, shutting out as much daylight as possible. She appeared to be in a sound sleep except her once sparkling hazel eyes were wide open, fixed, staring blankly into space.

Dad's whereabouts were still unknown to Sonny and me. Almost all our furniture was sold. I knew something disastrous was happening to our family. I just didn't know why. What I did know was that I yearned for my old life because I hated everything about living this big new life. Our new "to the moon you are gonna love the big life" as Dad would say, should get lost in space.

PART 2
California–Chicago Area, 1957–1958
Bad Things Can Happen to Good Kids

Chapter 11
Rancho Cordova, CA,
November 4, 1957–December 21, 1957

Uncle Gil, Are You Here?
❧

At last, we arrive at the Sacramento airport. It is already dark, around nine o'clock California time. It feels like eleven to me. My body thinks I am still in Chicago. This is the first true day of my "you're gonna love the big life", all on my own, with only Sonny.

I am worried. I am bewildered. I am sad. I am anxious. I am apprehensive. I am curious. All my crazy feelings rise as I hear the landing gear lower and we begin our descent into Sacramento.

We land abruptly with a big bounce and a loud screeching sound as the plane slows down and taxis to the gate. The stewardesses get ready to open the big door and send us off on our various journeys. I am thinking so many thoughts fraught with emotions I can't control. I am so overwhelmed by everything that's happening and stressed about what lies ahead—even within the next ten minutes. My mind won't stop with the questions. *What if my uncle is late? What if he has changed his mind about having us? What if he doesn't show up? If he is here, how will he know what we look like? It's been at least two or three years since he last saw us. What if no one wants Sonny and me? Dear Jesus, please wake us up from this horrible nightmare.*

I cling to Sonny's sweaty hand as we make our way down the steep airplane stairway. My heart's pounding so hard I can hardly breathe.

I think I may throw up. All the while, I am scouring the crowd in search of my uncle's face. There are so many people waiting for the other passengers, making it hard to see. Halfway down the airplane stairs, I pull on Sonny's hand, "Look, there he is! The tall man in the front. He's smiling and waving his arms. It's Uncle Gil. He did come to get us. He looks just like I remember him. Don't you think he looks a little like Grandpa? Let's hope he is as nice."

We walk on the tarmac along the yellow line through the metal gate to where everyone is waiting. Our uncle runs out to greet us. He gathers both of us into his arms in a huge hug and gives us a loving kiss on the cheek. He smells good. He bends over and exclaims, "I'm so happy to see you guys. Aunt Sue wanted to be here too, but she had to stay at home with your cousins who are sleeping. She can't wait to see you! Come on, let's go home." With one arm wrapped protectively around each of us, he guides us to where we claim our shared suitcase, and head to the car. I notice the night is a lot warmer here than Chicago was this morning.

I don't know how long it takes us to get to our new home. Exhausted by the ordeal of the day, the motion of the car has lulled me to sleep. Suddenly I feel Aunt Sue gently trying to wake me up and help me into the house.

They show us where our room is. We are sharing the room with our two-year-old cousin who is sound asleep in his crib. Sonny and I have a black metal bunkbed and a few drawers in a small dresser. He says I can have the top bunk if I want it. I do. As Aunt Sue tightly hugs us, she whispers, "I am so happy you two are here. Uncle Gil will wake you in the morning and take you to your new schools. Sweet dreams."

After washing my face and hands, and brushing my teeth, I am so tired that it takes every ounce of energy to pull my PJs on and climb up the ladder onto my new bunkbed. Either I am too young or too tired to grasp the gravity of how quickly my life has changed between waking up this morning in my big pink bedroom suite with a king size bed and private bathroom to now going to bed in a shared small child's room on the top of a black metal twin bunk bed. However, I am not too tired to ask God: "*Since Dad left us, we don't know where he is or if we will ever see him again. Mom doesn't want us anymore, so she sent us away. Does that mean Sonny and I are now orphans?*"

In what feels like minutes, it is morning. Warm bright sunshine streams through the windows, making me squint as I open my eyes. It takes a few seconds for me to process my unfamiliar surroundings and remember where and why I am on the top bunk of this black metal bed in this strange bedroom. To my right is a crib with a sleeping baby in it and beneath my bunk is Sonny, out like a light. The house is so still. I am afraid I will wake everyone up if I climb down the metal ladder to use the bathroom. Quickly, I decide it isn't a choice, nature is calling, signaling that I need to find the bathroom, now. As quietly as I can, I climb down and tiptoe across the wood floor, hoping the door won't creak as I open it. If I wake them up, they might decide I am too much trouble to keep.

There is a soft knock on the bathroom door. It's Aunt Sue. As I open the door I contritely whisper, "I am so sorry for making noise or getting up before I am allowed. I don't know the rules yet."

She comes in, gently closing the door. Her warm arms wrap tightly around me as she softly explains, "Honey, you are just fine. Thank you for being so considerate. Do you need help with what clothes to wear? What do you like for breakfast? I want you to know that you can trust and talk to me about anything whenever you want. I am happy that you and Sonny are here with us. This is now your home too." The whole time she is talking, she has picked up the blue hair brush from the bathroom counter and is tenderly brushing my hair. She tells me we will wash and set my hair tonight and she will teach me so I can set it myself anytime I want. I almost start to cry. It seems like forever since anyone was this kind to me. I wish I could spend the whole day alongside her.

With our new routine and everything else happening so fast, I completely forget one major detail. Sonny and I are going to start our new schools and Uncle Gil is going to take us this morning. In the afternoon we will ride the school bus home. As I dress, I realize we don't know where the schools are. I also realize we are the new kids in school for the second time in less than two months. Sonny is going to his second new high school and he won't know where any of his classrooms are. At least at his first new high school in Chicago he had a day or two to learn about that stuff before real school began. I'm nervous and I'm only going to my second sixth grade school. I am lucky because I stay in one room the whole day. I hope someone at his new school helps Sonny find all his classrooms.

Uncle Gil is so nice. He keeps us talking on the long ride to our new schools, which are over twelve miles away in a town called Folsom. I am not thinking about the name until I see a road sign stating: "Folsom State Prison: 8 miles."

That sign got my attention! *Are we going to school in a prison?*

I nudge Sonny and ask, "Did you see the sign I just saw?"

He murmurs, "What sign?"

I figure he didn't see it. I don't want to make him anxious so I simply shrug my shoulders and say, "Never mind." But holy moly, my insides are freaking out! I am too afraid to ask Uncle Gil about the prison and school thing because he might think I am not appreciating how nice he is trying to be.

It seems my elementary school is either on the way to the high school or my new school starts first. The school building doesn't look anything like my past three schools. It looks like a factory. There're hardly any trees, not much grass, and no flowers. School must have already begun because there aren't any other kids around. We park in front of the main door and Uncle Gil tells Sonny he will be right back. That makes me a little more nervous because I think I will have to register myself and I have no clue about my new address or the phone number.

As we climb the school steps, my stomach begins to hurt again. Uncle Gil walks me into the office informing the lady behind the counter that I am the new girl for the sixth grade. With that, he pats my head and says he will see me tonight. He turns and hurries out the door. I guess he wants to make sure Sonny won't be late for his new school.

The lady behind the counter asks me a few questions, then tells me to follow her to my new classroom. As I walk behind her down the hallway, I notice there are no statues of Jesus or the Saints. Also, no big pretty stained-glass windows. Nor do I spot any policemen, windows covered with jail bars, or people who look like prisoners anywhere.

Quickly, we arrive at my new classroom. My new teacher greets me at the door and welcomes me in. She's looks kind of old, but seems quite nice. She introduces me to the class and shows me to my desk.

I can feel the other kids staring at me, so I take a deep breath, look around and smile, pretending I am happy to be there. I busy myself organizing my stack of books, pencils, crayons—you know, school stuff—to put into my desk when I realize these desks are like the desks I saw in my mother's old school pictures. My seat is attached to the desk behind me and my desk is connected to the girl's seat in front of me. The top of the desk doesn't open and has an empty inkwell in it. I wonder, *Where do I store my stuff?* As I try to solve my dilemma, the recess bell rings and all the kids stand up and beeline it to the door. There is no before-recess prayer or silently lining up waiting for permission to go out into hall. Geez, everyone just races out the door and can talk!

My new teacher sweetly asks me, "Do you wish to join in recess or settle in?"

"I'd like to settle in then go out to recess after lunch," I reply.

While showing me the cubby for my stuff, she tosses out questions about when and where I moved from, plus what have I been studying in my previous school. I do not want to tell her that I haven't been in school for over a month or that I didn't know I was moving to California until yesterday morning, and by the way, my parents no longer want my brother and me anymore, so now we might be orphans. Therefore, I lie, but feel guilty. I know lying is wrong as I explain, "My parents bought a new house for us in Rancho Cordova but we can't move in yet. They sent us ahead to stay with my uncle and aunt." A loud bell rings, which ends our conversation because recess is over and the other kids are returning from the break, and may I add, in a most disorderly loud way. I notice there is no after-recess prayer, either.

The class settles down and Mrs. Teacher assigns a few pages in our workbook. I am in luck. I have already learned this lesson and am able to whiz through the assignment. I feel a bit better now; at least there is something familiar to me in this new school.

The rest of the morning flies by and it is lunch time. Aunt Sue made me a bag lunch today. Sadly, I can't eat because my stomach is all knotted up and hurting. However, I think she is a smart aunt, knowing that everyone brings their own lunch and eats at their desks.

I guess there's no cafeteria. We all finish eating and head out to the playground, which is a big dirt field.

I assume I will be alone at recess, but surprisingly several of the girls in my class come over to talk with me. They are curious about where I came from and where I live. I give them my same lie for an answer. They are so nice and friendly. One girl doesn't say much, so I start talking to her. She looks at me strangely and answers in Spanish. I have heard Spanish before when I went with my grandmother on her Missions of Love to the inner-city Chicago neighborhoods, but except for a few words, I don't understand it. The other girls explain to me what this girl named Marta has said and inform me that Marta speaks little English. I tell Marta that I don't speak any Spanish but want to learn so maybe she can help me with Spanish and I can help her with English. We could do this during our recess time. Marta smiles and nods. Right then, we start learning words from each other and becoming friends. Marta is my first friend in my new life.

The rest of my day goes well. My teacher is nice, my school work easy, and my class is small enough that I sort of meet everyone.

Next challenge of the day is going to be finding and riding the bus "home." I never rode a school bus before and I don't quite know where I live, just that it is somewhere in Rancho Cordova. My teacher must have observed my anxious face and asks, "How are you getting home today?" My lips tremble as I shakily explain my situation. She says not to worry; she will find my bus and introduce me to the bus driver. Whew, this takes a huge load off my mind, maybe this guardian angel thing really does work!

School ends and I board my bus. The bus driver is nice, plus I have a seat all to myself. The bus pulls away from my school, but doesn't go down the road the way I thought we had come in this morning. Instead we go to the high school and the best surprise of the day gets on my bus. Sonny! We both have survived and are safe. This bus is for every student that lives in Rancho Cordova. The second-best surprise of the day is how entertaining our bus driver is. She teaches us silly songs all the way home. Our entire bus of elementary and high school kids sing these crazy funny tunes together for the whole ride to Rancho Cordova. The twelve-mile trip goes by so fast and is so fun, I can hardly wait to do it again. I know tomorrow will be easier than today.

Fortunately, we find our aunt and uncle's house. We finish unpacking, do our homework, and sit down to dinner. My aunt and uncle never pray before eating, so I say mine fast in my head. In the middle of dinner, I can't wait any longer. I've got to find out about the prison school thing.

I boldly ask, "Is my new school a prison school or is it just a regular school near a prison? Oh, and do any kids of prisoners go there?" They both look at me and want to know why I am asking. I shyly murmur, "Ummm, I saw a Folsom Prison sign pointing the way to school this morning, but I never saw any jail bars on the windows, or policeman or prisoners in cells at school."

My uncle looks like he is going to choke because he is laughing so hard. Grinning, my aunt patiently explains, "No honey, your school is not part of the prison. The poor children of prisoners may go there, but I don't know that any do." With that information, I feel a little more comfortable with my new school despite the fact it is unlike any school I have attended before.

True to her word, after washing my hair and taking a bath, Aunt Sue sets my hair before I go to bed. When she hugs me goodnight, she sweetly says, "I will help you comb it out in the morning." Before I fall asleep, I fret about all the lies I told today. I thank Jesus for Sonny, my aunt and uncle, and that this day is over. I fall asleep still wondering if Sonny and I are orphans.

The sunbeams shining through the window feeling like warm caresses across my face wake me up. Maybe it is the brightness of the day compared to the midwestern grey autumn morning skies, but I feel a touch calmer than I have in a while.

The bus ride to school goes by fast and is just as fun as it was yesterday afternoon. Even this early in the morning, everyone sings those crazy songs. I find my new classroom without any trouble, place my stuff in my cubby, and chat with the other kids until class starts. I feel sort of normal. I like feeling this way and love the new hairdo Aunt Sue created for me this morning. I do miss not having a morning prayer, but at least everyone stands and recites the Pledge of Allegiance to the same flag. At recess, Marta and I teach each other a few more new words and I no longer worry about the prison school thing. All in all, it's a pretty good day. I feel safer than I have felt in a long, long time.

Sonny and I have instructions that after school, we are to change our clothes, go out to play, and unless it is raining, we are not to come back in the house until five o'clock. We don't know why, but it is their house and their rules. Both of us are rule-followers and instinctively know not to ask any questions.

We are excited. There is so much new territory to explore and we just made friends with another brother and sister down the street who ride our bus. And guess what? They are our exact same age. Cindy is in the other sixth grade classroom next to mine and Jake is a freshman in the same high school as Sonny. We pass their house on our way to our new home. Today, we stopped at their house so they could change their clothes. While we waited on the front porch, I peeked through the screened door. Their mom was home, but she looked kind of strange. She had all the curtains closed and was lying on a white furry chaise lounge staring at the TV, looking just like the movie star magazine photo of Judy Garland with her dark hair, a drink in her hand, and a cigarette hanging from her bright red lips. She saw us waiting for our new friends, but she never said hi or seemed to care we were standing there. It was a little freaky because it reminds me of what we left behind in Chicago.

At six o'clock, Uncle Gil isn't home as we sit down to dinner with my Aunt Sue and two cousins, Kammie, a sweet five-year-old girl, and Scout, a rambunctious, adorable two-year-old boy. Aunt Sue is not saying why our uncle isn't home yet, just that he'll have a special surprise for us when he arrives. I am curious about what kind of special something it is and apprehensive because I've had my fill of surprises this week.

The front door opens and in walks Uncle Gil with my grandmother. I am surprised—sadly, not in a good way. Startled, I get up to hug and kiss her. Unfortunately, my stomach reveals the real story—the horrible ache has returned. All I want is to go to my bunk to be alone and think. In the couple of days that I've been here with Aunt Sue, Uncle Gil, and my young cousins, I feel safer, secure, wanted, and loved again. The appearance of my grandmother reminds me of all the ugliness, fear, and sadness that I want to try to forget, at least for a little while. I wonder, *why is she here? What about Mom and Dad? Where is my beloved grandfather? Why wasn't he our special surprise?*

I don't remember Grandma being all that excited about seeing me. She hugs and kisses Sonny and Kammie, sort of hugs me, pats the top of Scout's head, and murmurs a cold hello to Aunt Sue who has draped her arm protectively around me. Uncle Gil explains, "Aunt Sue needs extra help now with four kids. She took off a couple of days from work while we all got settled and now she must go back to work at the bank in the Safeway shopping center. Grandma has come all the way from Chicago to help out and she needs your help too."

With all due respect to Grandma, I am sure her idea of retirement doesn't include taking care of her alcoholic daughter's responsibilities including flying out to the West Coast to be a nanny to her son's young kids, all because her son-in-law up and magically disappeared. In addition, I remember hearing when my mother was still my old mom, that Grandma never liked Aunt Sue, but Grandpa did. When I asked her why, Mom quipped, "Because Aunt Sue married Uncle Gil, Grandma's favorite child." Enough said.

Aunt Sue continues helping me set my hair and comb it out every morning. She teaches me about girls growing up stuff, like bathing regularly and using deodorant. She buys one just for me. She checks my homework while praising my grades and tells me how smart I am and how proud she is of me. She begins to hug and kiss me when I go to bed and whispers that she loves me. I know she treats Sonny in the same loving way. Grandma, on the other hand, doesn't like Aunt Sue and I don't think likes that I adore Aunt Sue or how excited I am each evening when she gets home. I try to stay out of Grandma's way; I never want to incur her wrath.

A few evenings later, Uncle Gil says he needs to talk to me, alone. We go sit on Sonny's bottom bunk. He looks right at me and says, "I am very sorry we have to have this talk, but Grandma complains that you don't listen to her, refuse to help and talk back to her when Aunt Sue and I are not around."

I am stunned and completely crushed. I start to blubber, "Everything Grandma told you about me isn't true. I swear! I did not talk back to Grandma and I will always help if she asks me. I am not

63

sure how to help her because when I ask her about anything, she orders me to go outside and not cause any trouble." Secretly, I think, *Grandma never asked me to do anything because if she had, I would have helped her even if I didn't want to. What if she convinces Uncle Gil that I'm bad and makes him drop me off at an orphanage?*

I hope and pray Uncle Gil believes me. As he leaves, he hugs and kisses me on my cheek, adding, "You're a good girl, just try a little harder to please Grandma." Relieved, I run to find Sonny, thankful that Uncle Gil isn't sending me away.

We'd been with Aunt Sue and Uncle Gil for twelve days when I turned eleven. It was the first time my birthday wasn't a big deal and pretty much forgotten. Sonny wished me a happy birthday as soon as he woke up, but neither of my parents called nor sent a card or a present. Mom had always made my other birthdays so special. They started as soon as I woke up and found my favorite breakfast food, including the stuff with tons of sugar and red jelly, waiting for me. A big family birthday party and another party with my friends topped off my celebration. I could count on Mom to make sure my birthdays were "princess" worthy.

This birthday, there was no birthday breakfast surprise awaiting me when I entered the kitchen. I think Grandma was still angry and maybe she chose to ignore my birthday. Uncle Gil and Sonny are going to the gym at the air force base. Aunt Sue is going to the local farmers' market, but asks if I want to come along. You bet I want to tag along!

Alone in the car, she wishes me a happy birthday and informs we aren't going to the farmers' market today. Instead, we are going to Sears Roebuck shopping, just the two of us, for my present. We decide I need slippers since Mom hadn't sent any in our suitcase. She helps me pick out a pink and blue fancy pair and then we celebrate my day with a chocolate cupcake and lemonade. Funny, but for all the incredible birthday celebrations before and the many beautiful lavish birthdays I've celebrated since, this simple eleventh birthday remains one of my favorites. All because of an aunt I barely knew, cared enough to see *me*, my pain, and make me feel so special. I learned that day that birthdays aren't about the "present" but about who is "present" for you. This beautiful life lesson was an incredible birthday gift from God.

Thanksgiving arrived, but it wasn't like past Thanksgiving holidays, where our entire family, including anyone my grandmother knew who was alone, joined us for the grand feast. She prepared every traditional and some not-so-traditional Thanksgiving dishes along with an enormous turkey. After overstuffing ourselves, everyone, young and old, sat together around her big dining room table playing card games, telling jokes, laughing, and talking. I always knew that I wanted to do the same when I grew up and hosted Thanksgiving.

This Thanksgiving, Sonny, Aunt Sue's two nieces, and I went to see an Elvis Presley movie. Both were a first for me; attending a movie on Thanksgiving Day and learning who Elvis was. Dinner at Aunt Sue's sister's house was good, but I sadly missed my other Thanksgivings. This year, Thanksgiving Day didn't start with Mass. In fact, it had been months and months since I was anywhere near a church. I missed it and as much as I liked my new teacher, I missed the nuns more.

Chapter 12
Rancho Cordova, CA,
December 1957

$1.50

೧೨

I think the strangest revelation of all, is when I realize I don't miss my parents. In the beginning I thought about them and sort of missed them, but not the gut-wrenching heartbreak that I felt the day I left Chicago. As each day and week flies by with no communication from either of them, I find that I am pretty happy living with Aunt Sue, Uncle Gil, Kammie, and Scout. I also get the idea that if Sonny and I are together, we can handle anything.

One day after school, we scout out an old orchard with our new best friends, Cindy and Jake. During our adventure, we glance up and see what looks like mistletoe growing on the old withered tree branches. We manage to grab some off a branch and after closer inspection decide it must be real mistletoe. On the way back home, the four of us come up with our entrepreneurial idea. We will come back tomorrow, pick as much as we possibly can, and package it in small bundles wrapped in saran wrap. Next week, we will go door to door throughout the neighborhood and sell it for Christmas.

At dinner we can hardly wait to share our fabulous new business idea. Aunt Sue and Uncle Gil listen intently to our plan.

Uncle Gil suggests, "Why don't you have a business meeting with Aunt Sue to make sure you do this correctly?"

Aunt Sue proposes, "After school, go check out the Safeway and figure out the cost of your needed materials. Afterward, bring a sample of your mistletoe along with your 'business plan' to me at the bank and during my break, I will help you complete your plan and apply for the money to fund the saran wrap and ribbon."

We are thrilled and can hardly wait for our meeting at the bank.

Heeding her instructions from last night, Sonny and I complete our scouting work at Safeway before we walk over to the bank. We decide we need to borrow one dollar for the box of saran wrap and fifty cents for a big spool of red and green crinkle tie ribbon. The actual product, mistletoe, is free. We will sell small bundles for fifteen cents each and larger ones for twenty-five cents. We proudly enter the bank right on time. Aunt Sue is all set up for us in her private office.

Reflecting on that day, I don't know how she kept a straight face while we conducted our business deal. After an in-depth presentation of our plan, she had us wait while she found her boss and discussed our loan. Returning, she seriously stated, "This bank isn't in a position to loan money to minors; however, I will be your personal banker for this business venture." With that, she named herself as the lender on the loan contract then typed our legal names as the borrowers. She said her "fee" for loaning us the money was a large package of mistletoe. We agreed and signed our names on the dotted line. She handed us the one dollar and fifty cents in cash. After thanking her and shaking hands, we ran out the door back to Safeway to purchase our packaging materials. I skipped alongside Sonny all the way home, planning to give Aunt Sue a huge thank you kiss after dinner.

For the next few days, we hurried to the orchard right after school. Singing Christmas songs as well as the funny bus driver's songs, we merrily gathered our fresh merchandise. Once satisfied we had enough to begin packaging the mistletoe, we set up our assembly line on our aunt and uncle's patio: one person making the bundles, one person cutting the saran wrap and ribbon, another placing the bundles in the saran wrap, and the fourth person tying the red and green ribbon around the top of the package and pricing it. We were now ready to take our product to market.

Our timing was perfect; Christmas was maybe two or three weeks away. Our house-to-house customers were receptive to our sales pitch and holiday packaged mistletoe. We sold out quickly and were able to pay Aunt Sue back the first day, including giving her a double fee: two large packages of mistletoe instead of one.

I don't exactly remember how much money we made on this venture, but it was incredibly fun and a positive first business learning experience. This was all made possible because Aunt Sue took the time to help us feel the joy of self-accomplishment and that we were worthy of her trust.

Both she and Uncle Gil made it quite clear:

"You are not bad kids, you just have bad things happening to you."

Chapter 13
Rancho Cordova, CA,
December 20–December 21, 1957

The Parents Who Stole Christmas

❦

F riday, December 20, 1957, was the last day of school for the year. Christmas vacation was finally here. Our whole school bus sang Christmas carols all the way home. Everyone was shouting "Merry Christmas" and "See ya next year" as we waved goodbye to our friends and bus driver. We were full of Christmas spirit walking home. It felt great because nothing that had happened to us this year had been good. It felt like everything was changing, including Sonny and me. I secretly thought we'd grown up a lot since arriving in California six-and-a-half weeks earlier. Living there made us happy; we felt at home.

We were going to make Christmas cookies and the next day, take Kammie and Scout to see Santa. They were little and all they talked about was Santa Claus and his elves. Their little eyes sparkled each time Santa's name was mentioned. I wasn't a little kid anymore, so it was fun playing along about Santa. This Christmas would be another kind of special Christmas and I could hardly wait.

Some nights I thought about past Christmases. I wondered; *will we ever again celebrate Christmas with our whole family or sleep over at Grandma's on Christmas Eve? Where's Dad, who loves Christmas, and went all out making our entire house, inside and out, look like a little Christmas wonderland? This year Sonny and I won't be helping him with the outside decorating or having a snow ball fight. Oh, I am going to miss making snow angels, too. We'd be so cold and Mom was always waiting with marshmallow hot chocolate as soon as we finished.*

Will we ever have our favorite family tradition decorating the fragrant fresh-cut Christmas tree? Where the music of Christmas carols, a cozy warm fire, snapping and crackling in the living room fireplace, and a plate of newly baked Christmas cookies still warm from the oven started our evening? Mom, Sonny, and I ate the holiday treats while watching Dad struggle to get the tree through the door, set it straight in the green and red metal tree stand, untangle and test the lights, then finally string them on the tree, often uttering some non-Christmassy, not-very-nice words that we weren't supposed to hear. I think I'm too old now to entertain them with my specially choreographed Christmas dances, while singing along with the Christmas carols. Hmmm, I wonder what Mom did with all our treasured multicolored glass ornaments that we so carefully placed on our special tree?

If I close my eyes, I can smell Christmas cookie baking day. I loved it, but probably not so much Mom. Somehow, despite Sonny and me wearing aprons, our hands, clothes, the counter, the floor, and likely every other kitchen surface was sticky and gooey from all the sugar and frosting we used to artistically embellish the sweet holiday confections. Even I, who love all things chocolate and sugary, got a little sick of so much sweet!

Will we ever do our oldest Christmas tradition day when Mom, Grandma, Sonny, and I get dressed up to take the trolley, bus, and EL train to downtown? The splendor of all the State Street holiday-decorated department store windows filled us with so much merry Christmas spirit. At eleven and fourteen, there are no Santa wish lists safely tucked in our pockets, or the desire to sit on his jolly lap. Gone is my napping on my mom's shoulder during the cozy long train ride home, which ended the perfect day and created so many beautiful memories.

Now we've grown too old for Santa, played by Grandpa, who arrived early on Christmas Eve to deliver one small gift to both Sonny and me as Grandma plunked out Christmas carols on her old upright player piano and everyone ate, drank, and sang along. I twirled and danced, of course! Sonny and I used to get up at dawn on Christmas mornings, then gleefully race to the tree, eager to discover what surprises Santa had brought us. Along with Santa's presents, we always found Grandpa waiting with his infamous sixteen-millimeter camera already in action, capturing our Christmas morning excitement and joy. The rest of the family remained snug in their beds, fast asleep, while glasses of wine still danced in their heads.

However, my most treasured of all Christmas traditions was the celebration of baby Jesus' birthday. Grandma constantly reminded me that Jesus was the "reason for the season." The presents we received from Santa and others were *because* Christmas was baby Jesus' birthday. Sweet baby Jesus chose to celebrate His birthday by *giving His gifts to us*! As a lucky recipient of His birthday gifts, I felt that was a nice thing for sweet baby Jesus to do! I mean, baby Jesus received millions of birthday gifts, but chose to give them away to Santa to deliver to all the children in the world. And that's why Santa brought some of baby Jesus' presents to Sonny and me. When I was six, I asked Grandma, "How come baby Jesus got a lot of girl presents?" I don't think she ever answered.

I knew I might be a little sad this Christmas season. I missed Grandpa and Aunt Lulu a lot. I didn't make any Christmas wish list nor did I expect any presents. Presents didn't seem as important as other years. All I wanted was to feel safe and normal. The absolute best thing about living with Uncle Gil and Aunt Sue was that I wasn't invisible to them; they saw me and made me feel valued and safe. This was the best present I could ever ask for.

This afternoon, I was bursting with Christmas joy as I opened the front door, inhaling the fresh Christmas wreath fragrance while smiling at our mistletoe hanging from the foyer light. I felt such warmth within as I realized I no longer cared if I was an orphan, I loved my aunt and uncle and felt loved by them. Life was better than it had been in a long time. I could let my guard down. Christmas was just a few days away and I felt like a normal eleven-year-old girl: safe, happy, and carefree.

Unexpectedly, I heard people talking in the kitchen. Voices I recognized; Mom and Dad. The familiar cold dread in my gut feeling was back; this instant reaction frightened me. *Shouldn't I be thrilled to see them? Why is my gut signaling I may not want to be with them anymore?*

Instantly, I was petrified what their arrival meant for Sonny and me. *Will they take us away from this happy life with Aunt Sue and Uncle Gil? Will we be forced to go live with them? What if we don't want to? Maybe we should run away until they leave.*

The shame of my thoughts made my insides feel sicker. The two voices I thought I longed to hear sent cold chills through me. What was wrong with me? These were my parents. Why was I not racing into the kitchen throwing my arms around them, kissing and hugging, making up for lost time? Deep down, I knew why. Mom and Dad wouldn't make me feel safe or normal or loved anymore. I looked at Sonny and wondered if his thoughts mirrored mine. The look on his face said they did.

Plastering a smile on my face and trying to be excited about this latest surprise, I breezed into the kitchen and kissed and hugged them both. I hoped I sounded happy when I told them, "You guys are a special present I wasn't expecting."

I quickly excused myself, claiming I needed to use the bathroom. They didn't know that I needed a moment to get away and take a breath. I hadn't had a chance to talk with Sonny about his reaction to this unexpected event and I felt guilty about my bad thoughts.

These parents were different, both thinner and tired. Mom looked older, with dark circles and bags under her eyes. Her arms looked like two fragile sticks and she acted like we weren't her kids. She didn't throw her arms around us or tell us how happy she was to see us. She didn't tell us she had missed us or that she loved us. She barely spoke, never asked any questions about our new schools or friends or anything. She pretty much ignored us, behaving like some stranger, not caring or loving like a mom or even an aunt. I didn't know this cold unloving woman. I felt no connection with her. It was like her body shell sat in this kitchen, but the mom I used to know had vanished.

I sat down right next to her and tried to hold her hand, to hug her, but she'd stiffen up and pull away. I attempted to talk to her about my new hair, our mistletoe business, anything to get her attention and have her look at me, but she never saw me; she looked through me. I was invisible to her. She made me feel like a strange kid she had never seen before and didn't like. She just stared at the window, posed and frozen in the chair like a mannequin in the Marshall Fields department store. I had so hated leaving her six-and-a-half weeks ago and now I hated that she was here. I didn't want this woman to be my mother and I no longer wanted to be her unloved invisible daughter.

I hadn't seen Dad since early September. He was a lot thinner. He's eyes had shadows, but he did look at me. He acted like he was happy to see Sonny and me. I didn't feel I could trust him, and still felt he had abandoned Sonny and me. My head overflowed with tons of old and new unanswered questions. *Where and why did he disappear to in the middle of the night? I know Dad lost both his parents before he was thirteen. Surely he remembers how that felt. But even that wasn't the same as how he left us—his parents didn't choose to die, but he chose to leave us. Why did he leave Sonny and me to be orphans? How come everything seems so confusing now? Why did you come now? How long are they going to be here? Will they be here for Christmas? Are we going to have to go with them when they leave? If we must go with them, where are we going? Does this mean we won't get to go to our new schools anymore? Why can't we stay here with Uncle Gil, Aunt Sue, Kammie, and funny little Scout? I love them, they make us feel safe, normal, and loved. Don't we get to pick now? At least Dad seems warmer and happier to see us. But how long will this last? What if they get tired of us and dump us somewhere else in a few weeks or months?*

By bedtime, we knew the plan. We had to go with our real parents. We were leaving in the morning right after breakfast. Sonny and I were not making any Christmas cookies, or going to see Santa with Kammie and Scout. We were not spending Christmas with Uncle Gil and Aunt Sue. Instead, we had to go to a place called Long Beach. It's still in California, but near Los Angeles where all the movie stars live. We will be changing schools for the third time this school year. Once again, our lives were turned upside down. The comfort of living within a safe and stable environment was instantly taken away from us when they walked through the door, rocking our world once again. It felt like being kidnapped by strangers, who just happened to be our parents. My stomach was seriously in pain.

Saturday morning, breakfast over, we packed the car to head South. It was fast. The agonizing part was saying goodbye to this wonderful family that took such tender loving care of us. The quote "Parting is such sweet sorrow" is a lie because we were not experiencing anything "sweet" about leaving our haven that represented family and home to us for the last seven weeks.

Sonny and I climbed into the backseat of the car, only this time it wasn't a shiny new car, but an old, beat up car. Unlike the past, we did not go directly to our self-claimed corners, but sat in the middle, right next to each other, hands and legs touching. No one talked; the silence was eerie. I put my head on Sonny's lap and fell asleep.

When I woke up, Sonny lay down with his head on my lap for his "get away from it all" nap. This was all new because in the past, Sonny always let me nap with my head on his lap, however, when he wished to do the same with his head on my lap, I drew an imaginary line down the middle of the seat and told him not to cross over the line onto my side. Consequently, he napped sitting up. My attitude was changed. We no longer needed separate spaces; my lap was his lap; whatever I had, he had. What we needed more now than ever before was each other and a lot of help from heaven.

Chapter 14
Long Beach, CA, Christmas Eve 1957

Gee, Mom and Dad, Thanks for Sharing
❧

Times were different during the late 1950s and early 1960s. Children could certainly ask questions of their parents. However, if your parents were silent, choosing not to respond, that meant ..."Do **not** bring it up again!"

Those first few days in Long Beach are sketchy. On that 1957 Christmas Eve morning, our parents called us into the motel bedroom for a chat. As Sonny and I stood at the foot of their bed, Dad announced, "Mom and I've changed our last name. From this day forward, you may not ever talk about or refer to our real last name. Forget that name. Both of you will only answer to and use our new fake name in all circumstances. You won't have any contact with our relatives or past friends. Everyone you meet now will know us only by our new last name. Mom will register you at your new schools under your new identity."

Neither Sonny nor I cared about our last name. We never liked the sound of our real name but we did like the new fake last name. With the initial shock of the new fake last name, the obvious "elephant in the room" question we asked was: "Why are you changing our name?"

77

Mom said nothing, just stared ahead with no expression. Dad calmly explained, "We are running and hiding from the FBI and some other really bad people. We can't let anyone ever find us."

I started to ask "Why?...Who?" but Dad held his hand up which meant "do not talk," so I didn't.

He continued, "We changed our real name to become a different family. We must live undercover and undetectable. Our whereabouts has to stay unknown to everyone we ever knew before today."

Again, I opened my mouth with another question, but quickly closed it remembering Dad wasn't taking questions.

"You two must never talk about this with anyone, not even your grandparents or aunts and uncles."

My brain silently revolted, *What! We can't talk to Grandpa, Grandma, Aunt Lulu? How long? Forever?*

"Don't forget," Dad reinforced, "no one can know our little family secret or our whereabouts. If the FBI or others find us, I'll go to prison or worse things could happen to the four of us. Remember, we're all in this together. We are a family!"

Abruptly, this intimate little family chat was over. No questions allowed. Dad's "you're gonna love the big life" plan had gone to hell in a hand basket just like everything else in our universe. There was no more discussion, no loving sentiments, no "We love you kids, we are so sorry. Do you want to live at Aunt Lulu's or back with Uncle Gil and Aunt Sue?" Nope, just three cold words: "You are dismissed."

I so wanted to testily talk back in my nastiest voice, "By the way, dear Mommy and Daddy, thanks for the fun little merry Christmas Eve chat!" I may have only been eleven, but I knew when to fold.

Sonny and I stumbled into the motel unit's efficiency kitchen in complete silence. Stunned, I whispered to him, "Can you believe this? Who are they? What happened to them? Don't you want to scream, 'Why do you hate us so much? You don't love us or care anymore, so just let us go back to Aunt Sue and Uncle Gil or Aunt Lulu's?"

Sonny remained quiet while my head was exploding with a million I-need-to-know questions: *What kind of family are we? Running and hiding from the FBI and bad guys? Are they crazy? Are we now fugitives? Will our family's pictures be hung on the post office wall as most wanted criminals? Who are these parents? Where did our real parents go? These are not the parents I so loved last Christmas. What did they do? Why are Sonny and I being threatened? Are these the same bad guys in Chicago Mom thought would kidnap us? How can our parents put us in this danger? We're only kids—helpless, petrified, panicked kids with a new fake name, no home, and no escape.*

I felt numb. I wanted to run away and hide somewhere, anywhere. I needed to get away from them. My mind screamed at me, "*These new name parents are so mean and unfair. They are crazy strangers and we are their captives. They are so cruel, which proves they don't really love us anymore.*" The reality of this big, new, "shoot for the moon, you are gonna love it" life was beyond my capability to understand. I looked at Sonny, mouthing and gesturing, "What are we gonna do? Let's go somewhere we can talk and they can't hear us." He nodded and out we went feeling deeply hurt, confused, and hopeless. In that moment, our despair was overwhelming.

We left the room and sat by the dilapidated, deserted, motel pool. Our parents' total detachment regarding the impact on Sonny's and my life or our reaction to this news or even about our feelings was devastating to us. We agreed we didn't trust our own parents who had uprooted and placed us in this terrible situation. We realized we had no support in this whole wide world except each other. We pinky swore, "We'll always be here for each other, share all our feelings and worries, look out and stick up for each other no matter what. We are one; what is mine is yours and what is yours is mine." We extra-sealed the deal with a big hug. Sonny and I understood we were trapped with no way out, but at least we were trapped in this life together.

Later, still racked with fear, I was reminded by that gentle inner voice that spoke: "You are never alone. Do not fear, I am right here with you. Trust in me."

My world went blank shortly after the bombshell revelation of our new situation on that Christmas Eve in sunny Southern California.

Chapter 15
Long Beach, CA, Christmas Eve 1957

All I Want for Christmas

I n 2016, I found my old childhood memory box where, during my very early years, I had kept treasured personal memorabilia. This small taped together blue box has been moved at least twenty times and was stored on a top shelf in the back of a closet. Frankly, I had forgotten all about it. It was like opening a Pandora's box of my young childhood. My First Communion prayer book, complete with holy cards from 1954, and my Daily Missal, an Easter gift from 1956, in both cases pages all yellowed and fragile, a couple of grade school report cards, special notes—all hiding in this frayed, blue, ordinary box. As I examined my Daily Missal, a tiny folded-up piece of paper fell out. It was my Christmas prayer from that hopeless Christmas Eve in 1957. I had forgotten all about it!

Dear Jesus,

Merry Christmas Eve.

Tomorrow is your birthday. Happy Birthday.

On your birthday you always give me gifts.

This year I don't want those kinds of gifts that we usually find under the tree. I need something only you and your Father can give. The Sisters taught me that you can always see me, dear Jesus. I know you can hear me too, even if I only pray in my mind. I know because you love kids that you love Sonny and me even if we are not sure our real Mom and Dad do anymore. I know I can trust you. Baby Jesus, everything is so scary. Please help our family and especially Sonny and me not just for Christmas but for a little while longer. We don't know what's going to happen to us now that our Mom and Dad came back and took us away with them. We are both very worried. Please help keep us safe.

I love you and your Dad.

Thank you. Amen. Diana S.

P.S. I really do hope you have a Happy Birthday and Merry Christmas.

P.S.2. I'm so sorry we don't go to Mass or communion anymore.

I promise when Sonny is 16 and gets his driver's license we will come back.

Chapter 16
Long Beach, CA,
Christmas Day, 1957–January 2, 1958

Seven Tacos for a Dollar
ᴄ෮

O ur family skipped Christmas that year, and on Thursday, January 2, 1958, we moved into a rental house in Long Beach. The front and back yards were landscaped with a few green and brown weeds decorating the insect-infested dirt. The house came complete with creepy crawly creatures, smelly furniture, and pet-stained, worn carpet. I was sure it could win best of show for "worst house" ever. It featured three tiny bedrooms, one yucky bathroom, a teeny kitchen, plus a small living/dining room area. I seriously didn't know people could live in a place this vile.

Adding to the charm were a ton of fleas, cockroaches, a carpet that reeked like a cat's never cleaned litter box, and a moldy smelly bathroom with lots of black stuff around the tub, sink, and toilet. I was so freaked out about this whole house, that I decided to sleep on top of the disgusting bedspread, not in the bed. Each night, I covered the awful pillow with my sweater and placed a dingy bath towel over the bedspread. I only slept on my back, fully dressed in the clothes I wore to school. Each morning, I switched to cleaner clothes. The bathroom posed a different challenge for me, so I'll let you imagine, rather than me describe. Sonny hated the house as much as me and he had the added treat of sharing his room with a family of fleas.

I did learn a life-changing "ah-ha" lesson in humility due to my new circumstances. Previously, we only shopped at high-end stores. This new "big life" caused a major shift in our shopping habits. We now shopped in thrift shops or the dime store. I was nine when a less materially fortunate friend asked me to go shopping with her to buy a slip. I said sure and off we went. I expected to go to Bradley's upscale department store or the high-end children's specialty shop where my mother shopped for me. When we marched into Woolworth's and she purchased her slip, I felt that was a bit déclassé and shamefully thought I was a teeny bit better than her.

Now, was my new life ever an eye-opener! Suddenly I was ashamed that I ever assumed I was better than anyone else. I thought, *Look at me today! I live in a nightmare, running scared from the FBI and other bad people. I have strangers for parents that I don't trust and live in a filthy house with fleas and cockroaches. Even shopping at the dime store is a big treat!*

Often, our main food for the day was seven tacos for one dollar from a local roadside taco stand—two for my dad, three for Sonny, one for Mom, and one for me. Sometimes, the only other food we'd have for the day was a shared banana.

Lesson of the day: No one is any better than anyone else.

Chapter 17
Long Beach, CA, January–March 1958

Liar, Liar, Pants on Fire

I began my third new sixth grade class with my new fake name. When my mother registered me, my old real name was on my previous school records. She quite believably explained, "I recently remarried and moved here to California. My new husband wants to adopt Diana so he and I decided she should use his last name. After all, it will legally be hers in a couple of months."

I was thinking, *liar, liar, pants on fire*, and suspected Mom might go to hell for telling such a whopper lie. Really, Mom should have won an Academy Award; her performance was Oscar-worthy.

The school secretary sitting behind the desk agreed with her, stating, "I understand and it's no problem. It makes perfect sense."

I wanted to interrupt her and tell her the truth. I mostly wanted to run away to Aunt Sue or Aunt Lulu. A little part of me wondered if the lady thought my real dad died or if they got divorced.

By now I was a real pro at changing schools. I followed the secretary to my new classroom. This school was a little different from my other schools because it didn't have hallways. Here, you stepped outside to get to the next classroom.

My teacher, Miss Hatcher, looked young and cute and smiled at me a lot. I didn't think she was much older than the last babysitter I had. I liked her instantly. She introduced me to the class and asked me to tell everyone a little bit about myself. I plastered on my now-fake-but-it-looks-real smile, declaring, "I just moved here from Chicago but I came here when I was six and always wanted to come back." Most of this was true because I didn't want to add more lies to all the lies I had been telling. I mean, every time I said or wrote my new name, I was telling a lie. My whole reason for being in California was a lie, so I tried to keep this story truthful. Sure, I wanted to come to California, but only to go to Disneyland. I also wanted to meet Doreen and Annette from the Mickey Mouse Club, but I never wished to move here.

My classmates were nice and friendly, but the surprise air raid drills freaked me out. In the middle of geography, a siren blasted and everyone immediately ducked under their desk, covering their heads with their hands. I copied them until we heard the all-clear siren. When it was over, I learned that this was a practice test in case we were bombed. Attacked by bombs? I'd never heard about this before. Just one more reason I wished I was back in Chicago with Aunt Lulu.

Meanwhile, life at the disgusting house was pretty disgusting. Dad had a job teaching evening dance classes and during the day, he sold used cars. Mom and her old friends, bourbon and Salem cigarettes, were best friends again and that's about all of our "old Mom" that we recognized. Her loving, sweet, "I love you kids so much" self never resurfaced. She continued to be disconnected and detached as she looked right through us, probably imagining and hoping we weren't there. She clearly resented having to do much of anything for us. Most days, Mom shut us out, preferring to stay in her own dark little world behind her invisible wall. I felt bad for her, but I felt worse for us. I didn't want Sonny and me to be invisible.

Dad was working one Friday evening and Mom laid on the couch with her new brown bottle and smokes close at hand. Uncharacteristically friendly, she watched TV with Sonny and me. When the program ended, Sonny and I headed to bed. Mom, enjoying her "best friends", stayed up, preferring their company over ours.

Sometime around midnight, I felt Dad shaking me. He was pretty upset and told me, "Get up! I need your help, *now*!" I shot up off the bed and followed Dad into the scuzzy bathroom where I found Mom completely nude in a bathtub of water and vomit. She looked dead. Dad splashed cold water on her face and Mom's glazed-over, unfocused eyes fluttered open for a second, but she passed out again. Together, we struggled, lifting her slippery body out of the tub and carried her to the bed, dripping wet. I spread a blanket over her for warmth. Dad, extremely upset, left the room, murmuring he was going to clean up the couch and bathroom. I positioned myself between Mom and the side of the bed, watching her, wondering what triggered tonight's nightmare.

Without warning, Mom, in her drunken stupor, woke up and tried to climb off the bed, screaming, "I am getting the hell out of here" as she attempted to push me off the bed. I was having none of that, so I hopped on her, my arms pinning her shoulders down while I straddled her hips. No way was I going to let her up to run down the street, buck naked and drunk. As she was shrieking and thrashing, trying to kick me off her, she repeatedly slapped my face, hard, back and forth, with both hands. Despite the abuse, I refused to let her up, crying, "Mommy, you can slap me all night long, but I will not let you up, no matter what you do."

In that moment, with total clarity, I knew "Mommy" was truly gone from me forever. Our roles had reversed; I had become her keeper. Maybe Mom realized it too because she stared at me, looking defeated as she gave up her fight and passed out again.

I sat on the bed thinking about the mother I had lost until I was convinced she was asleep then went to find Dad. He'd just finished hosing off the couch cushions. I whispered goodnight and went back to my bed. Tomorrow would be a new day.

Climbing back on top of my towel-covered bed, I began to sob softly, hoping no one would hear. Begging for help, I silently prayed to Jesus: *Dear Jesus, I am an eleven-year-old girl, trying hard to get my real mother back so she'll choose Sonny and me over her bourbon and cigarettes. Tonight, something awful changed and I've lost her. Would you please help Sonny and me because I am scared stiff and don't know what to do. Please make sure my guardian angel stays right with me. I need her too.*

Chapter 18
Long Beach, CA, March 1958

Holy Cow! I Need a Plan

❧

I woke up around eight. The house was completely quiet. I slipped into the bathroom. It was spotless. Dad must have stayed up late cleaning. In the hall, I bumped into Sonny. He seemed oblivious to last night's drama. Changing out of my Friday clothes and into my Saturday clothes, I heard my parents talking in their bedroom. In this horrible tiny house, you pretty much heard everything. Maybe not exactly everything they were saying, but you certainly knew they were awake. This morning, there was no guessing what they were talking about. Their voices were loud and nasty.

Dad was yelling, "I'm sick and tired of dealing with your drinking. All you care about is getting drunk and you totally ignore the kids. You don't even cook for them anymore!"

Mom was crying and spitting out slurs. "You ruined my life. I hate you and anything connected with you. I drink because of you. I don't want to feel or care anymore, about anything. I just want to be numb. You ruined it, you deal with it, you fix it. The kids can take care of themselves. I'm done. I need to try to get through my own life because I'm trapped here with you."

And so it went on. I'd heard most of it before. Well, maybe not the part about being done with Sonny and me, but we kind of had figured that out on our own.

I grabbed the box of cereal from the kitchen counter and headed to the backyard. I didn't want to hear about or relive last night. I knew I would never forget it. Right now, I wanted to wipe everything out, except Sonny.

As I opened the door to the backyard, I saw Sonny already sitting on the broken-down dirty picnic table. A former tenant had left it behind. Wise choice, the table matched the house. With the half-empty Cheerio's box in hand, I went to sit and share the dry cereal with Sonny, wondering if he knew what had happened last night.

I found him hunched over, his face buried in his hands with tears dripping down his wrists. Obviously he was aware. Sonny—my rock, my protector, my best friend, the best brother anyone could have, who saved me when I was five from drowning in the country club pool—was crying. It hurt me to see my hero so sad and broken. I knew deep inside that now I had to be strong and the one to comfort him. Instinctively, I put my hand on his knee and snuggled up to him. Just having my leg, hip, and arm touching him gave me courage and strength. I was positive that together, we'd figure something out. Besides, God would take care of us; we only needed to trust in Him.

Perched outside on the hard picnic table all morning, we hardly spoke. The fighting and ugly name-calling became louder. Mom blamed Dad, "You caused all this; you ruined my life. I want out of here ...to hell with you and the kids."

The more Dad tried to quiet her the louder she ranted. I cringed. *Don't they realize we can hear everything? The neighbors probably can, too!*

Just when I thought life couldn't get worse, it did.

I turned to Sonny quietly, spilling all my fears. "Do you think Mom and Dad love us or want us anymore? I wonder if we're kind of like orphans. I mean, if kids live with their real parents but their parents ignore them, don't take care of them, and act like they don't love or want them, does that make the kids orphans? Mom and Dad don't show us love and act like we're a nuisance; maybe they both wish they didn't have us. I bet that's how orphans feel. I feel like that ... like an orphan. Do you?"

Sonny sat still as a statue. I figured he didn't hear me. Then slowly he turned, his eyes welled up with tears. He sadly whispered, "Yes, I do too."

An image of a cracked vase popped into my head. It reminded me of our family; we were like a cracked vase. If we collected all our broken pieces and glued them back together, our vase would remain fragile and weak. These cracks could never be concealed and our vase could shatter again at any moment. Now our cracks were out in the open, too many and too deep to hide or ignore any longer. For years, Sonny and I had been innocent bystanders as our home life cracked and fell apart. Sadly, we weren't the right glue to hold it together. Our family had been cracked, but now we were shattered.

The two of us sat close on the old, broken down picnic table waiting for the raging storm in the house to calm down, both of us silent, lost deep in the sea of our own thoughts.

I realized I'd never thought about what I wanted to be when I grew up. Maybe a nun who taught kindergarten or maybe not, because I also wanted to be a mom. Before we moved to Chicago, every day was a carefree, happy day. I knew my loving parents would always be there to guide and take care of me until I decided on my future.

Well, my circumstances had changed. Instinctively, I knew that whatever was to be, it was now up to me. Today, what I desired most was to get away from my parents and this bizarre, dangerous life they've created for Sonny and me. I understood I was stuck with them for a long time; I was only eleven and in sixth grade. So, what did I need to do to survive until I graduated high school and could be in control of my own life?

Deep in thought, I remembered my trip to Marquette University. I didn't remember why I visited, but I had loved it and came away determined to go to college. As this memory of the university flashed through my mind, I knew this was my means of survival and how I'd escape from Mom and Dad. All I had to do was come up with a way to get there. Even if things got worse, I'd keep my focus on college. It was my goal, my "get out of jail" card.

The picnic table was starting to hurt my bottom. Knowing I needed to stay away from the house, I hopped off the table for a stroll through the prickly weeds sticking out of the bug-infested yard. I asked myself, *"How can we survive and overcome the obvious problems? One: our crazy parents. Two: Not getting caught by the FBI or bad guys. The good news is, I'm not alone. I have Sonny, who I'm sure is right now working on his own plan. Plus, we both have Jesus and our guardian angels. Sonny still is luckier; he only has to live with them for three-and-a-half more years."*

Feeling desolate, I pressed myself to dig deep for an idea, hoping Jesus would jump in and help. I thought, *what about my love for reading and my passion to learn things? I truly want to go to college but know it cost lots of money. I remember Sister once told me about a poor, yet smart student. She went to college because she earned something called a "scholarship" and didn't have to pay for college herself. Huh, maybe that could be me. I get A's. Could I be smart enough to try for this scholarship thing too?*

I recognized, right then, I couldn't do much except work hard to get top grades. I promised myself I'd do my best in school and try to act like my life was the same as the other kids'. I realized this might not be the whole plan, but for that day, it gave me hope and was a start.

Feeling calmer now that I had my plan, I still jumped when I heard Dad beckoning us to come inside. I thought, *what now? Please, not another surprise. I never want any surprises from you ever again.*

Once inside, I noticed they were still in their pajamas and not looking good. My smarty pants side wanted to preach, "It's past noon; you should learn to sleep in your clothes like me, then you'd already be dressed for the day." Fortunately, my brain overruled my mouth.

We all gathered around the scratched, rickety table. Mom, now a shadow of her old self, stared blankly at the far wall. Her eyes were empty and she never looked at me. Dad, who spent little time at home, rarely spoke and always seemed angry, looked beaten up as he began our cheery little family meeting, "Kids, your mother and I have worked out our little disagreement. Everything is going to be just fine, so forget all about last night and this morning. Remember we are a family and we have to keep our old name, where we lived and anything else about our family or past a secret from new friends and everyone else. We also can't ever contact or tell Grandpa, Grandma, Aunt Lulu, or people we knew from before about our name change, where we now live or anything else about us. I've already explained what will happen if you don't obey me on this. Let's pretend none of this happened, so go now and do whatever you do on other Saturdays."

I was disgusted as I left our little meeting, thinking, *Here we go again. No explanations or apologies about our new horrible "big life" or last night, the absolute worst night of my life—way worse than all those dreaded nights sleeping on Grandma's couch in her scary dark living room.*

Back in my room, I relived the events of last night and today over again. Somehow, we were expected to erase everything that happened in our past, especially the last twenty-four hours, from our minds and act as if this dreadful life-changing event and Mom's hurtful words never occurred. We had been threatened and ordered to never bring it up, discuss it, or expect further explanations.

My eleven-year-old interpretation of Dad's command was: *"Only use your new fake last name, which means lying every day to everyone. Keep your mouths shut about our past. Watch out for FBI guys and the other bad people who are after us meanwhile, pretend we are the happiest family in the whole world."*

My heart heard, *"Take everything you love from your entire life, including family and friends, and forever lock them away in your mind's memory box of top-secret secrets. Throw away the key and don't ever open that box."*

My obstinate side reared up, questioning Dad's demands. *What were they going to do if I didn't obey all the rules? Cut my tongue out? Do their "now you see us, now you don't" routine? Been there, done that. Love the "don't see you" part. Hey, Uncle Gil and Aunt Sue, can we come back? Or how about, you're safe with your parents; oops, no you are not! Sonny and I are living that scary life every moment.*

Thinking these testy thoughts made me feel like I was fighting back, but it didn't change anything. This was my life and I had to live it. Today's event merely reinforced the dilemma I struggled with each day: our parents no longer love us, so why do we continue to love them?

Chapter 19
Long Beach, CA, March–June 1958

Mom Was a "No-Show"

❧

A week later, we moved out of the horrible house. They found a nicer one and we could stay at our same schools. One morning, I left the horrible house, and six-and-a-half hours later, I returned to a new house.

I liked it. It was clean and bug-free. My room had two twin beds and was pink. Sonny's room didn't have any fleas, so he was thrilled. The living room was bigger, plus it had a real kitchen where we all could eat. The yard had flowering trees and real grass. Hooray, I could practice my cartwheels again! However, the best thing about this house was the three classmates who lived right across the street. The only bad stuff was that Mom and Dad barely spoke and most of the time acted like Sonny and I were invisible or a nuisance.

Our perilous predicament forced us to keep the sickening secrets and continue telling the sinful lies. I had to choose between obeying God's commandment to obey my parents, even if it meant lying for them, or do I obey God's other commandment, "Thou shalt not lie"? I didn't want to lie, but I didn't want the bad guys to find Sonny and me either.

For a while, it seemed life improved. Dad quit his dance instructor job and only worked at the car dealership. He had to work some evenings there too. Mom certainly enjoyed her two friends, bourbon and Salem, each day, but not quite as often as before. In some ways, she seemed a little more like our old mom. There were nights when she made us dinner and the house was clean. My guess was she hated the other house too, but didn't want us to know.

My personal mission to be the best in my class was going well and I had lots of new friends. Miss Hatcher helped by often giving me extra credit work. I liked her a lot so asked Mom if Miss Hatcher could come to the house for lunch one day.

My old mom showed up and said, "Yes, I'll pick you two up, serve a nice chicken salad lunch, then return you both to school." It had been a long time since I was this excited. The day came and everything was all set. Mom promised she'd be waiting for us in front of school right when we got out for lunch. The bell rang and Miss Hatcher dismissed the class and followed me out to Mom's car. Unfortunately, Mom was running a little late but I was confident she'd be there any second. She'd promised me. We stood on the sidewalk waiting for quite a while, but Mom never showed up. I felt so embarrassed that I wanted to fall in a hole and die right then.

My sweet teacher told me, "Don't worry, your mom probably had a flat tire, so let's go find something to eat in the teachers' lounge."

Trembling on the inside, I somehow managed to hold myself together through the long afternoon. My mother didn't show up, but my good old stomach ache did. Mom never arrived to pick me up after school either. Magically, one of the girls who lived on my street saw me and said her mom could drop me off.

Surprise! Sonny's home. Mom's not. She was a no-show for dinner too. We called Dad at work; he had no idea she was AWOL all day. Dad raced home, bringing us tacos for dinner. Sonny and I did our homework, then hit our beds. Later I woke up to a huge argument between Mom and Dad. Of course, I knew what it is about: bourbon and something or someone else.

There was never an apology or explanation. Mom acted like she'd done nothing wrong. Crushed and hurt, I couldn't believe this strange Mom was so mean and uncaring. In my eleven-year-old heart, this was absolute proof that she didn't care about or love me anymore. Again, I thought, *if she doesn't love me, I don't want to love her, but why can't I stop?*

Mom was sometimes home after school and sometimes not. I never knew which. Each morning before I left for school, I asked, "Are you going to be home when I get home after school?" She outright refused to answer, always acting as if she never heard me. This put my stomach in knots all day because if she wasn't home after school, then she wasn't home for dinner, and that caused huge arguments with Dad when she finally showed up, drunk, hours later.

After too many Mom no-shows, I worked out the way to walk home by myself. It was a long walk, but better than always being the girl who waited in front of school for the mom who never came. After all, how many times could I make up another dumb excuse for my mom's failure to show? I was a little nervous, but I knew my protective guardian angel was beside me all the way home.

For the record, I did meet Isabelle, who shared Mom's same "interests" on those days when she wasn't at home. They would start drinking before lunch and continue through cocktail hour and dinner until the restaurant, lounge, or bar closed. Isabelle would finally drive Mom home long after Sonny and I were in bed. I hated her because Mom always chose Isabelle over Sonny and me. Isabelle must have treated, because Mom didn't have that kind of money.

Due to my disappointments and distrust of Mom, I promised myself that I'd never ask, count on, or depend on her for anything, ever. I also vowed when I grew up, I'd be the mom I wished I had. I would never, no matter what, be like my weird mom. My children would always know how much I loved and cherished them. We'd do all the kinds of fun things I wanted my mom to do with me. I'd always be there waiting for them after school. Every night at bedtime, I'd hug them, kiss them, and tell them how loved they were so they'd fall asleep feeling safe and secure. I'd never lie to them. They'd never feel invisible because I would always lovingly be there for them.

We stayed in this house almost until the end of the school year. Apparently the landlord's elderly ill mother lived up the street. The landlord had moved in with her to care for her. She rented her home to us until her mother passed away. The month before the school year ended, her mother died. Now the landlord wanted to move back into her own home, the one we were renting. A deal was struck and we swapped houses and moved up the street into her mother's house. It was okay, clean, but I liked the other house better. Here, I had the mother's old bedroom. That meant I slept in the mother's old bed, the one she died in a few days before. I was creeped out. I had nightmares about the mother's ghost being in the room and that same old dark presence visited me nightly.

A couple of weeks before the school year ended, unknown to our zoned-out Mom, Sonny was practicing pulling the car in and out of the garage. A nosey neighbor called the police. Knowing he was not yet sixteen, she reported that the car's tires were on the public sidewalk and Sonny was an underaged driver. The police came to our door. I thought my mother was going to faint when she saw who was knocking. She opened the door and explained that her almost-sixteen-year-old son had a learner's permit and was just practicing for his driver's test. She assured them he would not do it again.

One minor point I noticed: while Mom was speaking to the police, she lied. Sonny was fourteen-and-a-half and he did not have a learner's permit. However, I could have personally sworn that he was an excellent driver and had been driving for years.

Chapter 20
California to Illinois, Summer, 1958

Drive Fast, Run Out of Gas!
❧

Finally, the school year was over. Summer vacation began. This summer was different for Sonny and me. We packed up all our belongings and drove east, two-thirds of the way across the USA, sleeping in off-the-beaten-path, seedy motels. Sometimes, when Dad failed to find a motel rate cheap enough, we simply slept in the back seat of the car as Dad sped eighty miles an hour through the dark night down an endless two-lane ribbon of road. Dad called this family vacation our "shoot to the moon" summer adventure. It was a different kind of vacation from any others we'd taken before we started to live the "big life."

Dad stopped at some cool places like Las Vegas. Mostly though, we drove fast, only stopping for bathroom breaks when the car desperately needed gas and if the bathroom was in a gas station on our side of the road. A few times, the car suddenly started chugging, which meant we were running out of gas, even though Mom cautioned, "Honey, we need to fill up because the gas gauge is a hair from empty."

Dad was defensive and would answer, "I told you the gas gauge is off." We all knew he was being stubborn because he was determined to clock his daily six hundred mile driving goal within x number of hours. Therefore, we'd run out of gas and pull off the road. The three of us tried hard not to laugh out loud. We'd watch him get the gas can out of the trunk and hitchhike down the middle of nowhere highway toward the nearest gas station, often several miles ahead. This glitch in his schedule sometimes took almost two hours. I don't think he included his walking and hitchhiking miles in his daily time tally. Often, I wanted to ask him how his miles behind the dial time race was going when he returned with the gas, but even I wasn't that brave. It is a good thing we were blessed with strong bladders.

This adventure trip was educational. Along with geographical and historical sites, names of the states and their capitals, we learned unique vocabulary phrases from Dad. For instance: "put the pedal to the metal." The four letters on the "STOP" sign mean, "skid tires on pavement," or "do unto others before they do unto you." He consistently spewed lots of other gems. It appeared Dad's had one for every occasion.

The best thing about this adventure trip was that it seemed mostly worry-less and carefree. We knew no one could possibly find us because half the time, we weren't too sure where we were either. Briefly, it's a better time for Sonny and me. Our parents were a little more like they used to be. We laughed, joked, and talked without one word spoken about our recent circumstances or why we were traveling far off the major direct routes on the map. Mom was more her old self, bourbon safely packed in the trunk, out of sight and reach. We laughed while speed reading the Burma Shave signs whizzing by and played guessing games as we headed to nowhere in particular. It was like taking a cleansing breath and we forgot about our real-life circumstances, even if it was if only for a few days.

Our adventure road trip included picking up Grandma from her friend's house near Wickenburg, Arizona. Grandma suffered from bad rheumatoid arthritis and this year wintered in the warm dry Arizona climate with her best friend, Elda. We were bringing Grandma back to Chicago for the summer.

The trip across the desert was boiling hot. We drove with the two little front triangle side window vents open and the back windows cracked. If we left the windows all the way down, the wind and blowing sand got into our eyes. It was a beastly hot and long, boring, flat ride past the yuccas, Joshua trees, and barrel cacti. Grandma complained while profusely sweating in the backseat with Sonny and me. Several times she'd moan, "My arthritis is acting up; look how swollen my fingers are. There's no air and I can hardly breathe. *Por Dios*, my clothes are sticking to me and I am stuck to this seat."

Sonny and I were miserable as well, but we stayed quiet.

Then, it happens. Dad runs out of gas. Mom warned him, all of us heard her, but he ignored her. There we were, stranded in the middle of nowhere, sweltering in the extreme heat, at a dead stop on the side of the desert road, out of gas, with not even a road sign to tell us where the next town is.

Mom testily informs Dad, "I don't want you to start walking down this nowhere road because the sun and the heat are so intense and we can't tell from this map exactly where we are or how far the next town is. I'm not going to sit here stranded with you lying dead somewhere down the highway."

After enduring the front seat's less-than-pleasant confrontation, they decided the best plan is to put the hood up, keep all windows and doors open, then hope and pray for any car from either direction to come by, preferably soon. It didn't matter if the closest town was behind us if it meant we could fill up the gas can.

By now, Grandma wasn't only overheated, she was boiling-over mad at Dad and let him know it. The two of them went at it; the hotter we all got, the hotter their argument got. Both the temperature and they were insufferable. Finally, we spot a car. It looked like a shimmer on the far horizon. At least, we hoped it was a car and not a trick, like a mirage glimmering on the distant pavement.

Thankfully, it's a car and it stopped. Dad, along with his only friend of the moment, Mr. Gas Can, hopped in, heading back toward where we were a while ago. Grandma began praying we don't die before he returns. While Dad was gone, Mom and she made some "Dad's not going to be happy" decisions. When he finally returned with the gas, we silently drove to the next town. After finding a motel, we ate in the local diner, then raced to our air-conditioned rooms. Sonny and I shared Grandma's room, leaving our parents alone to have a private discussion.

Later in the evening, Mom and Dad knocked on the door. I noted a bit of tension as Mom explained the new plan. "Tomorrow, before dawn, we're gonna leave and drive in the cool of the morning to New

Mexico. Your father will stay there. Grandma, Sonny, Diana, and I will drive on to Chicago." No one gave us a clue why or where Dad was going and once again, the conversation concluded.

After kissing Dad goodbye, we learn we are spending the first few weeks at the lake with my grandparents and then at Aunt Lulu's. Toward the end of our time in Chicago, we'll stay a couple of nights with Mom's long-time best friend, Aunt Babs. There is no mention of when or where we will reconnect with Dad or what the plan is for us when our stay in Chicago ends. Mom reminds us that the rules stay the same: "Don't ever tell anyone we've changed our names, where we lived, or anything about our life. You kids may not reconnect with any of your old friends either. Do you understand?"

I'm thinking, *of course Sonny and I understand, but doesn't Grandma now know as well? I thought no one could know.* Anyway, I'm just happy that I don't have to use my lying fake name. Actually, except for with Sonny, I'm too embarrassed to ever talk about the FBI, bad guys, jail, Mom's strangeness, her drinking, or our parents' constant fighting. I know we are safe with our grandparents and Aunt Lulu. I've missed my little cousins and find myself excited when I see the sign indicating Chicago is fifty miles ahead.

Chapter 21
Chicago Area June–July 1958

How Stupid do You Think I Am?

ԑ৽

The carefree summer days with Grandpa, Grandma and Aunt Lulu fly by. Sonny and I feel protected, safe, and loved. My grandfather did a lot of remodeling on the lake cottage since last fall when we hid out here. Now they have a real stove and washing machine. Sonny and I have fun painting Grandpa's rowboat bright red and white. We can go by ourselves across the lake to swim and to play on the raft and lounge on the sand beach each afternoon. It's easy to find fun things to do here. Our much-adored grandfather has enclosed the front porch. On rainy afternoons, we play a marathon of Canasta card games with my grandmother. Sonny and I are pretty good Canasta players and soon catch on to Grandma's cheating so she can win. We pretend that we don't notice, but together laugh about it in bed at night. We love playing card games with her.

We also love roasting hotdogs and marshmallows on the fire pit that Grandpa built. When the sun fades into the shimmering lake, we run around, catching mason jars full of lightning bugs. Once breathing holes are poked through the jar's tin lids, we bring the captured lightning bugs in our room to be our nightlight. I never understood how they could "blink" their bodies on and off at night and why they were dead in the morning. It was like their batteries wore out.

A large bookcase had been added to the main room of the cottage. Grandma filled the shelves with her huge collection of *Reader's Digest* hardbound books. I remember thinking Grandma had so many of these books, she must have been collecting them since she was a child. I loved reading and passed many hours with my nose buried in between the pages of all these condensed novels. My wonderful grandpa quietly surprised me with a flashlight for my secret late-night reading under the covers. I've never figured out the mystery of how he knew, but his thoughtfulness I'll never forget. He was extremely courageous because he was taking his life in his hands going against Grandma's bedtime rules.

Meanwhile, Mom was kind of lost in her own world of booze and cigarettes. It was okay at my grandparents' because I felt safe and didn't think I needed to watch Mom so closely. She was with her own parents, so I assumed they took over watching their daughter when we were with them.

I also loved spending time at Aunt Lulu's house. I don't even remember what we did because the most important thing for me was that I was with my most favorite person in the whole wide world. I didn't worry about Mom there either; Aunt Lulu took such great care of everyone. She would sing funny songs with me, hug me, kiss me on my head, and make my life feel like fun.

I loved playing the older sister to my two cousins, Marie who was four, and two-year-old Kevin. Lucky for me, a new family had moved in next door to my aunt's house and had two daughters. I was right in the middle of both the girls' ages. Finally, I didn't have to tell any lies or make up cover stories about anything, because to them, we were just their next-door neighbor's niece and nephew visiting from some other state.

Late in the summer, we went to Mom's best friend's house. Sonny loved it because Aunt Babs had a son who was nine months younger than him. They had been friends their whole lives. While the two boys weren't mean, they were not interested in having a "little sister" tag along with them all the time. That left my mother stuck with me. She'd set me up with a book to read in another room while she visited with Aunt Babs. They talked loudly and I—absolutely cross my fingers hope to die if this is a lie—couldn't help but overhear every syllable of every word they uttered, even when they whispered. I accidentally learned some inappropriate juicy things that weren't found on the pages of my book.

All went well until the last night before we were leaving Chicago. It was a Saturday night. Sonny and Robby were going to some "boys only" thing and Mom, Aunt Babs, and Uncle Rob were going to a neighborhood friend's cocktail party. The plan was for me to go to the party with the three adults for a little while. At nine o'clock, Uncle Rob and I would pick up the boys, take the three of us back to their house, then Uncle Rob would return to the party. The whole plan went off without a hitch. Since Aunt Babs only had two bedrooms, my mom and I slept on the pull-out couch in the living room. Around four-thirty on Sunday morning, I woke up, then noticed my mom had not come to bed yet. I got up and checked the whole house, but she wasn't anywhere to be found. I went back to bed, wondering where she was and fell asleep. I awoke again around six-thirty and heard Mom and Aunt Babs whispering in the kitchen. Naturally, I got up to join them.

When I saw Mom, I noted she was in the same fancy party dress she had worn the previous night. I asked her, "Why are you still dressed for the party?"

Aunt Babs quickly jumped in, saying, "Your mom didn't want to wake you for early Mass with her, so she quietly put her same clothes back on and just now returned."

I thought, *oh my gosh, how stupid do you two think I am?* First, we hadn't been to Mass in way over a year, and, out of our whole family, she was the least likely candidate to return to church. Secondly, her party dress wasn't the kind of dress that you could wear to church. Something smelled rotten and not just the cigarette breath laced with bourbon emanating from my mother's mouth. Irritated, I retorted, "I don't think so." Turning on my heel, I proceeded to get dressed, then pack up my things, thankful we were leaving Chicago later that afternoon.

As usual, my automatic stomach sensor alerted me. *Danger! Danger!* Mom had gone off track again. Way off track. This summer of feeling protected, safe, and loved with a calm, happy stomach had now officially ended.

While I gathered my stuff together to pack in my bag, I couldn't help but overhear their conversation continuing in the next room, a mere four feet away. Jim, the man who lived right next door, was mentioned several times. Suddenly, I wanted to tune out everything they were talking about. Instinctively, I knew Mom had morphed back into the strange awful mom I didn't like. I had seen her flirting with Aunt Babs' next-door neighbor, Jim, last night. I thought she was being way too friendly. I'd grown up a lot in the past twelve months and knew enough to think there was more to this story and it was shameful. Hearing Aunt Babs and Mother talking about the fun party, how Mom left the party early with Jim, and now knowing what time she came home this morning confirmed all my thoughts.

Later, as I was putting my stuff in our car, the lady next door, who was Jim's wife, came out of her house. She stood in her yard, staring at me. I could tell she was quite upset; rivers of tears ran down her cheeks. We both stared at each other as if we were frozen in time. She called my mother an unspeakable name. Unfortunately, I knew what the word meant.

In all these years, I've never shared what I knew or the name that distraught woman called Mom, not even with Sonny. How could this nasty woman who tells these lies and hurts people be my real mom? My world stopped for a moment as I realized my precious old mom, the mom I had so adored a few years ago, would never have been guilty of such shameful actions. How had she turned into this selfish, uncaring, sinful woman? For the first time in my life, I felt ashamed to be her daughter and then ashamed of myself for feeling that way. How I could ever trust or respect this selfish, distant, awful person? I wondered, *how is it possible to miss and grieve for my mother, who is still alive and I live with every day?*

My happy summer vacation ended, leaving a painful lasting memory. I knew I would need a lot of help from above in my role as my mother's keeper.

Chapter 22
Redondo Beach, CA, Late July 1958

Busted! Mom's on Notice

❧

We left Chicago, arriving in St. Louis as the multicolored dusky sky faded into night. Sonny had sat in the shotgun seat while Mom drove. I was thrilled to have the backseat all to myself so I could rewind the events of this day in my head. Basically, no one said much during the whole ride.

We checked into the expensive Chase Park Plaza hotel. For some reason, Mom felt compelled to explain, "We are staying here because it's the safest place to stay since Dad isn't traveling with us." After checking in, Mom decided to take a bath then locked herself in the bathroom for most of the evening. The next morning, I noticed a letter on the hotel room dresser next to her purse. She'd addressed it to Jim, the man who lived next door to Aunt Babs, however, the actual street address she used was Aunt Babs'. I supposed Aunt Babs was going to secretly slip the letter to him. We checked out early that morning and I assume Mom mailed the letter in the lobby.

The rest of the trip was benign. In fact, I don't remember it at all. It was only the three of us and no one did much talking. We ended up in Redondo Beach, California a few days later. Dad was waiting for us in his cramped one-bedroom efficiency furnished apartment. Thrilled to see him, yet troubled what to do with the "Jim secret" I was harboring, I was unsure if I should tell Dad about last Saturday night's events or protect the deceitful woman who had taken over my mom.

I was encouraged by the voice inside me to keep quiet. The real story was not mine to tell. However, I desperately wanted Mom to know she was busted. I was not stupid and I did know what she had been up to.

The morning after we arrived, I climbed onto Mom and Dad's bed. Dad asked me how Chicago was. Smiling, I answered, "It was lots of fun at Grandpa and Grandma's and Aunt Lulu's." Suddenly, I couldn't stop myself from adding, " Mom has a boyfriend at Aunt Babs' house. His name is Warren."

I knew "Warren" wasn't Mom's last Saturday night's "date's" name; plus, Dad had once met Aunt Babs' other neighbor, the real big and pretty fat almost-bald Warren. I figured he would know Warren was not Mom's type and think I was merely teasing him. On the other hand, I wanted Mom to know she was busted. I was not stupid and I did know what she had been up to.

Dad simply laughed. "Really? Warren?"

Then I zipped up my mouth, locking my secret away, hoping that someday my real loving mom would return and I would forget last Saturday night had ever happened. Apparently those memories were harder to forget than I had thought.

Our stay in Redondo Beach lasted only a couple of days. It was time to move on again.

PART 3
San Diego 1958–1960
Catch Us If You Can

Chapter 23
San Diego to Chicago to St. Louis
to San Diego, August 1958

The Birds and the Bees in the Canyon
❧

W e headed south down the coast to San Diego. Dad had rented a brand new three-bedroom furnished duplex situated on the edge of a huge canyon in a new developing area. I sort of liked it. The uncomfortable, wannabe-modern furniture was cheap and sparse, but new and clean. I can't remember if there was even grass in the mini front yard, but there were a few other kids our age to explore the canyon with. When I think about it today, we should never have gone exploring through the deep canyon's brush and huge sharp rocks hiding all kinds of poisonous snakes, scorpions, tarantulas, and who knows what else ... including some strange people that were living right there in the canyon.

My new best friend, Sherry, had just turned eleven. She was almost a year younger than me. We became good friends and spent a lot of time in the canyon talking. Sherry may have been eleven months younger, but her voluptuous body looked three years older than mine. She was a hundred times worldlier, and shared, in explicit detail, everything she knew about boys and the birds and the bees. I was easily embarrassed by the sex talk and blushed a lot, but I certainly came away well-educated. I guess I would title the summer of 1958 as my summer of enlightenment. Some things I learned were good, some were bad, and some sad.

I was entering seventh grade, which in California meant junior high for grades seven, eight, and nine. This was a new concept for me since my other schools were always kindergarten through eighth grade. I knew in junior high, I would have to change classes, buildings, and have to take Physical Education. I was okay with the buildings and class changes. I was even okay with Physical Education class. What I was not at all okay with was learning about the mandatory girls-open-showering-together rule after every day's PE class. I didn't know any of these girls and being ordered to shower naked with them stressed me out every time I thought about the new school and new school year starting.

The first day of school, my parents took me to the junior high and Sonny to his new high school out in a southern suburb of San Diego. These weren't the San Diego city schools that we were currently zoned for, but my parents wanted to move out to that suburb, so they used the address of a friend from the car dealership Dad worked at for our school enrollment purposes. This way, Sonny and I wouldn't have to change schools when we moved there. I dreaded that first day of junior high. It hung over me like a black cloud. If I had my old mom, I would have confided my fears about it, but this new mom was detached and I was invisible to her so she never noticed how anxious I was.

They registered me and I got a card with my class schedule, buildings, and classroom numbers. The bell rang and I was off, with no idea where to go. No one knew I was brand new to the school because several elementary schools fed into the junior high. Since it was the first day of a new school for all seventh graders, the only kids anyone knew were the kids from their elementary school. Since they didn't know anyone else yet, they hung with the same kids they knew from before. Everyone else was a stranger to them. I was a stranger to everyone. I didn't make even one friend that day and assumed the next day would not be any better.

Back at the canyon duplex during dinner, Mom and Dad informed us they had found a nice house in Chula Vista. We could move in right away. Sonny would stay at his new high school and I would start at Chula Vista Junior High tomorrow morning. Chula Vista was a cute little town seven-and-a-half miles south of downtown San Diego and seven-and-a half miles from the Mexican border. It was also known as the lemon capital of the world.

I was excited to switch schools because I thought it couldn't be any worse than today, and maybe this school would be better. As it happened, I loved Chula Vista Junior High and the friendly kids immediately.

We moved into the new house. It had a quaint enclosed patio with a tiny yard in a nice, normal neighborhood. Life actually was okay. Mom cut way down on her bourbon and glimmers of our old loving mom would peak through. Dad worked at a car dealership and had a regular schedule. Sonny liked his high school, especially because of the ROTC program. Since living with Uncle Gil, Sonny wanted to become an Air Force pilot. Joining ROTC was a major part of his escape to college and freedom plan.

I made quite a few friends, loved my classes, and worked hard toward my goal of getting a scholarship to college. Mom even enrolled me in the community center's teen modeling and etiquette class. We started to feel like a normal family again. At least, as normal as a family with a fake name who is running and hiding from the FBI and assorted bad guys could be. In fact, Sonny and I went trick-or-treating and enjoyed a small, but traditional family Thanksgiving. This year, we had a Christmas tree, celebrated Christmas Eve, and went to Mass on Christmas Day. The end of 1958 looked brighter. I hoped and prayed 1959 would start and be more like life was in Wisconsin, but with a little less liquor and smokes.

The expression, "Don't get your hopes up" was perfect advice for my hope of a more normal life. Shortly after 1959 began, we moved again. This time, to a small, two-bedroom, nondescript, minimal apartment. It was in the same school district, so thankfully we didn't have to change schools. However, something was going on with the FBI or "bad guys" because we had to remain undercover. Around midnight every Sunday night, we would pile into the car and drive to a seedy downtown area. Dad would randomly choose a phone booth and make a call to someone back East. I think it was his attorney. Whoever he called would give him the latest news on the FBI hunt for us.

Diana -12, Sonny -15, Chula Vista 1958

Chapter 24
San Diego, CA, Late February 1958

Midnight at the Phone Booth

ℰℛ

I t was a Sunday at midnight late in February, during one of these late-night phone call capers, when Dad got the news that the FBI or bad guys were hot on our trail. Driving home, Mom and Dad were quiet except for an occasional whisper between them. Sonny and I were kept in the dark regarding the danger alert from the phone call.

Monday morning began as usual. Sonny and I left for school at the normal time. Around ten-thirty, during my English class, I was summoned to the administration office. Of course I thought, *What did I do to be in so much trouble to get called into the office? This has to be a mistake. I would never do anything to spoil my college chance for a scholarship.* Curious, but nervous, I hurried to find out what now awaited me.

As I entered the school office, the office lady looked up and asked, "Are you Diana?"

I replied with a nod.

She continued, "Your parents called and told me to get your school transfer papers in order. They'll be here shortly to pick you up. I need you to gather your PE belongings and clean out your hall locker then come back to this office. Be quick about it."

Stunned, I turned and walked out the door. The voice inside me screamed, *what now? Not again!* As I scurried around, gathering my things, I desperately tried to keep my emotions in check. I kept asking myself, *why do our parents continue to do awful things like this to Sonny and me? I don't know any other kid that has such crazy uncaring parents, so why do we? What exactly did we do to them to make them so mean? Why were Sonny and I born to them? Surely there were other loving people who wanted children that would have been happy to have us born to them instead. After all, we're pretty good kids.*

It struck me as funny how, on this day, my mom showed up right on time to whisk me away from this school and my friends. I must admit, she looked exhausted and scared to death. "I've been up since dawn packing up our things. As soon as we get back, Dad and Sonny will quickly put everything in the car. We have to hurry up and leave California by this afternoon."

I kept quiet while thinking, *Leaving beautiful, sunny, warm California near the end of February to go to wherever, which I am sure is someplace cold, is stupid. On the other hand, everything they have done in the last year and a half has seemed stupid to me.*

Sure enough, as soon as Mom parked the car in the apartment parking lot, Sonny and Dad appeared. It was then I noticed a car carrier attached to our car's roof and immediately they began loading our stuff into it. I didn't have any time to get the scoop on this surprise event from Sonny, but I could tell he was angry and smartly trying not to show it. Well, at least there was one thing to look forward to: Sonny giving me his theory on why we were on the run and how he felt looking down the track at high school number six within the past eighteen months.

All packed and loaded before one p.m., we were off and running. I mean literally running, racing down the highway toward the Arizona border as fast as we could. I didn't know where we were headed—I just knew it was East, where it was still winter and cold.

Later that night, at a sleazy motel somewhere in Arizona, Sonny and I had a chance to talk about today's shocker. I asked, "Do you have any idea what's going on? Did Dad say anything about what the guy on the phone last night said?"

Sonny shook his head, "No, I don't know anything. Dad just picked me up from school and said we were leaving today."

Okay, so he knew nothing more than me. His knowledge plus my knowledge equaled no knowledge. Once again, our parents offered no explanations for these radical actions. We were captives of their plight and two confused and scared passengers on their flight. In my esteemed twelve-year-old's assessment, I pictured Sonny and me as kidnapped innocent fugitives.

I am certain that because it was winter season at its best, we stayed on the main highway roads and took the most direct southern route to wherever my dad was taking us. Even on this southern route, we ran into some nasty snow crossing New Mexico and maybe in Texas, too. By the time we reached New Orleans, the weather was nice. With all those miles behind the dial and hours on the road, our parents remained silent about where we were going and what the plan was. I began to wonder if they even had a plan. I did know I was getting bored with this trip, feeling like a rubber mannequin molded into the back seat of the car. I almost asked the famous question, "When are we going to be there?" but I wisely chickened out. They weren't in the best of moods; in fact, they hardly talked. The old lesson learned of "speak only when spoken to" came to my mind. This was an excellent time to practice it.

After a flyby through Memphis, we landed in St. Louis. That evening, at a hamburger place, Dad made the announcement that he was leaving again. Mom would drive us on to Chicago in the morning. We were going to live with Aunt Lulu and Uncle Steve.

Upon hearing our fate, I was secretly elated. Going to live with Aunt Lulu and Uncle Steve was my dream come true. Then it hit me: Mom was going with us, which probably meant she was going to live with them, too. The horrible nightmare from the Saturday night last summer at Aunt Babs' came to mind. I felt like throwing up.

We only stayed one night in a cheap St. Louis motel. I hated the dirty, smelly cabin room so much that Sonny slept on his stomach and let me sleep on his back because I didn't want the bed to touch me. I'm sure he had a delightful night's sleep with my ninety pounds of dead weight on his back. He never complained or made me get off him.

The Big Life

We finally arrived in a northern Lake County suburb of Chicago in icy rain and fog. Perfect! The gloomy Chicago weather matched my mood. I always adored Aunt Lulu and had prayed that I could live with her ever since Sonny and I got on that plane to California. However, my dream was that Sonny and I could live with Aunt Lulu, Uncle Steve, and our little cousins like we had lived with Uncle Gil and Aunt Sue—meaning, without Mom and/or Dad. I justified my stance by thinking that they needed to finish their awful fugitive lives on their own. It was something they did that created this petrifying life, not Sonny or me.

I was stymied and pondered my own thoughts. *Why won't our parents just go away and leave us alone with our aunts and uncles? Mom and Dad aren't loving parents to us anymore. Ever since they decided to move back to Chicago eighteen months ago for the "shoot to the moon big life", neither of them bothers to pay any attention to how we feel, think, how we progress in school, or take any interest in getting to know who we are inside. When we're with them, the only thing they share with us is the actual physical space we live in. They hide in their own distant selfish world, leaving us to figure everything out by ourselves, whatever the circumstance or crisis requires. They may be there physically, but we both feel invisible and abandoned in every other way.*

Shortly before we arrived at Aunt Lulu's, I knew I had to settle myself down. I had to believe things would get better. All I needed was patience, hope, and to remember the tons of help from my guardian angel.

Chapter 25
Lake County, IL, March–June 1959

Thank You Mrs. T, Wherever You Are

Aunt Lulu and Uncle Steve were watching for us and when we pulled into their driveway, they all came out to hug and kiss us. It felt so good to feel Aunt Lulu's arms around me again. I loved her so much and I could feel her love envelop me. At this moment in time, all was well in my world again. I could be the true version of the twelve-year-old me.

Since we were going to be staying longer than a couple of weeks, Aunt Lulu had put a twin bed in Kevin's room for Sonny. Kevin would be turning three in a couple of weeks. I would share a double bed with my mother in Marie's room, which already had a twin bed. I wasn't keen on sleeping with my mom, so most of the time, Marie, who was only five, and I slept together in her twin. She seemed to like it as much as me. I liked to pretend that she was my own little sister. I truly loved her as one.

On Monday, Sonny and I started our sixth new school within an eighteen month period. He was a sophomore at the high school in the next town and I was a seventh grader at the local elementary school. It was only about a block and a half walk to my new school. This was great because I knew I would never have to worry about my mom not showing up after school and I got to walk to school with the two girls next door that I had become friends with last summer. On the not-so-good side, I was surprised that for the first time ever, I was behind in a key school subject, English. This was seriously of significant concern to me. I had my college scholarship goal fixed in my mind and this lack of English class knowledge could set me back.

One day as I labored over diagraming compound sentences, dangling participles, and future, past, and perfect tenses, my new English teacher, Mrs. T., asked me, "Diana, would you please stay after school for a few minutes?"

When the bell rang and the class cleared out, she closed the classroom door. I was curious but not alarmed. As Mrs. T. sat in the wooden desk across from mine, she asked me, "Would you like some help with these assignments? I noticed that you are fine in all your other subjects but are troubled with the English homework."

I explained, "I never learned any of this and I am having trouble. I need to get a scholarship to college so I must do well and get the best grades now and all the way through high school. I am worried that I won't master this subject enough to get an A."

This sweet teacher, who didn't look sweet at all, offered a solution. "Diana, if you could come in thirty minutes early each morning, I'll come in early too and help you so you will understand it and get your A."

"Of course I will. In fact, I'll come in sixty minutes early if you want me to," I quickly answered.

Mrs. T. smiled. "Thank you, but thirty minutes will be just fine."

I was so appreciative of her help that I wanted to hug her. I didn't because she didn't strike me as the hugging type, so I thanked her and told her I would work hard for her. I ended the year with my coveted "A". That proves how a good teacher can make a huge difference in a child's life. Why else would I remember her name?

Chapter 26
Aunt Lulu's House, Lake County, IL, March–June 1959

Everyone Should Have an Aunt Lulu

❧

Home life was crowded and wonderful. It felt like I belonged to a big loving family. Marie and Kevin were always cracking me up and of course, there was Aunt Lulu at home to greet me after school with a hug and a kiss, asking about my day. I felt so safe and loved. I no longer spent every few minutes in school hoping Mom wasn't drinking or worrying that I may have accidentally slipped and said something that would bring the FBI or bad guys running to our door. At night, when I went to sleep in Marie's bed, I wasn't awakened by crying and fighting. Best of all, it was fun to see Sonny more like his old self. He even playfully teased me again. Just like he used to when I was five and he would tell me I was adopted. I would defiantly tell him no, I wasn't, and he would cunningly ask why I was the only one in the entire family with straight blonde hair. I would well up with tears and he would laugh and say he was only teasing. I thought I hated him then, but I so dearly loved him now. Sonny and I were wrapped in a warm, snug, safe time—at least, for a little awhile.

Living with my aunt taught me so much. I learned that I loved to sew. It began with the fact I had outgrown all my old winter clothes that Mom had saved when we moved out of the "you're gonna love the big life" house. Then, because I wanted my first straight skirt like the teenagers wore on TV, Aunt Lulu took me to the fabric store to buy the skirt pattern and material. I was so excited. On Saturday, she taught me how to lay out the material and then cut the pattern out. I diligently watched her every move each step of the way. She even let me sit at her sewing machine and sew one side. I loved the idea that you could make anything you wanted out of a fabric you got to choose. She took so much time with me even though I know she had at least a thousand important other things to do. My love of sewing was born and has continued throughout my life.

Aunt Lulu never acted like I was in her way or being a bother. This sweet Aunt took me to get my dress for the end of year seventh/eighth grade school dance. Frankly, I didn't quite know what a seventh/eighth grade dance was. I went because I thought we had to. Fortunately, Aunt Lulu knew because she fixed my hair, took my picture in my new pink dress, and when I arrived at the dance and saw all the other girls, I felt I had the prettiest dress there. It had been a long time since I'd had anything new or felt even a little bit special.

The teachers gave each girl a decorated card attached to a ribbon that tied around the girl's wrist. They called it a "dance card." Whenever a boy asked you to dance, he had to sign his name on your dance card. Again, this was unfamiliar territory for me, but it was my new adventure so I was going to enjoy it. And boy, did I ever. The dance ended before I hardly knew it had begun. I glanced over at the side of the gym and there was Aunt Lulu, watching me and smiling. I remember wishing with my whole heart that she was my mother; I loved her so much. We walked to the car and she headed in the opposite direction of home. I was puzzled, "Where are we going?"

She smiled her amazing, sweet, infectious smile. "We're celebrating! Let's go get an ice cream sundae at the drug store soda fountain. You can fill me in on all the juicy details of tonight. From what I saw you looked like you were having a ball."

As I twirled left and right on the soda fountain counter's stool, savoring every bite of my hot fudge sundae, I dished out every minute detail of my evening. Showing her my dance card, I gleefully pointed out, "Look Aunt Lulu, every line is filled in with a boy's name. That means that I danced with all these guys. I'm so surprised. I never thought about any boy asking me to dance. It was so fun and I got lots of compliments on my dress. Thank you so much. I think it was the prettiest dress at the dance."

I went on and on about what other girls wore. I even spilled the name of the boy I maybe had a crush on. Aunt Lulu and I sat there talking and laughing well after our ice cream dishes were empty. Her kindness, love, and caring at a time I so desperately needed some, brings tears of gratitude to my eyes even as I write this all these years later. Sadly, I can't remember anything about my mother that night, but when we arrived home, Sonny teased me about dancing with all the boys. It was like the old good times and I loved it.

In no time at all, June arrived, signaling the end of school. I was proud that I managed to continue with my string of straight-A report cards due to the hard work of one devoted English teacher.

In 1968, I learned from Aunt Lulu that during those months we lived with her had been frightening. The FBI would come to her house when we were at school and question both Aunt Lulu and Mom as to Dad's whereabouts. Aunt Lulu said their phone line was tapped and at times, she was certain the FBI was following her by car. Apparently they were only interested in Dad. Mom continued telling them she had no idea where he was. As ominous as that sounds, I was glad it was the FBI and not the bad guys finding us. I guess these FBI agents were finally convinced Aunt Lulu and Mom didn't know anything, because the day after school ended, we left Aunt Lulu's. As before, Sonny and I didn't have a clue where we were going. I'm sure that's so we couldn't accidentally tell Aunt Lulu. Therefore, if the FBI visited her again, she honestly wouldn't know where we were. Leaving Aunt Lulu that day was one of my most painful memories of that time in my life. The saving grace was that I knew I would see her again, someday.

With school number eight left behind, it was "hello" to my next new school, number nine, come September. This would be Sonny's twelfth new school, in case anyone's counting. Once again, the sixty-four-thousand-dollar question: where in the world are our new schools going to be and when will this craziness end?

Chapter 27
St. Louis, MO, June 1959–December 1959

And the Definition of Insanity Is?

❦

"On the Road Again" by Willie Nelson should have been our theme song. The reality was, every three months or so, we were uprooted and off again, destination unknown to Sonny and me. This one turned out to be St. Louis. Not just to pick up Dad, but to live there. The pattern was the same: rent a house, Dad got a job, enroll in a new school, make some new friends, and then suddenly overnight we were on the road again to an unknown destination, starting over once more.

So, while everything was ever-changing on one hand, nothing was changing on the other.

Mom's best friends continued to be bourbon and Salem cigarettes. When we were living with Dad, running and hiding out from the FBI or whoever else the bad guys were, Mom and Dad either fought a lot or were lovey-dovey to each other. We never went to church. When we weren't physically living with our grandparents or Aunt Lulu, we could have no contact with them and they couldn't know where we were. Our future was ever fearful and unknown.

Driving to St. Louis, it dawned on me that regardless of how many middle-of-the-night moves we did or where we ran to, our circumstances always remained the same. Isn't the definition of insanity doing the same things repeatedly, yet expecting a different result? Had our parents thought that through? Or maybe, they simply were bona fide crazy.

Meanwhile, Sonny and I were clearly left to our own devices, doing our doggone best to cope and fly under the radar screen. I always found comfort in knowing that we had each other's back and that we, together, were on alert for Mom and Dad's next unwanted surprise.

We met up with Dad at our new St. Louis house in a suburban neighborhood. The house, set up on a hill, was an older, smaller two-bedroom bungalow but had a cool breezeway and a nice unfinished basement. My poor brother had to sleep on the couch in the front room. I got the teeny second bedroom with one twin bed and we all shared the single small bathroom. Dad told us that we would live here and not just be passing through.

Sonny and I spent the entire summer never seeing anyone our own age in the whole neighborhood. We did see a lot of old people, though. Bored out of our minds, we entertained ourselves watching TV game shows, Bonanza, and our personal favorite, Dick Clark's *American Bandstand.* Sonny and I would practice the show's latest and greatest dance moves together. We'd laugh a lot at our crazy antics and it took our minds off the insanity of the life we were living. I thought more than once, if only we had moved to Philly, Sonny and I could have tried out for the TV teen dance show!

Since I loved chocolate so much, I learned to make brownies from a box, Betty Crocker's devil's food chocolate cake with chocolate frosting, and chocolate pudding cream pie. Sonny was my biggest supporter and told me he was eating these treats to prove how good a baker I was. True or not, I loved the compliments. However, the absolute most exciting event of the year was Sonny being old enough to get his driving learner's permit. He turned sixteen in late August and passed the driving test on his first try. Remember, he was already a great driver back in the good old days when he was twelve, but now he could, officially and legally, drive me around!

September arrived and we were off to new schools. Junior high, eighth grade for me and a junior in high school for Sonny. Dad worked as the manager of a car dealership's used car lot and had gotten a much-used car for Sonny to drive. Since my junior high was across the street from his high school, Sonny would drive us both to and from school every day.

This junior high was a lot more rigid than the one in California. Furthermore, they placed me in all the honors classes taught by a no-nonsense faculty. One more time: thank you Mrs. T. for the early morning English tutoring.

I immediately made friends, enjoyed the academic challenge, and settled in to the eighth-grade routine. School was great, except for one teacher, Mrs. P., who for some unknown reason absolutely loathed me. Her science class was scheduled right after lunch, prompting my old anxiety-caused stomachaches to return. As soon as class began, she would belittle me and point out every mistake I made. Oftentimes, she credited me for mistakes I didn't make. If I went to talk to her about the issue after class, she would tell me to get out of her classroom. Naturally, I never mentioned any of this to my parents.

At the end of each quarter, a blank report card was given out to every student in morning homeroom. We each would hand our card to the teacher at the beginning of their class. They would mark them and return them to us in the last minutes before class ended. I was proud that I was ringing up all A's for subjects and all A's in character. That is, until I reached Mrs. P's science class. She returned my report card with a D for science and an F in character. I was shocked; I always had received A's and I always had teachers give me the highest grade in character. Most of the time, the teacher would write a complimentary note about me as well. I didn't share this awful grade with anyone as I proceeded to my next class, where the history teacher was also my homeroom teacher. He collected everyone's report cards while we started on our homework assignment. About halfway through the class, he asked me to join him out in the hall.

In the hall, he explained, "Diana, I think there is a problem with a grade on your report card. I'm certain Mrs. P. made a mistake on your science class grades. I urge you to have your parents investigate this. You are a straight-A student in all your other classes and it is unlikely for a student like you to receive this low grade in any class. You are a pleasure to teach and you are well liked by your fellow students and all the teachers. Please have your parents look into this."

Embarrassed, I thanked him and decided to think about telling my parents. I didn't mention this to Sonny on the way home.

Once home, I went in my room to look again at my report card. I was proud of it, except for the mean and grossly unfair science teacher. I had made all A's with one B+ on her science tests and turned in every homework assignment promptly. Because I disliked and was afraid of this teacher, I only spoke in class when she called on me. Now this mean woman threatened my ultimate college scholarship goal. I also realized one parent would have to sign off on the report card before I could return it to my homeroom teacher. My intuition told me to have Dad look at it, then sign it.

Right after dinner, I approached my dad with my report card in hand for him to sign. I didn't say anything about the grades or science teacher. As he looked at it, I saw his jaw tighten. I knew this was not a good sign. Was he mad at me or maybe mean old Mrs. P.? Surprising me, Dad pulled me close and hugged me while praising my all-A's report card, then he asked me to tell him about my science class and the teacher. That's all it took for me to have a major meltdown, complete with hiccups, while spilling all the beans about my science class experience. And that's all it took for Dad to tell me not to worry. He, himself, would take me to school in the morning and have a discussion with the principal and Mrs. P. I was not to worry anymore about her or my science grades.

Sleep came and went that night. I was nervous but grateful that Dad was coming with me in the morning. I left Dad at the school office and walked to my homeroom. I informed my nice homeroom teacher of my current situation as I handed him my signed report card. He told me he was glad my father had come in.

Lunchtime rolled around and my stomach started to hurt again. I was going to have to face Mrs. P. in science class. When I entered the classroom, I thought Mrs. P. looked upset. She didn't look at me, speak to me, or call on me during the whole class. I was relieved when the end-of-class bell rang and I headed to my next class, history. My nice history/homeroom teacher informed me that my science class grade had been changed. It was now recorded as an A for subject with a C for character. I still despised her, and she did her best to ignore me for the rest of the semester. I don't know what my dad said or did at school that day, but it was a win for me. My ultimate college scholarship goal remained intact.

Meanwhile, back at the bungalow on the hill, the saga continued. Three noteworthy events: one small, one good, and one life-changing were in the works.

The small event was my thirteenth birthday. My parents had forgotten my last two birthdays, but recently recalled I was soon turning thirteen and somehow this was a milestone birthday. They offered to let me have a boy/girl party in the basement as their present to me. I loved the idea and invited most of my classmates. We celebrated with pizza and birthday cake at my *American Bandstand* themed party. It was a great night; my parents acted normal and didn't embarrass me even once. Of course, my best friend Sonny was there. He didn't act at all like a big high school snob and danced with me a lot. Our *American Bandstand* dance practices paid off. I thought we were the best dancers at the party. Everyone had so much fun that night. It felt like our family was a normal family like everyone else.

The good event started a couple of weeks prior to my birthday. I didn't notice the change right away. It began with Mom drinking a little less and being more engaged with Sonny and me. Dad and Mom seemed to be getting along better. There hadn't been any big arguments and they were nicer to each other, sort of like a polite dance, sometimes even lovey-dovey. Whatever truce they had made, our life was a little better.

The third, but huge event came a couple of days after the party. Mom asked Sonny and me to sit down at the dining room table. She had something she needed to discuss. Both Sonny and I were holding our breath. In the past, these types of surprise conversations hadn't gone well for us. I could tell Mom was nervous as she sat across the table.

Finally, she asked the question, "How would you feel if we had a new baby in the house?"

As I looked at Sonny to see if I could read his expression, I wondered if she meant adopting a baby or we were going to babysit someone else's baby, or if this meant she's pregnant and she is having a baby. Okay, now I knew why they were holding hands and kissing again. Despite all the chaotic thoughts and unasked questions running through my head, bottom line, I loved babies. I had wanted and prayed for a little brother or sister when I was younger.

I guess Sonny felt the same way because we both smiled at Mom as we excitedly responded, "Really? Yes!"

We accompanied her to her first doctor's appointment, sitting anxiously in the waiting room, hoping for a positive confirmation. She came out with a smile. We were having a baby in late June!

Chapter 28
St. Louis to California, December 1959

Sick of Route 66

And then guess what happened? We moved. Back to California. As soon as Christmas vacation started, we packed up and were on the road again. The major difference this time was that we took two cars. Mom and Dad drove our family car while Sonny and I drove a car that Dad wanted to sell in California. He claimed he could get a much higher price out West. Sonny and I followed their car down the never-ending highway, Route 66, right through Christmas Eve and Christmas Day. Dad said we would celebrate Christmas on New Year's. He was back on a mission to quickly put as many miles as possible between St. Louis and us for a new trip time record. However, we did have to take a few extra bathroom breaks because of Mom's new condition.

Finally leaving Route 66 for a more southern route, Dad experienced another road trip interruption that impeded him from achieving his record-breaking St. Louis-to-San Diego time goal. This occurred early one cold and rainy Sunday morning in Yuma, Arizona. As usual, Mom and Dad were in the car in front of us with Sonny and me following close behind. Dad was driving faster than the speed limit through the Yuma city streets. A stoplight was already yellow as my dad made a quick left turn without any blinker or warning. Poor Sonny had no directions about the route and had followed right behind Dad throughout the trip. If we lost sight of them, we were truly lost. We had no money for gas or even a map. When Dad pulled over, we pulled over. When Dad's car needed gas, we filled up. So when Dad turned left, Sonny immediately followed, turning left. The difference was the yellow light had now become a red light and Dad hadn't had a garbage truck charging at him as he made the turn. We did.

Bam! The garbage truck hit our car, full force, right behind the front passenger door post.

There were no seatbelts in 1959. Since I was seated in the front passenger seat, I flew up and hit my head on the roof and crashed into Sonny, crushing him into his door. The car teetered on the two driver's side wheels, threatening to turn over. According to the police, if the truck had hit us two inches forward it would have killed me and probably Sonny too. Miraculously, Sonny and I were left a little stunned, but totally unhurt. The car was one-hundred percent drivable, however, a lot of body work was needed once we arrived in California. Our parents appeared shaken, but as soon as the police report was written and Sonny was handed his first ticket, Mom and Dad returned to their car and told us to follow. We climbed back into our now-crunched-up car and were back on the road with no map, directions, or money. Dad didn't want to lose any more time and we didn't want to lose sight of them.

Aside from my slight headache, my head was bothered by a few questions as we sped down the highway toward the Arizona/California border. Why, during this whole cross-country trip, were both my parents driving in one car while Sonny—who had just gotten his driver's license a little over three months ago—and I driving in another car? Why didn't Mom or Dad drive the second car or let Sonny drive the car having a parent in the passenger seat? Why didn't Dad stop at the yellow light and wait until it was safe for both our cars to turn left? Was Dad's trip time record more important than Sonny's and my safety?

Mom and Dad didn't care or bother to ask us if we wanted to take a moment to settle our insides down after the crash. We were told to hurry up and get going. I honestly thought their lack of concern for us hurt me more than my headache or stomach.

Why did Sonny have to get the ticket? I thought Dad should have gotten the ticket. I mean, I know Sonny was the person driving, but Sonny had been instructed to keep up, follow Dad, and not to lose sight of them, under any circumstance. This was awfully unfair to Sonny; he didn't deserve the ticket or the blame.

I wondered if the FBI would now be able to track us and find us. The police did have our information. They could alert the FBI. Maybe that's why Dad was in such a rush for us to leave Yuma.

The main issue that continued to confuse and nag at me was about our parents. It was a question from my heart. How or when had our parents become so irresponsible and selfish? Had they always been this way? Am I just now old enough to notice? I asked myself, *had they been lying to us all these years, maybe never wanting to be our parents?* The beautiful, caring, loving parents I had always thought they were now seemed to be like my old imaginary friend, Meeka ...just something my imagination made up, was never real, and then—*poof*—disappeared.

All these questions and doubts made my headache worse and my heart heavy. The one thing that did comfort me was my unwavering belief that God had saved Sonny and me in the car crash this day. I knew He had a plan for each of us, so I guessed that we hadn't finished His plans for us yet. My mind must have rested the next 175 miles because I remember nothing else until we arrived in San Diego.

Chapter 29
Chula Vista, CA,
Late December 1959–August 1960

Lovin' Livin' in Chula Vista

❧

S an Diego is such a beautiful city. The air is the perfect blend of sweet fragrant flowers and salty ocean air breezes. Just one deep breath of her oxygen offered me a small sense of peace. My spirits were uplifted and my heart felt a little lighter.

Our parents found a cool duplex complex in the same area that Mom and Dad had wanted to live in before. It was brand new, complete with a big swimming pool. I liked our apartment location because the back of the kitchen eating area had a large sliding glass door right out to the pool. We had a little patio with a couple of stepping stones through the grass onto the pool deck. I almost felt like it was our own private swimming pool. Sonny and I swam every day, even if it was a little chilly. This was our little taste of heaven, treating us to rare moments of freedom from our anything-but-normal life. Even swimming in cooler temperatures was way better than being trapped inside with Mom and her new friend, wine, and old friend, Salems. Her demons were taking charge again. Sonny and I shared a room with twin beds and my parents had the other bedroom. I loved sharing a room with him. We would talk about everything from current music hits, movies, school, friends—anything—but not much about our circumstances that we knew were unable to do anything about yet or how it all affected us. It wasn't like we were mad or hated our parents for this bizarre unsettled life, but we both were bewildered and disappointed in their poor choices. Consequently, Sonny and I each had our own "escape plan and college goal" that we worked hard to achieve. We kept these plans a secret, just between the two of us.

We ended up never having our Christmas celebration and moved right on through New Year's. We started school on the first day after the Christmas break. New year, new schools again—well, not exactly new schools. We reenrolled in our previous Chula Vista schools. It felt rather weird that they moved us to National City, but put us in Chula Vista schools. When I questioned them about this, they responded that Sonny and I had both loved the Chula Vista schools so they wanted to let us return to them. I was happy that they cared about what made us happy, but forgot to ask them what Chula Vista address they gave the schools. Of course, returning to the same school with past friends would be great. But it was the adding of more lies to the long list of lies that we were forced to live and tell since we began "living the big life" that became increasingly disturbing to me. As my list of lies kept growing, so did my concerns about my inner conscience. School was a bit surreal. On one hand, everything was familiar, yet on the other hand, everything was different. Some of my old friends were surprised to see me and curious why I had just disappeared one morning without a word. They asked a ton of questions regarding why I left, where I went, and if I would disappear again. Boy, these challenging questions were tough to answer. I hadn't prepared my story and I knew I could never tell them the truth that my parents had the FBI and some nasty people after them. Yes, I might disappear again.

So, I kind of, sort of lied by telling them a family emergency came up and we had to immediately go back East. Things were better now, so we were able to return. Basically, there was some truth in the statement, so I decided to give myself some wiggle room on my made-up, teeny tiny lie to whopping big lie scale, allowing this lie to weigh in a little heavier than a tiny white lie. However, my early Catholic school years taught me that a lie was a lie, regardless of its size. They're all counted the same on God's personal list of the lies you have told.

Everything was going along well until I was, once again, pulled out of class and told to report to the front office. *This must be a sick joke.* I had this same thing happen to me last year in seventh grade—same school, even the same month.

Trembling inside, I gathered my books and headed to the office, dreading what bad news or who might be waiting for me. This time, it was the principal who greeted me "You, young lady, are being expelled because you do not live within the school district boundaries for Chula Vista Junior High. You should be attending National City Junior High. I have spoken with the NCJH principal and he is expecting you tomorrow morning. Your parents will be picking you up momentarily."

My heart sank and my stomach lurched into my throat. This could not be happening to me *again*. Plus, I had hated National City Junior High the one day I went there last year. I was so distraught, even the fragrant San Diego air couldn't lift my spirits.

Right on time, Mom and Dad whipped into the parking lot and I climbed in the backseat. I didn't want to look at or talk to them. I had asked about this very subject when they reenrolled me and had been brushed aside with a "don't worry about it." *Well, I'm still worried about it and now I'm paying the price of you two not worrying!* Also, where was Sonny? He was at Chula Vista High School, which wasn't the correct school district either.

Amid my misery, Dad assured me, "Diana, quit worrying. I've fixed the problem right before we picked you up. This happened because the old bat in the duplex across the pool from us works in the National City Junior High School office. She saw there was no record of you attending. She was curious when she heard you talking about Chula Vista Junior High with Sonny at the pool."

I would call her a nosey busybody, I thought. *Make that a nosey busy body with huge nosey ears, who should mind her own business.*

He continued, "Apparently she felt it was her duty to inform Chula Vista Junior High of your illegal enrollment, so she made the call to the principal. The problem is no longer a problem. I called our duplex management company and found out they have an identical duplex community right here in Chula Vista. A furnished unit exactly like the one we now live in became available this morning. We can have it right now and it will be an even exchange with the National City duplex. Mom and I have just come from the new duplex office and completed all the paperwork. We'll swap out duplexes over the weekend. We are moving there in two days."

Since he had the newly signed Chula Vista lease in hand, Dad got out of the car and went straight into the office, settling the out-of-district problem before any paperwork was completed. I was to return to Chula Vista Junior High in the morning as if none of this ever happened. Fortunately, Chula Vista High School never found out about the wrong school district issue and Sonny was left out of this whole debacle. A huge surprise for me was that my best friend from school, Valerie, lived a couple of blocks up the street. Her house was on the way to school. I would meet her at her house in the morning and we would also walk home together. It was great. It felt normal. We spent time with each other after school doing homework, looking at movie magazines, and mostly talking. Sometimes we even talked about cute boys.

Valerie took modern dance lessons at a dance studio on Third Avenue. She went on Tuesday evenings after dinner. I was always invited to go with her each week. I would sit on the big window seat of the studio and watch her dance class. I loved going to watch her, then going home and try to remember all the routine's steps. This dance routine was to a popular 1960 Peter Gunn movie song and somehow we owned the same record album so I could practice the routine with the actual music. This went on for weeks.

Then, one evening, the dance teacher asked me, "Diana, would you like to join our class?"

I was thrilled at the offer but quietly whispered, "Thank you so much. I would love to, but I don't have the two dollars to pay you."

She sweetly smiled, "It's okay. If you would like to try dancing with the girls tonight, I am not going to charge you."

I was so excited and jumped in the back row in my normal clothes and bare feet. Of course, the other girls had special shoes and leotards, but I didn't care. I was going to participate and get to dance the routine tonight. I was confident about my dancing abilities. After all, remember, I was the grandniece of a famous Vaudeville 1920's Follies dancer and I had taken six years of ballet and tap until we moved to the "you're gonna love it" house in Chicago. I was ready and this was my big moment.

I would love to tell you that I was fantastic, the absolute best in the class. How the teacher raved about my talent and because I was so gifted, I could dance every week for free. Except that would be telling you a lie. A teeny, tiny bit short of the big whopper lie. A lie that rated at least a nine-and-one-half out of ten on the whopper lie scale.

The truth was, I was so nervous that I had two disobedient feet. My memory of the dance steps cha cha'd right out of my head. I destroyed the rhythm of the dance routine. The nice dance instructor patted my arm while telling me that I had done well, but in my heart of hearts, I knew I had been awful. She was a lovely person who didn't want me to feel bad. Despite my dancing disaster, I still loved going with Valerie each week and hoped that maybe next year I could ask for dance lessons for my combined birthday and Christmas gift.

Mom was getting pregnant looking and didn't always feel great. By the end of every evening, she would perk up after having had considerable time with her wine and Salems. She and Dad got along well most of the time. Meanwhile, Sonny and I tried to stay out of their way. During the week, we would spend most of time at the pool, but on the weekends, Sonny would drive the two of us and sometimes a couple of friends to nearby Imperial Beach where we would play on the sand, swim in the Pacific, and do a little homework while we caught some warm California rays. It was the perfect way for the two of us to spend two or three hours on a weekend afternoon away from our parents. I think Mom and Dad welcomed the time alone as well.

Chapter 30
Chula Vista, CA, April–July 1960

Please God, We Need a Miracle

❧

I t was early April 1960 when Mom and Dad first took us to Mass at the Mission San Diego de Acala. This "going to Mass at the Mission" excursion came out of nowhere to Sonny and me. We had only been to one Mass since May 1957, close to three years ago, so we wondered what was up with this. The Mission was beautiful in a Spanish, old world kind of way with the Mass simple in style, basic in message. Even the San Diego air felt purer and more fragrant on the Mission grounds set majestically overlooking the blue Pacific bay.

But the big question was, what would have prompted Mom and Dad into going to Sunday Mass again, especially so early, every single Sunday morning? It was a long drive across the city. Was the FBI getting close? Was Dad going to move us again? Was he getting ready to maybe take the family and new baby across the Mexican border to live? Was something wrong with the baby? Why now?

During this whole nightmare, which I mentally referred to as Dad's "big life," I had never seen neither Mom nor Dad pray about anything. Years ago, I'd sometimes see them pray, but now I figured they'd quit praying because they were mad at the failure of their "shoot to the moon, you're gonna love our new big life" plan. Lots of bad stuff had happened to their dream and bad stuff continued. We needed to keep running from the FBI and/or the bad guys; we could have no contact with anyone we knew or loved from back East; we used a fake name and told tons of fake stories (lies), lived in furnished rentals, and had no money. In my opinion, their "I'm sorry, God; please help me and make everything bad go away" prayer ship had sailed long ago. If any prayers were being offered up, they were a whole lot too little and a whole lot too late.

We didn't need to wait long before we found out the truth why early Sunday Mass mornings had become their obsession with mandatory whole family participation. The answer to the big question was born six-and-a-half weeks early, in May 1960: a precious, almost four-pound baby boy. Apparently Mom and Dad had been cautioned that there could be major complications with the baby. Sadly, there were, causing a lifesaving emergency C section. We almost lost both. Mom recovered quickly, but baby Johnny was touch-and-go for a few weeks. While Mom came home in about seven days, Johnny stayed for more than a month. Most days, Sonny would pick me up from school and we would drive to the hospital so we could stand outside the special baby nursery window and look at our miracle teeny baby brother connected to tubes and being kept alive in an incubator. Both of us felt such a strong connection to this helpless little guy who had so many hurdles to overcome. We had been told he was blind and that was just one of his many serious health complications. I think it surprised us how much we loved him and wanted to protect him. We could do nothing more than hold hands peering through that nursery window, silent in our own thoughts and prayers, willing him to be strong enough to live and come home. So great was our concern for him, that our other "big life" horrendous circumstances seemed to pale in comparison.

Mom had closed herself off from us and usually had been drinking long before we arrived home. She was overcome with grief, I guess, or maybe guilt. Dad went to work and tried to be supportive of Mom. He also may have been dealing with his own demons. They both had to be worried about their new little son's future and how they were going to care for him. That worried me too because they weren't doing a great job taking care of the kids they already had and we were easy and pretty much self-sufficient.

Miraculously, the day came. Johnny had barely survived, but now was strong enough to come home. Our parents were just pulling up in the car with him when Sonny and I arrived home. It was the last day of school, summer vacation was just beginning, and so was a whole new dimension to our lives.

Baby Johnny was so small, wrapped up tightly in his tiny blue baby blanket, that we could hardly see him. Finally, after all these weeks, Sonny and I each got to hold him. As young as we were, it was an emotional moment for the both of us. He stole our hearts. I think we both felt we would do anything for him. He was so helpless and innocent.

It wasn't long before we were doing a lot for him. Johnny needed to be fed every two to three hours. Each of us had our own shift. Mom would mostly take care of him during the day. Dad would take the morning shift before he left for work and the late-night shift. Sonny and I would alternate with the two a.m. and four-thirty a.m. shift and help Mom throughout the day. It may sound strange, but we didn't mind and since he needed to be fed about ten times in a twenty-four-hour period, Mom needed our help. Besides, he looked like a little angel, was fun to cuddle, and so easy to love. He took our minds off our "what's next?" situational problems as we focused on him. For a while, he became the new adventure.

The school year ending was rather anticlimactic due to Johnny's arrival. I got my all-A's eighth grade report card, so my college scholarship/escape to freedom plan was right on track. I would be a high school freshman in the fall with only four more years to go. Sonny was still in ROTC, did great in his classes, and had one more year of high school left. Johnny was growing bigger and more alert each week. He weighed almost six pounds. His health seemed better and even I could tell he was stronger. Mom still drank and smoked, but maybe a little less. Dad worked a lot. So far, things had worked out to be better than I would have thought a few weeks earlier. I had learned not to think too far ahead, but to be thankful and enjoy today. After all, you never know what adventure may be waiting around the corner for you tomorrow.

Mom and Dad were having Johnny christened at the Mission in mid-July. My Aunt Lulu and her family were coming to California to see us and meet Johnny. Grandma was staying in Fallbrook, where her wonderful family friend, Elda, had built a cedar and stone ranch home in the orange and avocado orchard covered hills. Fallbrook was around sixty miles north of San Diego. The plan was to have the christening on a Sunday morning at the Mission and then everyone would go up to Elda's home for the afternoon celebration.

On the day of Johnny's christening, I thought I figured out why we had been driving across town to the Mission for Mass every Sunday despite the fact they had ignored and dismissed God for the last few years. In fact, I was certain they blamed Him for their financial fall, dreams crashing, and all the other ugly "shoot to the moon, you are gonna love it" stuff. While in their unborn baby crisis, they became desperate and with nothing else left, turned to praying for their unborn infant with the hope that he would be healthy. If he survived, they would dedicate him to God and he'd be christened in this historic Mission church.

Well, it appeared their prayers for this baby, at least, were being answered. Johnny was doing well. The last testing report indicated that he may not be totally blind. So, I was grateful that if any of their prayers were going to be answered, it was these prayers for our little baby brother. Whether or not they would continue with attending church and prayers was up to them and only time would tell.

On the fun side, the next morning, our entire family went to Disneyland in Anaheim. Aunt Lulu, Marie, Kevin, Mom, Dad, Sonny, and I would go for the day, while Grandma and Elda babysat Johnny. We would pick Johnny up in Fallbrook on the way back to San Diego. This was the first day we had done anything fun like this since we left our old life behind.

It was such a happy carefree day, especially with Aunt Lulu's family sharing it. Sonny and I went on all the little kids' rides with Marie and Kevin, then many of the big rides by ourselves. We never saw any Mouseketeers, but that was okay. I was way over The Mickey Mouse Club with Annette and Doreen by then. Dad took tons of movies commemorating this special day. I don't think neither Sonny or I wanted it to end. For the moment, we felt like we were living in a wonderful dream, instead of our usual nightmare.

As all fun days do, our time in the park had to come to an end. Dad filmed the day's final memory with us all leaving the park's train station waving goodbye to Disneyland. We headed out to the huge parking lot in hopes of remembering where we'd parked the car. Once we found it, we also found a bag with two boxes of new movie film sitting on the front seat. Dad was stymied by this discovery and looked in his camera's film chamber, only to find it was empty. His cinematography skills were wasted, because the film needed to capture our epic family day for posterity had never been loaded into his camera. We may not have any movies, but we still had a great day and fabulous memories to last forever.

Chapter 31
Chula Vista, CA, Late July 1960

Guilty Till Proven Innocent

Another set of Chicagoan guests came to visit us shortly after Aunt Lulu's family departed. Aunt Babs, Uncle Rob, and their son, Robby, came to California to see Johnny. Both families stayed together in our two-bedroom, one-bath duplex. Including Johnny, there were eight of us. Aunt Babs and Uncle Rob stayed in Sonny's and my room. Sonny and Robby slept on the living room floor and I slept on the living room couch. One night, the four adults decided to go out for a nice dinner. Sonny and I were told we would babysit Johnny so they could have a fun evening. After we fed, changed, and made sure Johnny was asleep, Robby, Sonny and I laid on the floor watching some TV beauty pageant, then talked until the three of us fell asleep. Just as a matter of chance, Robby was between Sonny and me on the floor. This was normal; he was like a brother to both of us. We had all been together a lot from the day I was born. In retrospect, it seemed like Robby was sort of a visiting half-brother.

The parents came home and we must have been zonked out. Not one of the three of us had heard them come in. Sometime in the middle of the night I woke up and moved onto the couch.

Early the next morning, my mom woke me up. "Get up and come into my room right now, alone!" she hissed. "We need to have a little chat."

Believe me, this was so strange. Usually she hardly acknowledged me or Sonny unless she wanted us to help her with something. I was baffled. Of course, I followed her into their room.

Dad irritatingly said, "Close the door."

This was getting spooky. They proceeded to question me: "Why were you asleep on the floor next to Robby when we came home last night? Don't you know better?"

Truly, I had absolutely no idea what they meant. I had enough sense to know they were upset with me, yet was clueless as to why.

Dad asked me, "Do you know what happens to girls who act like you acted last night?"

I thought, *How did I act any different last night from any other time?*

Stunned, I answered, "Honestly I don't know what I've done wrong. Would you please explain what you're accusing me of? Why are you so upset with me?"

Inwardly, I wondered if Sonny was in trouble too. I tried my darnedest not to freak out. I wanted to run to Sonny and ask him if he knew why they were being so mean to me, but I didn't dare walk away from them. They never explained what shameful deed I was guilty of but, told me I was punished. Until Aunt Babs' family left, I was not to look at, talk to, or sit by Robby. I was not to be alone with him under any circumstance. I had to ride in the car with the four adults and the baby while Sonny and Robby would take another car by themselves.

In my indignant thirteen-year-old mind, I thought, *this is America, where everyone is innocent until proven guilty. Here, in my own family, I am automatically guilty and being punished for an unknown crime that never happened. They've made up a phony charge, which I have no knowledge of what the charge is, and furthermore, they haven't given me one single moment to ask questions, explain, or defend myself. They didn't even wake up Sonny and ask him about it. I have no doubt whatsoever that they've violated my constitutional rights. I know all about these rights because I just studied this in my eighth grade US Constitution class. If they had ever asked me, I would have proudly informed them that I aced the Constitution test. This whole stupid incident is a figment of their dirty evil minds. I'd like to remind them that they are the ones that the FBI and bad guys are looking for, not me.*

Underneath all my bravado, these falsely perceived accusations stunned and hurt me. How they could come up with these dirty little ideas, much less think I would be guilty of any kind of improper behavior? They were disgusting and I was crushed and angry. I was only thirteen-and-a-half-years-old, but I had a deeply ingrained sense of right from wrong. Something that I surmised was sorely lacking in my parents' own character. Look at the indiscretions and misadventures of theirs that even I knew about. Surely they could never think I wanted to be anything like them at all. Back in Wisconsin, when Mom, crying and drunk, would climb in bed with me, I knew I never wanted to be like that. Sonny and I had discussed this very topic several times. What would they think if they knew of our escape plans? How might they feel if they knew we wanted to get far away from the two of them and this insane life of madness as quickly as we could?

I wanted to scream at them, "Look in the mirror! I'm not the one guilty of anything!" because I knew neither of them could say the same about themselves. I think right then, I hated them, losing more respect every time I thought about our early morning "chat." I vowed to myself that I would follow my inner spirit's guidance and disregard anything they ever would accuse me of or insist I had to do. It's not that I was going to disobey them on purpose, after all, like it or not, they still were my parents. However, I would decide, based on my own sense of right or wrong, what path I would follow to become the honest, caring, and best person I could be. When I was younger, I trusted and respected them. I had thought they were the people I now so wished they were. It no longer mattered who or what they were or what they did or didn't do. I may not be able to change them, but I wasn't going to become like them, apologize for them, or most of all, allow them to keep me from being the person I desired to be. It was *my choice*! I would be the one to choose the kind of person I would become. I just had to listen to my inner voice to guide me down my path. I also realized I wasn't mad at them, but was more disappointed by and for them. Knowing, but hating to admit to myself, that I did love them dearly and despite everything, I was more fearful about their future than Sonny's or mine.

All these thoughts raced through my head as I looked at their lips moving, but by now, I refused to have ears that listened. When they stopped talking, I left the room without a word, thinking how to survive the many days left till I went far, far away to college. However, my task of the moment was calculating how many hours till Aunt Babs, Uncle Rob, and Robby would leave and I could share my "little chat" with Sonny.

After our summer company left, I did have one question and one concern. If we were not allowed to tell anyone from back home where we were, how come so many of those people had come and visited us here in California this summer? My concern was the same as it had always been. Couldn't the FBI or the bad guys easily find us now?

Within the next few days, the familiar and infamous decree was declared: "We are moving." Now my immediate concern had just become a non-concern. Obviously, it was okay for our guests to know where we lived because we weren't going to be there any longer. We would vanish into the proverbial night and my life here will become just another memory filed away in my mind's box of lifetime secrets. But hey, we had lived here around nine months—an eternity by our recent standards.

For the record, Sonny was entering his senior year and his ninth high school move. I didn't care where we were moving; I just hoped wherever we were going, Sonny would be able to graduate from that high school. I was entering my freshman year and had zero hopes of graduating from that same school in four years. In fact, I had no idea where in these contiguous forty-eight United States I might receive my high school diploma. Funny, how the "where" didn't matter to me anymore. What *did* matter was that I would successfully achieve my goal. I'd earn my scholarship and be off to a faraway college or university. I just needed to stay focused and survive four more years of this turbulent insanity and my perplexing parents.

It was then that I realized how Sonny and I were the lucky ones in our family. We would get to leave them and this dysfunctional crazy life of theirs. For the rest of their lives, both Mom and Dad would have to live with who they were and what mayhem, hurt, and pain they had caused themselves and the rest of their family. Deep inside, I sort of felt sorry for them, but mostly I worried about my innocent sweet baby brother, Johnny, and his future.

So, we packed up all our cares and woes along with our belongings, including a new baby, lots of baby things, and a baby car bed. The car top carrier was so full that Sonny and I had a secret bet if Dad would get it closed enough to lock, then would it stay closed as we sped down the road through the scorching hot desert and over the mountains to who knows where. We all piled into the overstuffed four-door car. Mom and Dad in the front seat, Sonny behind Dad, Johnny in the middle in his car bed, and me behind Mom. The backseat was also loaded with a diaper bag and a little cooler to keep Johnny's formula bottles cold.

We left beautiful San Diego in the crisp coolness of the breaking dawn. By high noon, we were in the middle of the hot desert. I have no idea how high the actual temperature was, but I thought there was a chance we all could die. Real worries of the engine overheating and then us literally being baked out there on the almost-deserted desert highway were valid concerns. Early in the afternoon we stopped and spent the day in an air-conditioned motel room, cooling off and resting. Dad bought a window cooler that you carefully filled with water and placed over a slightly opened back window. It had a pull string that would send a somewhat cool spray on us (mostly on Johnny) and it did help. However, after that first day, we only traveled the desert after sundown and switched to a more northern cross-country route.

Once again, our destination was unknown to Sonny and me. I knew we were still running from the FBI, but when were we going to have the right to know why we were on the run again; our lives being constantly uprooted? We'd played this same running game before, and it was growing tiresome and old.

PART 4
St. Louis, 1960–1962
Hallelujah Highschool

Chapter 32
St. Louis, MO, August 1960

Been Here, Done This

❧

Newsflash! History repeats itself. The third time is a charm! St. Louis, here we come, right back where we started from ... two days before last Christmas. Yep, we were back in St. Louis. Dad was going to work for the same Ford car dealership he had worked for before. And the definition of insanity is ...?

We stayed at a nice Holiday Inn the first night. Dad, Mom, and Sonny went shopping for some furniture for our new abode. They decided to rent an unfurnished place this time and retrieve the stuff Mom had locked in a Chicago storage facility three long years ago. I was in charge of babysitting, so I remained at the Holiday Inn. While Johnny was sleeping, I called my best friend from school last year, Laura.

"Hey Laura, it's Diana! We're back in town. My parents are looking for a place to live right now. Oh and my mom had a baby boy in May!"

Laura squealed into the phone, "What? You're really moving back here? Guess what? My mom had a baby boy, too. In June. Will you come back to school? We'd be in high school together!"

Excited just to be talking to her, I replied, "I'm not sure, but I hope so. It would be so cool to be at the same high school, but I don't know where we're going to live quite yet. I'll call and let you know as soon as I know where we'll be living. I can't wait to see you!"

We chatted a little longer, then hung up, promising we would get together regardless of where I lived.

Sonny and my parents arrived back a short time later. They had bought some furniture and rented a house in the same school district where we had lived before. Dad excitedly told me, "We'll all go back to see the house tomorrow, register you both at school, then the Chicago movers will deliver all our belongings the day after tomorrow."

I quickly realized the "day after tomorrow" just happened to be the first day of high school. This sure sounded good to me; maybe there would finally be some kids our ages in the new neighborhood. I asked the address of the new house. They gave it to me and I immediately called Laura. "Laura, my dad got us a house on a street named Ferndale Lane. The number is 7108. Do you know where that is or how close to your house it is? And guess what, the new house is in the same school district as you. We will be able to be in the same high school. Sonny, too!"

When I gave Laura the address, she started screaming. "Ferndale Lane? That's my street! I don't know exactly where 7108 is, but it's got to be pretty close to my house. We can go to school together. Maybe we'll be in some of the same classes like last year in junior high."

We hung up, agreeing that I would call in the morning to let her know what time we would be on her street. I would stop by and see her.

Now I found myself more excited about moving back to St. Louis. Sonny had reconnected with his old buddy, Ted, as well. We both felt better; each of us had at least one person we knew from before. We wouldn't be total strangers and we would be going together to the same school once again.

The next morning, I could hardly wait to see where we were going to live. First item on the day's agenda: registering Sonny and me for school. Everything went okay, except I left the school counselor's office a little nervous. It was a big school and I wasn't sure if I would find all my classes on time. I was also anxious about being placed in their top college prep curriculum, especially since a more advanced version of algebra was part of that college prep track. I had never had any algebra, so this could challenge my all-A's goal on my college plan.

Fortunately, Sonny was able to get every class he would need to graduate in June. When I thought about him escaping home and being away at college by this time next year, I could feel my stomach tightening up. I was truly happy for him, but scared out of my mind for me. I could handle anything regarding our parents with him by my side, but Mom and Dad, on my own caused me to panic. At least I had several months before Sonny left to figure something out. Then again, maybe miraculously they would return to the parents of old. I could always keep on hoping.

And hoping that this new house was close to Laura's, was exactly what I was doing as we turned on to Ferndale Lane. It wasn't a terribly long street and I had no trouble finding her address. I decided I could walk back to her house after we went to see our new house. Dad pulled the car into the driveway next door to Laura's. I assumed he had missed our rental house and was turning around. But instead of backing out, he turned off the engine while announcing, "This is it," and he got out of the car. At first I thought he was teasing me, but when I checked the address, I realized this wasn't a joke. The house we rented was next door to Laura's, I mean right smack dab next door! I burst out of the backseat, sprinting across the two front yards right up to Laura's door. I didn't even bother to check out my new house first. This was better than perfect.

Laura had seen me streaking across the lawn through their big front room picture window. She was opening her front door when I got there. I excitedly told her, "My new house is right next door to you!" We both started screaming and hugging while we jumped up and down like a pair of sugared up two-year-olds. We caused such a commotion that her mom and Gram H. came running to see if there was a problem.

Laura's mom and Gram H. were so sweet. Gram H. stayed in with Mathew, Laura's two-month-old brother, while Laura and her mom came with me to meet my mom and dad. Laura's mom, Maggie, and my mom hit it off immediately. After all, they had a lot in common with two infant boys one month apart in age, and of course, two ecstatic and crazy freshman teenage daughters. Sonny just grinned at me and rolled his big brown eyes.

We spent the rest of the day cleaning the house, unpacking the overstuffed car carrier, hanging up our clothes, and putting everything else we had brought with us away. Tomorrow, some of the newly purchased furniture and all our old stuff from Chicago would be delivered. I was looking forward to seeing if any of my childhood treasures had survived Mom's packing.

As it ended up, my parents, Sonny, and Johnny went back to the Holiday Inn that night and I stayed with Laura. We would get to start our first day of high school together. The plan was, early in the morning Dad and Mom would drop Sonny off at school on their way back to the new house and wait for the movers. As I was falling asleep, I couldn't help but be thrilled; however, I felt sad that Sonny had to "go it alone" tomorrow. I hoped and prayed that this, his ninth high school within three years, was the last high school he would ever have to attend. I also wished it would be the first and last high school I would ever have to attend. Yesterday, Dad had sworn and promised me that I would be graduating from the same high school as Sonny.

Arriving together with Laura to begin our high school years was wonderful. The day was full of good surprises. First, Mrs. P., my last year's science teacher from the junior high down the street who despised me, had not taken a new job teaching in this high school. I had been a little concerned about that. Laura and I were in many of the same classes together, including the accelerated algebra class. My ace in the hole, I figured, was living next door to Laura. I remembered she was good in math; I could ask her for help. So, with that problem sort of solved, the rest of my classes sounded a little challenging, but manageable. While registering, my guidance counselor informed me that my accelerated college prep program was a good start toward college scholarship requirements. I was excited and encouraged. This, I told myself, was doable and up to me. I felt my future was looking up and was in my hands.

My first day of high school was exciting and time flew by. Sonny's friend, Ted, drove Sonny, Laura, and me home that afternoon. I loved being in high school with my brother. He was my anchor and I loved that I got to be his sister.

Chapter 33
St. Louis, MO, August 1960

You Remember Me?

❧

As we pulled up to the new house, the movers were finishing and getting ready to leave. New furniture had been delivered and Mom and Dad looked tired. Maggie, Laura's mom, had graciously kept Johnny at their house most of the day so Mom and Dad could concentrate on moving in. I went into my new room to put my books away and was speechless when I saw the new double bed with a white wrought iron heart-shaped headboard plus a double dresser with a big mirror hanging above it. A tricolored pink ruffled bedspread covered my already-made bed. The best part of all this was seeing my old dressing table with the same pink chintz skirt and matching boudoir chair from my tenth birthday waiting for me. My old dressing table lamps were turned on, making the room warm and inviting. I was overwhelmed at my parents' sweet gesture. We had left Wisconsin over three years ago and this was the nicest thing they had done for me since then. I hadn't had anything that was my own after that move. I ran out of my room to find them, hug them, and thank them. I hoped Sonny had found a wonderful surprise in his new room too.

We all helped to get more settled while enjoying being reunited with our past belongings. Mom had done an exceptional job, without any help from Dad, moving out of the "big life/you're gonna love it house," despite the terrifying circumstances of 1957.

It didn't take long for the reality of high school homework to set in; I never expected so much the first night! In fact, I had to stay up late to complete it all. Exhausted, I climbed into my new bed. Looking around my room, I found comfort merely by the sight of these treasured old things. Those "old things" reminded me of the happiness and security I had felt in my earlier days of innocent childhood. It was as if I was finally able to reconcile my younger, joyful, and loving past along with all the scars, lies, and fake stories of these last three years. In an odd way, these cherished old childhood belongings prompted memories that helped me recognize I was still the same good and honest girl inside, despite the lies and fake stories I was forced to tell. My different lives had finally merged together, reconnecting me to who I truly was, the girl I was created to be, and most importantly, the person I aspired to be. Deep in my soul, I had needed affirmation that I, the real Diana, was still an honest and good person with a sense of wholeness and hope. I was not the fake Diana, whom I hated being, always having to lie to protect her parents. Sadly, to the outside world, the lies and made-up stories that I so despised would have to continue. I vowed I would never make my children lie for me.

I awoke early, taking in the new surroundings with my old treasures validating that it was truly my room. It made me feel like I had been reborn or renewed into a more grounded version of the real Diana. Anxious for this day to begin, I hopped out of bed with big hopes for my future. I was ready to get back to working on my college goal plan.

Sonny drove Laura and me to school. Man, this was so much more fun than having a parent drive us. First class: homeroom. Today, the nominations for the new freshman class student council representatives would be announced. Somehow, there must have been a lot of students that remembered me from first semester eighth grade last year, because they nominated me. I was astonished when told I was in the running. Later, I was taken by surprise when my name was announced over the PA system as one of the newly elected four freshman class representatives to serve on the high school student council. This was a such great honor. I was dumbfounded and grateful for the opportunity to serve on the council. I hoped it would be helpful in my quest to receive that coveted college scholarship. Life and I were looking up.

Sonny got a job after school at Leroy's gas station around the corner and another job working at the used car lot on weekends. He also had a girlfriend who was a year older than me. I liked her; she was nice. We would all now pick her up each morning on the way to school. She would sit in the front seat next to Sonny. Laura and I would sit in the back. Before the girlfriend, all three of us would ride together in the front seat. Other than that, everything else stayed the same.

Homecoming was the first high school dance of the year. Both Laura and I were asked to go. I don't recall the guy's name who asked me, but I vividly remember how nervous he looked when he stopped by my locker and stammered out, "Do you want to go to the homecoming dance? I mean, with me?"

It was awkward, and thinking I couldn't afford a dress, I replied, "Thank you. I'll have to ask my parents."

Laura and I were beyond excited. We thought going to the homecoming dance was a big deal. Laura's mom took us shopping and Laura found the perfect dress. My mom said she didn't have any money for me to buy a new dress, so I wasn't sure I would be able to go. Laura told her mom my sad tale and her mom said she would sew one for me. Mom found the money for my material and took me and Laura to the store where we chose blue brocade material and a pattern. Each afternoon, I would go over to Laura's house (which I did anyway, as Laura and I were inseparable) and Maggie would have me try her creation on, make alterations, and continue sewing. When she presented my finished dress, I was thrilled and so thankful. It was just what I had imagined it would look like: a scooped neck with puffy sleeves and a swirly full skirt—sort of like Cinderella's dress for the ball with the prince.

I felt good about how I looked when my date picked me up. The homecoming dance was fun, even though my date was a bit boring. He hardly talked and didn't really want to dance. When he did dance, maybe two times, he stepped on my toes a lot. Mostly we stood together on the side of the gym while I watched and talked with friends. He was polite and an okay choice for my first dance experience. Overall, I assumed everyone's first dates were somewhat awkward, but we all must experience that first date so we can move on to a more exciting second one.

Life at home had begun to function almost like a traditional family. Dad had his work schedule at the car dealership. Mom spent the day at home taking care of Johnny. I don't think she was drinking quite as much as she was before he was born. Every afternoon after school, Sonny would go work at the corner gas station and I would be in charge of Johnny for ninety minutes or so until it was time for him to eat. Laura and I figured we would get extra brownie points from our mothers by taking both babies for walks when we got home. Trust me, this was more about us being able to spend more time yakking with each other than taking a special interest in walking baby brothers in their strollers. It also made the mandatory babysitting time go quicker. Obviously, we were going to have to figure out a more creative scheme if it rained or when the weather got too cold.

One afternoon, Laura and I walked the boys up to the drug store so we could buy something we each needed for a project. As we entered the store, baby brothers and strollers in tow, we ran into our English teacher. She looked at us, and frowning, asked, "Where did you girls get those babies?"

Taken aback, we answered, "They're our baby brothers. Our moms make us take them on a walk every day after school."

"Brothers or your own sons?" She scoffed at us, giving us a dirty look as she continued through the door. Laura and I thought our teacher was weird, but also decided right then that we would never again walk the boys anywhere except around Ferndale Lane.

Our mothers had become good friends, which worked in our favor. Before dinner, Laura and I would check out what each mom planned to cook for the night's meal. We'd decide who was having the best dinner, then show up for the more enticing meal. The same scenario worked with sleeping over, even on a school night. We'd just tell them where we were sleeping. It was like having a twin sister.

As much as I relished spending time with Laura, Sonny remained the most important and special person in my life. We were so close that one day we were shocked when we realized we didn't argue. We had become that considerate and dependent on each other. Since we both liked to be on the phone, we worked out a schedule where we each had one hour of uninterrupted private phone time at a designated hour each night. We respected these private phone times, making sure our personal conversations did not intrude or overlap into the other one's time. Sonny also liked spending time with Laura and me. He would tease her like another pain-in-the-neck younger sister and Laura adored him.

Chapter 34
St. Louis, MO,
August 1960–January 1962

Four Years and I'm Outta Here

❧

1 960 was the year I became aware of politics. It was an important election year and the presidential candidates were Richard Milhouse Nixon and John Fitzgerald Kennedy. I think I was interested in this election for two reasons. One: John Kennedy had a glamorous socialite wife, Jackie, and they were Catholic. I knew who Richard Nixon was because he was the vice president under the current president, Dwight D. Eisenhower, and he had two daughters, Trish and Julie. Julie was my same age. Two: The TV news talked about them a lot and the candidates debated on TV.

Other than that, I tried to focus one hundred percent on my freshman year of high school. I do have to admit regarding Mom and Dad, I kept looking over my shoulder, waiting for my parents to drop another proverbial bombshell.

The holidays came and went. They were uneventful. Johnny continued to grow, but was slower to sit up and do other baby milestone things that Laura's little brother, Mathew, was already doing. Dad began to disappear for a couple of days at a time again and it was quite apparent when I got home from school that Mom had begun drinking more. When I asked where he had gone, she never gave an explanation. Were they never going to tell us the truth? Sonny and I were so tired of being kept in the dark and masquerading as a normal, happy, loving family. Our entire knowledge of what kept driving this tiresome, nomadic, unpredictable life consisted of "we had to change our name because we were running from the FBI and other bad guys." They should have recorded those same words alleviating the need to communicate with us altogether.

After three-and-a-half years of Sonny and I having no choice but to live their chaotic life of fake stories and lies, how could they continue to discount our right to know the whole story? Perhaps they didn't want us to know the facts, which made me wonder just how bad the truth might be. Had they been feeding us lies all along too? Confusing and opposing thoughts kept plaguing me. How could I love them so dearly yet mistrust them at the same time?

Silently, in my fourteen-year-old opinionated head, I imagined me informing them, "You need to pay attention and know this! Sonny and I are tired of this sham of a life built on your false stories and deceptions. Sonny has only six months left of this imposed fugitive life and in three-and-a-half years, I'll be long gone as well, leaving you to run and hide wherever you choose."

My own life was going to be an open book. A life of no lies. The only problems I would have to deal with would be of my own making. And I didn't plan on having too many.

Despite all the "baggage" in our lives, Sonny and I were oddly happy and managed to create a few typical teenage memories. The one that stands out the most to me happened one weekend when Mom, Dad, and Johnny went to Chicago, leaving us home on our own.

Wahoo! We planned a party. I mean, it would have been teenage code-breaking irresponsible *not* to have a party when your parents leave you home alone for four whole wonderful days. There was no alcohol, no smoking, nothing immoral at all. Just a lot of friends, in a small house having soda, popcorn, potato chips with onion dip, and chocolate brownies. No marijuana included. In fact, I don't think any of us knew about marijuana yet. It was simply a time of innocent early-1960s fun with lots of dancing, loud Elvis music, and laughter. The worst thing that happened was our Saturday night party ended around two on Sunday morning and the house was messy, including a sticky, spilled Coca-Cola-coated kitchen floor.

In true teenage fashion, we went to bed when the last guest left, saving cleanup for later in the morning. Mom and Dad weren't expected home till around six that evening. Of course, we slept in, awaking around noon, lying around, and deciding around three that we should start to clean up. I don't remember whether we had decided we were going to tell them about the party, but in either case, we knew the house couldn't look like we had been partying all night into this morning. We ran around the house and yard, collecting and disposing of all the bottles and trash, stashing the stuffed brown paper bags in the trunk of Sonny's car to be thrown out at Leroy's corner gas station where Sonny worked.

We wiped tables and countertops, cleaned the bathroom, vacuumed the whole house, and tackled the sticky, icky kitchen floor. Here was the first problem: neither of us exactly knew how to wash the kitchen floor. We knew a bucket and mop were involved, along with smelly cleaner and water. We could get that handled, but how do you get up the soapy water and then rinse the floor and get the clean water up? Brilliant and ever resourceful, we grabbed every towel in the entire house and used them to soak up the excessive water off the floor. That solved the water-on-the-floor issue, but created another problem. What do we do with all the heavy, water-logged, dirty bathroom and kitchen towels? Ah, genius minds at work solved the sticky little dilemma by cramming all the soaked filthy towels into the washing machine and adding triple soap because the towels were so disgusting.

Truth or dare question: would you believe me if I told you the only thing the two of us knew about a washing machine was that it was in the garage and it washed stuff when you turned some dials? If you guessed "true," you win. By the way, there was also one other minor detail we neglected to consider: how long it would take for the towels to get washed, dried, folded, and put away like nothing ever happened. It was going to be close, but we hoped we still had at least ninety minutes before they returned.

Washing machine running, we set the stage for their arrival.

Current tunes on our favorite rock and roll radio station, homework and books laid out on the dining room table, a bowl of pretzels and coke in place for study snacking—*check*. Sonny and me sitting next to each other looking like we had been studying all day—*check!* Sonny facing the big picture window so we knew when they pulled in driveway—*check!* Boy, were we ever good, gloating like fools—*check!*

Fly in the ointment lesson: Don't count all your chickens before they hatch and don't underestimate "things" not in your control.

Oops #1: Mom and Dad pulling in the drive way sixty-eight minutes early, just in time to witness massive amounts of Tide soap suds escaping out from under the closed garage door, cascading down the driveway to greet them as they arrive home ahead of schedule.

Oops #2: Parents bearing pizza as our reward for being so responsible in their absence.

Fortunately, they must have had a great weekend. When we fessed up, told them the whole story, including our clean-up fiasco and now fouled cover up plan, they chuckled. We could have our pizza and eat it too—on the condition that we wash the garage floor and driveway tomorrow after school. We agreed and devoured the pizza, realizing we hadn't had anything but junk food since they'd left.

The year was flying by. For me, this was a good thing and a bad thing.

Good because we had lived here six months and there had not been a "we are moving" decree issued.

Good because I'd had a great school year so far, was up to speed in my college track algebra class and my straight-A record was holding.

Really good because this school allowed two Greek high school sororities and Laura and I had to become pledges of one of them.

Bad because we were still lying.

Double bad because Mom was back to spending her evening with her favorite drinks and Salems.

Triple bad because Dad didn't always come right home from work at ten every night, so huge arguments ensued.

Quadruple bad because Sonny would graduate soon. Wonderful for him; not so much for me.

The end of the school year signaled the quickly approaching senior prom. The anticipated event was all the buzz around school. Sonny was going, of course, with his girlfriend. I wasn't dating anyone regularly and didn't expect to be asked. I had learned that according to prom etiquette, a guy needed to ask a girl to be his date for the prom one month in advance. So when that four-week deadline passed, I assumed I would sit this one out. A week later, Sonny's good friend, Ted, was over. He asked me if it would be too late to ask a girl to prom. I replied that four weeks was the cut off, so yes, it was too late. He told me he had wanted to ask a girl, but was nervous, and accidentally let the time slip by.

A couple of weeks later, he called and asked if he could come over. I explained Sonny was working and wouldn't be home till later. Ted said he only wanted to talk to me. He came by and we went to Steak 'n' Shake for their fabulous chocolate milk shakes. I thought nothing strange about this as we were sort of friends, too. While sipping and slurping my way through my delicious creamy chocolate shake, Ted confessed, "Diana, you were the girl I wanted to ask to the prom but I chickened out and now it's too late."

Tongue-tied, a totally new experience for me, I looked at him, and bashfully responded, "That's okay, I would have loved to have gone to the prom with you. I am flattered that you thought of me."

Embarrassed and not knowing what else to say, I busied myself with slurping more of my chocolate shake. I thought, *Man, if only I had told him he could still ask the girl, I would be going to the prom!*

On one hand, I was quite flattered that Ted, a senior, would ask a lowly freshman, namely me, to go to the prom, but bummed that I had blown my chance. However, on the flip side, I was relieved it hadn't worked out because I didn't have the money for a fancy prom dress, shoes, or getting my hair done at the beauty shop, and would have died telling him the truth. If I lied and just told him, "No, I can't," he'd think I didn't want to be his date. Though disappointing, it worked out better this way. A few days later, he called and asked me if he could take me out to dinner on prom night instead. I said, "Yes!" and had a great, one-hundred-percent platonic evening with a good friend who just happened to be a senior boy and my brother's best friend.

Graduation night arrived. This was a huge deal for Sonny. My grandparents and Aunt Lulu's family came from Chicago for his big celebration. Watching him walk across the stage to receive his diploma was exciting for me too. I was so proud of him. Nine different high schools, unbelievable life challenges, and setbacks due to our parents' neglect and instability, yet he managed to have a great GPA, stay committed to ROTC, and now was heading off to the University of Missouri in three months. Even today, I can't describe how much I admired him with my heart bursting with joy for him. In that same moment, my bursting heart was also breaking, because come fall, for the first time in my entire fourteen years and nine months of life, my anchor and hero would not be in the same house with me. We had never been apart except for maybe five days max, ever. I now had to figure out how to manage living with these parents on my own.

To calm myself, I decided that I always could spent most of my time at Laura's—that is, when Mom wasn't having me take care of Johnny, who had just turned one. The truth was, I felt sort of responsible for this sweet little guy. He was so innocent and rather frail. I knew he had physical and mental challenges ahead of him and that our parents were ill-equipped to raise *any* children, much less a child with handicaps. I loved him and didn't mind watching him, especially when I could make him laugh or get him to give me hugs. On the other hand, it was like their problem became my problem, just like everything else they had dropped on us since November 1957. Sometimes, I thought I would suffocate living under their roof of disrupting and unsolvable problems. Now soon to be alone, without Sonny, they were going to become an unbearable heavy load.

The three months of summer passed quickly by. Along the way, I acquired a boyfriend named Cary, who happened to be best friends with Laura's boyfriend, Tim. They were going into their junior year and Laura and I were soon-to-be sophomores.

Late August arrived way too fast for me, but probably not fast enough for Sonny. On a Saturday morning, we loaded up Sonny's stuff into the car and drove to Columbia, where we dropped off my now-college-freshman brother at his new fraternity house. I had made a promise to myself: *I would not spoil his special life-changing opportunity and inaugural escape day with a sad, drama-filled farewell.*

As he hugged me goodbye, he whispered, "I love you .Call me if you need me. I will always come back to help you."

I appreciated his offer, but there was no way I would ever drag him back into this prison. We were both going to move forward and he was just a little ahead of me. We were survivors. Survivors conquer their obstacles and keep on moving forward to achieve their goals.

The ride back home felt strange without him. Laura's gram had stayed with Johnny, so I had the whole backseat to myself. My mind drifted back to remembering all the times when I was seven, eight, and nine that I had told Sonny he couldn't cross my invisible dividing line or that I wished I was an only child so I could have the entire backseat to myself. How awful and selfish I was to have treated him like that. I concentrated, counting down the days until his Thanksgiving break. Sonny would return home for a few days and I would apologize for my bad behavior and tell him how lucky I felt to have him for my brother. I was also eager to hear about his college life and adventures. His experiences would make my college dreams feel more real and attainable. Right now, I needed to remind myself that my immediate task was to survive one day at a time while simultaneously keeping my focus on my goals.

For the first time since fifth grade, I was starting the new school year at the same "old" school that I went to last year. I still lived in the same house right next door to my best girlfriend. Although, this year, our mode of transportation to school was downgraded to the big yellow school bus.

My sophomore year started out fantastically. I was reelected to student council, and had a nice and cute boyfriend. The college prep classes were taught by inspiring teachers and I belonged to a fun high school sorority of smart and cool girlfriends/sisters. We did good things for charity and plenty of silly things for fun. In some ways, it was a perfect life to be me, a fifteen-year-old teenager in 1961. Perfect, that is, until three-thirty every day when I arrived home.

Shortly after Sonny left, my parents had me swap bedrooms with him. His was a larger room with a big window overlooking Laura's side yard. When Laura couldn't come over or wasn't allowed to be on the phone, she would tell her Mom that she was "taking the garbage out" then sneak to her side yard and we would talk through the window. That is, until we heard her dad's irritated call, "Laura, quit talking and come in now." *Shoot*, caught again.

All my treasures made it into my new bedroom. I also inherited Sonny's big desk, which I loved. My days of trying to concentrate while doing my homework in the dining room, often full of distractions and noise, were over. This new arrangement allowed me more distance and privacy from Mom and Dad. In my mind, the new bedroom and Laura's house next door were my getaway sanctuaries. That said, regardless of how much I loved my new digs, I would have gladly traded in this new room to have Sonny back. Laura did not know my life was full of fabricated stories regarding my past and continuing lies to protect my parents. Only my brother knew my past life and my college plan for my future. I missed having my special brother around, the only person I could be one hundred percent real with.

Old patterns were repeating. Dad was out of town quite a bit of the time. I never asked where he went. I liked the respite from worrying about the arguments that happened when he returned home late from work and found Mom waiting up for him, drunk. When Dad was out of town, Mom drank herself into a stupor and passed out on the couch. I just ignored her, thankful I didn't have to deal with her. She was nasty and mean when awake and drunk. The negative was that she never heard Johnny wake up crying in the middle of the night, so I would get him and bring him into bed with me. I loved snuggling him, but I was a teenager who also loved her sleep. I often wondered if I wasn't around, would she continue to drink so much? Would she remember she had a helpless sixteen-month-old son to take care of? Due to her excessive drinking, I often questioned her judgment and her ability to make even simple decisions anymore.

And then what about Dad? Honestly, he was just as responsible as Mom was for Johnny and me. In fact, this horrific four-year-long debacle, called *our life*, was based on his own portfolio of lies and reckless decisions. *Would he leave Mom alone with Johnny at night if I wasn't there? What will they do when I leave? I want to have my very own life too. When I leave, will that make me selfish and irresponsible like them?* I decided I had almost three years to figure this out. I also knew just where I always found my help and answers. All I had to do was pray and ask.

The fall flew by and the once-vibrant red, orange, and yellow autumn leaves were lifeless brown and quickly carpeting the grass. I loved school and my extracurricular activities. Laura and I were together all the time, even if that meant I brought Johnny along with me. Cary and I were going steady and enjoying each other's company. Most importantly, my grades were good. The Thanksgiving holiday was soon to arrive and so was my big brother.

Sonny was only home for Thanksgiving Day, then went back to Mizzou due to work and studying for exams. His departure wasn't quite so upsetting this time, because I knew he'd be back in about three-and-a-half weeks for the Christmas break. For some reason, Mom and Dad took Johnny up to Chicago for Christmas early, before Sonny and I were able to go. I spent a couple of nights at Laura's until Sonny got home and then the two of us flew to Chicago.

The holiday in Chicago was a blur to me. Sonny needed to get back to school early and I was eager to return to St. Louis for New Year's Eve. My sorority sisters were having their annual New Year's Eve get together and we could bring dates. Laura and I wanted to bring our boyfriends. Our parents had decided to spend New Year's Eve together, so I was off the hook for babysitting. When the clock struck midnight, I prayed that 1962 would be better. I felt optimistic about it and hoped my wishes, and dreams for a great year would come true.

Chapter 35
St. Louis, MO, Late January 1962

I'm Not Okay, but Thanks for Asking
❦

T he school year of 1962 began and I was off to a great start. I knew this year was going to be the best. I loved all my teachers and classes. In fact, I loved everything about this school and was involved in as many clubs and activities as I could handle.

One cold wintry morning during Spanish class, I was summoned to the principal's office. He was a nice man and I had worked with him on a student council project earlier in the fall. He stood up as I entered his office and came around to give me a hug and fatherly pat on my shoulder. He held a chair out for me to sit in and then he sat in the chair directly across facing me. He reached out for my hand while he kindly informed me, "Your parents called me this morning." (Sound familiar?) "They'll be here to pick you up in a half hour. You're moving to Chicago."

I know I stared at him, frozen in place. I couldn't comprehend what he was telling me. My mind refused to process the information. I didn't want to accept what I was being told.

He took both my hands and said, "I am sorry, so sorry, but now you must gather your things and return your books to the office."

I sat, dumbfounded, unable to move. He tried to soothe my distress by telling me, "Change is like wearing a new pair of shoes. At first they feel strange, often even painful, but after a short time they become like home to your feet. They may even become your favorite shoes. So, while leaving this high school is painful right now, it won't take too long and you'll get comfortable and love your new school in Chicago as well."

I heard him. I appreciated his kindness and his words of wisdom, but all I could do was stare at him with quiet tears streaming down my cheeks. My emotions weren't only about leaving this school or Cary, my boyfriend that I may not even get to say goodbye to, or my sorority sisters or my even my best friend, Laura, it was about the lies! It was about all the broken promises, one after another. It was about the hypocrisy of my life, my world. It was about the shattering of my carefully mapped out college freedom plans.

Ultimately it was about my dad, who had sworn and solemnly promised that I would never have to change schools again. I would graduate from this high school, no matter what. He'd promised but like all his past promises, he broke it. Once again, I was a pawn, at their mercy, regardless of how hard I tried to pretend I could divorce myself from my real home life and be like a normal teenage girl from eight to three-thirty, five days a week.

In the last five years, I'd changed schools nine times. I had been awakened and had to flee into the night like a hunted criminal running from the FBI and who knows who or what else.

I had been promised that life would be normal. I had been promised that Mom would quit drinking. I had been promised they would quit fighting and arguing. I had been promised and promised and promised so many times and so many things that I wasn't sure if they knew what a promise meant anymore. Here I was, sitting in this kind principal's office, trusting his truths more than I did any words uttered by my own parents. I couldn't believe, trust, respect, or feel any kind of compassion for them or from them. I didn't know them, I didn't like them, and I was truly afraid of them and the consequences of the rash decisions they made. I hated the world of unreality that they lived in and forced me to live with and in. It was chaotic, unsafe, unstable, and if I was being truthful with myself, neglectful, uncaring, and unloving. I was trapped, susceptible to their crazy whims and harsh irrational directives.

Oftentimes I had pondered if they were sane enough to comprehend their own madness. Despite my angst over this new development, I was now seriously worried if they were truly mentally ill, incapable of rational thinking. What had triggered this spontaneous moving decision? Yet, while I detested what they did to us, in another way, I felt sorry for them. I also loved them both, but truly had no idea why.

I rose from the chair and thanked this kind man. I agreed I would gather my items and get my transfer papers from the office. I thanked him again, we hugged, and I found the door. On the way out, I also found my resolve. I was not going to let my parents bring me down, spoil my dreams, or get in the way of my goals. I was going to succeed despite them. They could throw anything at me, it could hurt, it even could briefly stall me, but they never ever were going to defeat me. I had my own plan and I had the best counsel living within me. I only had two-and-a-half years left. I had survived almost five years so far, so two-and-a-half more was doable.

Mom and Dad were both waiting in the car with Johnny as I reluctantly walked out the high school's glass doors and down the steps. I climbed into the back seat as calmly as I could. I would not let them see how demoralized or devastated I was. I just wanted to get going, get away from this high school that I'd thrived in. I needed to look forward—far forward, not backward—and stay focused and strong. Looking back at the school I loved and all I was losing would cause me to crumble. In my head, I kept a mantra going: "One step, one day at a time. You can do it." Right now, I was struggling with one minute at a time, but I would hold on. They could bend me, but I'd never let them break me. I could feel God's strength bolstering me.

We arrived home and I silently packed up my treasures. The movers would be there in the morning. Laura's mom already knew the plan so when Laura got home from school, she called me to come over. I quickly finished my packing duties and walked to her house next door. I lost my cool. Laura's mom hugged me, rocking me like a baby, her sweet tears mixing with mine. Laura's gram was calming Laura as well. It was a scene right out of an afternoon soap opera. We were all dramatic. Maggie told me I was spending the night with them.

Laura told me our sorority sisters were having a last minute going away party for me at the local pizza parlor. Tim and Cary would pick us up after that. We would come back to Laura's house for a while so I could say goodbye to Cary. Tomorrow, my parents and I would head to Chicago. The plan sounded good to me. I wouldn't have to talk or see my parents until tomorrow when I got in the car to leave. Laura whispered to me that her mom and dad had offered for me to live with them until the end of the school year, but my parents declined. I was incredibly disappointed, but not surprised. I wondered if anyone had informed Sonny of our new plight yet. I was happy he had been able to make it into college before this occurred. Ten high schools would have pushed him over the edge.

My sorority sisters and the pizza parlor party was so much fun that I almost forgot I was leaving in the morning. Saying the tearful goodbyes brought my circumstance back to reality. Right on time, Tim and Cary arrived to pick Laura and me up. We stopped at Steak 'n' Shake for one last double chocolate milkshake and it gave me some time to explain what had happened that morning at school. Laura's dad was a stickler about her curfew time, so there wasn't much time to say a final goodbye to Cary. It was hard to break up with someone you still liked and they still liked you.

Laura and I talked through most of the night. I tried not to think how hard it was going to be saying goodbye to Laura, Maggie, and Gram H. tomorrow afternoon when the movers finished. Living next door to them had been my major source of normalcy the past seventeen months and especially the last five months since Sonny was away at college. I loved tiny Gram H., who seemed to sense that I might need a hug or pat on the shoulder whenever she saw me. Maggie was like another mom to me. In fact, I often felt guilty because I liked and trusted her more than I did my own mother. And then there was Laura, whom I loved like a sister. I hated that I hadn't been able to be truthful with her about my family's past or what my real name was. There had been so many times that I wanted to bare my soul to her, but didn't; I knew I couldn't. I also knew I wouldn't, because unlike my parents, I would always keep my promises.

I babysat Johnny and hid out at Laura's the entire day until the movers left. Then came the moment I had been dreading. We were ready to pull out of the driveway and head to Chicago. I hugged Laura's family one last time.

I was so upset, sobbing, that I could hardly breathe as we drove off down the street. My dad pulled the car over at the end of our street and turned around to face me. Furious, he demanded; "Diana, stop your crying right now. You are acting like a spoiled brat, absolutely obnoxious. We are moving to Chicago; it's not the end of the world. You are not a baby anymore. Quit behaving like one. Your hysteria stops now. I don't ever want to hear another word about us moving. Do you understand?"

I nodded, but unfortunately, his stern words made me cry harder. Mom kept looking straight ahead, saying nothing.

We stopped to fill up with gas at Leroy's corner station where Sonny had worked after school. My parents got out of the car and went into the gas station for some reason, leaving a sleeping Johnny and a seriously hysterical me in the car. I must have looked terribly upset because Leroy, Sonny's former boss who owned the gas station, quickly came over while my parents were inside and asked. "Are you okay? Is there a problem? Do you need my help?"

Of course, I wanted to yell, "*No,* I am not okay," but instead tried to smile at him and hiccuped a "I'm fine, but thank you for asking."

My parents returned to the car, and I closed my eyes to shut them out. Hiding behind my swollen eye lids, I realized I had no idea where or why we were moving back to Chicago. I questioned how we could be returning to the very place we kept running away from. What about the FBI and the bad guys? Did this mean Dad was free, or maybe he was caught and now going to go to jail? I knew nothing more about the reason for this move than I did when I left for school yesterday morning, innocently thinking I would graduate from that high school in two-and-a-half years. Once again, I had no idea where my next high school would be or if there would be another one after that. Who knew what was ahead? I sure didn't and I wasn't confident that the two adults in the front seat did either. I didn't feel like asking them any details because how would I know they weren't lying? In fact, I couldn't even talk with them because I felt so betrayed and manipulated. I laid down, kept my eyes closed, hoping to fall asleep. Maybe I would wake up and find this was finally all a crazy bad dream.

PART 5
Chicago, 1962–1964
It's My Life

Chapter 36
Chicago, IL, February–May 1962

You'll Never Break Me

ɕɔ

Five years of Running, hiding, secrets, lies, nine new schools, and now we can come back? *Why? What changed?*

The two-story, three-bedroom brick house was on the outskirts of the suburb of Elmhurst. I hated to admit that I did like the house and neighborhood a lot. Aunt Lulu, her precious family, and my grandparents lived about twenty-five miles north of us. Dad's family was even closer. I loved that now I had family close by, but living in the Chicago area meant Sonny was a far four hundred miles away. I hated that. I missed him terribly.

My confusion over why we now could live back in the Chicago area after our fugitive life of running and hiding the last five years still bothered me. For one-third of my entire life, I had to lie, tell fake stories, hide like a criminal, and be uprooted several times, for what? Why and what had so miraculously happened, that now we could openly live in Chicago close to our family and old friends? In my mind, the only difference from five years ago was our name change and the addition of an innocent nineteen-month-old baby.

Inwardly furious but having to accept that some things were never going to be explained to me, I decided to fly under their radar screen, keep looking forward, and doing whatever I needed to do to stay on my plan. Therefore, I had to let go of my anger and frustration, put on my big girl pants, suck it up, and make the most of the first day of my new school. I mean, this was my twelfth new school. I could get a PhD in changing schools. I certainly had gathered enough material for my dissertation.

Putting my experience to work, I made my agenda for the first day of school twelve:

Night before: gather all school materials, take bath, wash and set hair. Choose best or favorite outfit for first day of school.

Morning of: Get up early and get dressed in my best outfit laid out night before. Carefully put on makeup and style bubble hairdo.

Be at front door early and ready for Dad to take me to register at new high school. Be quietly respectful and upbeat on drive to school. Register for classes and say goodbye and thank you to Dad.

Take a deep breath and smile at the student helper taking me to my first class. Give myself a pep talk prior to entering classroom. Do not be scared, remember His strength resides inside me, I am never alone, and think: *one step at a time.*

Lastly, warm friendly smile at teacher and classmates when introduced to class. Take assigned seat and proceed to focus and pay attention. Keep my eyes on my goals and remember I've done this before and I have got this now.

All went better than I could have imagined or planned. Everyone was extremely friendly and the teachers offered to help me in any way they could. Again, I was in the college prep classes and while this high school's required classes differed from my last high school, my counselor worked everything out and it was fine. Before lunch, I asked a friendly girl from the class if she would show me where the cafeteria was. She did much better than that and invited me to join their table and I did. At the table I was asked a lot of questions.

"Diana, where did you go to school before here? Where do you live? Do you have a boyfriend?"

I also found out that a few of the girls lived in my new neighborhood and offered to meet me at the school bus at the end of the day. This was fabulous since I had no idea what bus I should take. Two of the girls, Jan and Jen, were twins and both were JV cheerleaders. Two other girls at the table were also JV cheerleaders. I liked them all instantly and hoped they would want to become friends with me.

The rest of the day was just as good as the first half. As it turned out, Jen was in most of my same afternoon classes. She seemed smart and cool. The bus ride home went quickly as we all talked, getting to know each other. In fact, the three of us got off at the same bus stop and stood chatting for another thirty minutes. It turned out that we only lived about a block and a half from each other. We decided I would come to their house in the morning and then we would all walk to the bus together.

As I continued to my new house, I had to admit this was a pretty good first day and this high school was a lot better already than the proverbial new pair of shoes. Who knew if maybe the twins, Jan and Jen, would possibly become my new good friends? I hoped so.

Arriving at my house, Grandma was there, helping Mom unpack. I was truly happy to see her and noticed Mom had not started drinking yet. Maybe this move would help bring my beloved old Mom back. Then again, maybe not, but a girl can keep on hoping, can't she?

A couple of weeks into Chicago suburban living, I still missed Laura, Cary, and of course, Sonny. However, while no one would ever replace Laura, I had a great time with my new girlfriends. They immediately included me in everything. It was as if I always had been here at this high school and this high school did do cool things. Since four of my new friends were cheerleaders, I went to all the Friday night basketball games with them. I also met a lot of nice guys. As for Cary, I still liked him a lot and we exchanged letters, but he lived in St. Louis and I lived in Chicago, so I figured we both had to move on. I soon started babysitting around the neighborhood and was finally able to start to fund my secret college money box. I kept my accumulating stash in an old shoebox hidden in the bottom of my closet behind my special treasures box and the other shoeboxes. I didn't think anyone would find it there.

About a month after we moved in, Mom and Dad hosted a family Sunday dinner at our house. My follies dancer Grand Aunt V and her family came, along with my dad's brother's family and all my cousins on that side. Of course, Aunt Lulu's family plus Grandma and my now-frail beloved Grandpa joined us. Except for Sonny, for the first time in years, we were together again. It was a great afternoon. However, all my cousins were at least four or five years younger than me, so after a couple of hours we ran out of things to talk about or do together. I excused myself and went upstairs, claiming I had tons of homework to do, which was true.

Shortly thereafter, the doorbell rang and my mother announced someone was here for me. I had no clue as I came down the stairs and saw one of the guys I had recently met from school, so I invited him in and took him into the family room where it was quieter. As we chatted, the doorbell rang again and it was another guy from school that claimed he was passing by and decided to stop in and say hello. I also invited him to join us in the family room. Well, I don't know if these guys all planned this or not, but within the next fifteen minutes, two more guys from school arrived and followed me into in the family room where we all sat around talking about school, sports, and other friends.

After the fourth guy came in, my mom and dad asked to see me. They took me upstairs to their bedroom and started to grill me. "Why are all these guys coming over? Did you invite them? What are you doing that would make four guys show up on a Sunday afternoon? What kind of impression are you making that would draw four boys to come to your house? Did you give the impression you would be home alone?" Through clenched teeth, they continued, "Do you realize how bad this makes you look? What must all our relatives think of you? What kind of questionable reputation do you have at school?"

If their looks could kill, I swear I would have been dead. I was fuming inside. Once again, they were accusing me of whatever their immoral minds or own past indiscretions and memories dug up. Did they think that I should walk around with a scarlet letter on my chest? I hadn't done anything. I hadn't even accepted a date yet. One of the guys had the locker next to mine, another was in one of my classes, and the other two, I knew through other people. I mean, this was innocent on my part. I had no idea these guys or any guy knew where I lived, nor had I invited anyone, not even a new girlfriend, over this Sunday afternoon. Hadn't they realized I didn't invite anyone over, ever?

The reason? I never knew if my mother would be drunk and mean or passed out on the couch. I had to hide all the ugliness that went on inside our house, hoping none of it ever made it's way out the front door. I just pretended and smiled. Crying or feeling sorry for myself was a rare activity held silently under my covers.

In my heart, I would have loved to be proud of my parents and my home. I would have loved to have the peace of mind to be able to invite a friend over after school or say my parents would take a turn picking us up and taking us to the pizza place after a game, but I couldn't take a chance. Historically, they had proven unreliable and embarrassing.

Their insinuation was the ultimate insult and it stung me, badly. How could they think so little of me? There was nothing in my past that I was ashamed of except lies, fake stories, a drunken promiscuous unfit mother, and a running-from-the-FBI, lying, cheating, unfit father. But solely based on me and my character, I never had cheated, lied, been slightly immoral, disrespectful, or anything. I had my own personal code of conduct since I was seven years old. I was proud of who I was and who and what I wanted to become. It's funny, but in that moment, a silly childhood rhyme came into my mind, *"Sticks and stones may break my bones, but words can never hurt me."* I decided to go with that in my head while I turned away and left them standing in their room. I had guests to attend to and so did they. They could punish me after everyone left, but I could not leave four guys sitting alone in the family room any longer. The rest of the family probably hadn't noticed any of us were missing.

Coming down the staircase, I thought, *two years, two-and-a-half months until I graduate and leave for a faraway college.* I vowed to myself that I could do this; I would do this. Then I plastered a smile on my face and entered the family room where four guys sat watching sports on TV. After drinking a coke and munching on potato chips, we all said, "See ya tomorrow," and they left. I hugged and kissed my remaining relatives goodbye and climbed the stairs to return to the books, my commitment to my plan stronger than ever.

The expression "old patterns die hard" is certainly true in many cases. In our household, a better expression would be "old patterns never die; they just morph into worse patterns." At least, that was the case with Mom and Dad.

My life at school continued to get better and better. Distressingly, home life slid to a new historic low. Dad worked long hours and didn't show up at home for a few days at a time. Again, no response to my now old, familiar question: "Where is Dad and when will he be back?" Mom was almost always physically home when I returned after school, but the new twist was I often found her passed out on the living room couch while Johnny cried or sometimes hysterically screamed from his crib upstairs. He apparently would awaken from his nap around the time Mom would have dozed off into a liquor-induced semi-coma. I decided to make sure Mom knew if I was not coming directly home after school, fervently hoping that she would realize she could not start drinking so early in the day. She must have connected all the dots because when I came home late, she was relatively sober and the days when I came straight home, I found her "napping" soundly on the couch. Not an ideal set up for me inviting friends over, but at least I had some peace of mind regarding Johnny's welfare.

Chapter 37
Chicago, IL, April–May 1962

The Hot Guy with the '55 Pontiac

❧

O n all the other fronts, my life was special. I babysat a lot, squirreling my money away in the hidden shoebox. Classes were good, grades great, and my social life even better. I was dating, but no one special. So far I had been asked to the prom by three different guys. Two had been at my house that miserable Sunday afternoon. I had accepted the first offer and had separately put away enough money to buy a prom dress, shoes, and a boutonniere for my date. I couldn't afford a trip to the beauty shop, but I would do my popular 1960s bubble hairdo myself.

Jan and Jen encouraged me to try out for the next year's cheerleading squad with them. Practice was after school one week in mid-April. I was also good friends with another cheerleader who informed me that she had arranged a ride home for us on Friday afternoon. Cheerleading practice ended and we met this tall, cute guy in the school parking lot. He drove a 1955 green and white highly polished Pontiac Catalina with rolled and pleated interior. I had absolutely no idea, nor cared, what rolled and pleated interior was, and to my insensitive eyes, this was just an old car in good condition. Since I had been around cars all my life, I didn't have a particular interest in any car whatsoever, but obviously, these were massively important wheels to this handsome junior. He politely opened the passenger door and my friend Kate told me to slide in first. Feeling awkward, but wanting to appear "cool", I smiled and slid to the middle. Kate quickly jumped in next to me. I learned his name was Luke and then I remembered watching him play varsity basketball. I now realized this was the tall guy that I had thought was hot, but had never run into him at lunch or in the hallways.

He dropped Kate off at her house first, then I directed him to mine. I wanted to get to know him better, but couldn't invite him in when we pulled into my driveway because who knew "who" might be welcomed by a passed out, napping mother and screaming baby brother. We politely chatted for a few minutes then I thanked him for the ride and went into the house. I surprised myself that I liked him in a dating sort of way.

Kate called shortly after I got home, quizzing me about him. "Okay, what did you think about Luke? Isn't he so hot?"

I gushed, "He is *so* cute and nice. I think I could really like him. I can't believe I never ran into him at school before. I hope he asks me out on a date."

"Well," Kate went on, "I was thinking if you dated Luke, maybe he could help me get a date with his best friend, Mike. We could double date or something. There's a school orchestra concert and since Luke plays a mean saxophone, he has a solo. We should go hear him and then I might run into Mike. What do you think? Wanna go on Sunday?"

"Okay, that sounds like a neat plan. Let's do it." Now, I couldn't wait for Sunday to come.

I thought the school concert was exceptionally good. Actually, I thought it was the best ever because Luke appeared to be looking directly at me while he played his saxophone solo. He was one hot guy dressed up in sport coat and tie. I began to really hope he would ask me out on a date. He was sort of shy, which added to his appeal.

I was thrilled when he caught up with me after the concert and introduced his mom, dad, six-year-old sister, Karen, and eight-year-old brother, Michael. Michael and Karen were so excited and proud of their big brother. They were sweet and cute and anyone could see how much they idolized Luke. His parents were warm and friendly and the whole family reminded me of the popular *Leave It to Beaver* TV series. Right in front of his family, Luke asked if he could drive me home, meet my parents, and then take me to play miniature golf and dinner. Since it was Sunday and both my parents were home, I felt it was safe to say yes to meeting my parents and fairly sure it would be fine for me to go out with him afterward. Since they were not pleased with the guy I had been dating the past three weeks, they would probably welcome this well-mannered, new guy.

Mom and Dad were wonderful. They acted like normal, healthy, loving parents. I was proud to introduce them to Luke. I could tell they both liked this guy from the get-go. Mom kept smiling and winking at me behind his back. Both wished us a fun time and never mentioned what time I needed to be home. I was happily surprised. Life would be perfect if this was who they could be all the time. Thankful that this was turning out to be one spectacular afternoon, I blew them a kiss as we drove off.

It was a beautiful, warm, late-April, Sunday afternoon. However, being that it was spring in Chicago, the weather could change to cold in a minute. Luke suggested I bring a sweater for later. I assured him that I was fine, no sweater needed. We played a fun round of peewee golf, which I handily won, then went for a bite to eat at Howard Johnson's. We were seated across from each other in a booth for two. After the waitress brought us menus, Luke asked me, "What would you like? You can order anything you want."

I coyly replied, "That's so nice Luke, but really all I would like is a coke. I'm not very hungry."

"Are you sure you wouldn't like something more than just a coke? How about a hamburger or fried clams? In fact, I'm going to have the fried clam platter. It comes with fries and coleslaw. There's a picture of the fried clams platter on the menu. I think you'd really like it," he urged.

Making a face, I laughed. "Oh! Nope, thanks, I'm good with the coke. Besides, fried clams? "Aren't they slimy and icky?"

Luke chuckled and ordered his fried clam dinner with fries and coleslaw and two cokes.

When our order arrived, Luke showed me the platter and asked me again, "Don't you want to try just one of these fried clams or order something else?"

Again, I declined his offer, adding, "Okay, I take it back. The clams don't look slimy!" Secretly I thought those fried clams looked pretty good.

Luke graciously offered me a fried clam to taste. This time, I took him up on it and found the fried clam was delicious. I loved the fried clams so much that I proceeded to eat his entire dinner. Well, maybe not his entire dinner because I think I left a few French fries on his plate. I also must confess that the late afternoon did turn quite chilly and he gave me his sport coat to wear while he froze during the mini-golf game. Perhaps his shivering was the real reason he lost at golf.

I had a delightful time and I imagined he did too because he asked, "How about I pick you up for school in the morning?"

I eagerly responded, "That would be great, but are you sure you want to be here at seven-twenty? I mean, you live clear across town and school is smack dab in between us. You'll have to get up extra early."

Luke smiled. "I'll be here at seven-fifteen so we have time to talk before the bell rings."

Getting ready for bed that night, I thought about Luke and our date. I surprised myself because I felt a bit smitten with him and thought he was with me as well.

Luke picked me up bright and early and we did have some time to talk prior to the homeroom bell. As soon as he parked the car in the school parking lot, he turned to me. "Diana, I would love for you be my date for the prom. Would you go to the prom with me?"

Whoa, that caught me way off-guard. It also left me in a huge conundrum.

I looked up at him with my heart beating fast as I explained, "Luke, I would love to go to the prom with you, but there's a complication. Three other guys already asked me and I accepted the first guy's invitation. To do the polite and right thing, I must go with the first guy. If he has to cancel, then I have to go with guy number two, then three, however, if all the first three guys cancel, I'd be honored to go with you."

Of course, I wanted to go with him but just didn't see how I could renege on my acceptance to guy number one.

Luke was unfazed, stating, "I'm sure we will end up going to the prom together, so I'm taking that as a yes." The discussion ended because the bell was about to ring. Entering the building, I started to think he wasn't all that shy after all.

My prom date problem occupied my thoughts all day. When I arrived home, I found Mom sober, playing with Johnny, and asking me about my day. I decided to discuss my prom dilemma with her. I knew she would agree with me and confirm that I needed to go with the first guy I had already said yes to.

You could have knocked me down with a feather when she counseled, "You should go to the prom with Luke and just tell the first guy that you can't go with him."

I challenged her. "Mom, you've got to be kidding. If I go with Luke, that's saying to the other guys, 'thanks but no thanks, something better than you came up.' Mom, that's hurtful and selfish. I don't want people to think I'm that awful kind of girl because I'm not."

Mom continued, "Dad and I like Luke. He is the one you should date. Say thank you to the others, but be Luke's date for this special occasion. Prom is different from a regular school dance."

Her advice compounded my confusion and internal fight. My heart wanted to go with Luke, but my gut said it would be a slap in the face to the first guy and that didn't feel right. The prom was still six weeks out, so I decided to think on it for a week.

After two weeks of being driven to school and three dates later, I hadn't made a definite decision. It was clear Luke and I had become close friends—in fact, we had begun sharing small tidbits about our strange home lives. We walked to classes together and talked on the phone for an hour each night. Therefore, it would be weird to go to the prom with someone else when the only guy I was hanging out with was Luke. He continued to insist he knew I was going to go to prom with him. His prediction became reality when I finally decided he was kind of my boyfriend and the one with whom I should and wanted go to the prom. I felt so bad about guy number one and profusely apologized and explained the situation. I guess I didn't do a good job because he never spoke to me again.

With the "Dear John, I am sorry but I can't go to the prom with you" conversation behind me, I became excited about going to the prom with Luke. Mom was excited too and went with me to find the perfect dress. We had a fun day. She even took me out to lunch. This was almost the mom that I had adored when I was little. I had never stopped loving her, but I had stopped liking her. My heart hoped that maybe she was changing back so I would begin to like her again.

Aunt Lulu and her family came to spend prom night at our house so she could see me all dressed up in my first formal, take pictures, and meet Luke. She even helped me with my hair and makeup. Mom was so excited that she started her own "partying" way early in the afternoon. She was extremely "happy" when Luke arrived, movie star handsome, in his white tux jacket and his prized Pontiac. My dad had arrived home with a big surprise of a brand-new 1962 Thunderbird convertible for us to take to the prom. I knew Dad had only the best intentions to make it a memorable evening, but when he told Luke to leave his car and take the Thunderbird, I think he hurt Luke's feelings. His two-door coupe was his pride and joy and I believe he wanted it to go to the prom with us. Nevertheless, he thanked my dad and off we drove in the white convertible with red interior, reminding me of Prince Charming and Cinderella in the magical coach that turned back into a pumpkin at midnight. This whole event was feeling like a fairytale to me; fortunately, midnight was still many hours away.

Everything about the evening was perfect. I couldn't have imagined anything more special. I knew I'd made the right decision in accepting Luke's invitation. He was the only guy I would have wanted to share this wonderful evening with. It was so natural to be with him; we had become good friends, like best friends who trust each other enough with some bad and sad secrets.

When he held my hand, it fit perfectly into his. There were no awkward moments, whether talking seriously or laughing hilariously. Even when we danced we were in sync, plus he never tripped over my feet or stepped on my toes. Have I mentioned that he was cool: tall, handsome, and a gentleman? I felt so honored to be his date. All of a sudden, I realized, in that distinct moment, that he was a special guy and that I liked him in a way much more than a good guy friend.

Fortunately, for me, he liked me too and asked me to go steady with him. I was over the moon and I immediately responded, "Yes, I will!" He gave me his class ring to wear, then we finally kissed each other for the first time.

As I floated up the stairs with his ring on my thumb, I couldn't quit smiling and thinking about this glorious evening. Closing the door to my room quietly behind me, I began to search for my bag of angora yarn to wrap around his ring so it would fit my finger. Ever so softly, I heard a knock on my door and sweet Aunt Lulu's voice whispering, "Can I come in?"

Of course she could come in! I wanted to share the whole evening, including showing her Luke's ring. Together, we sat cross-legged, facing each other on my bed while I whispered and she listened to every magical detail of my evening. I couldn't have imagined the best night of my fifteen-and-a-half-years-old life ending any more perfectly than being able to relive it all again with my precious loving and caring Aunt Lulu, truly a guardian angel to me in so many ways.

Chapter 38
Chicago, IL, June–November 1962

The Parentification of Diana

❦

T he school year ended and I continued on track to achieve my long-term goal. Sonny came home from his freshman year at college for five weeks and worked at the dealership. I earned money by also working at the dealership and babysitting for three families, a lot. Having Sonny home, even if only for a few short weeks, was wonderful. We spent a lot of time together and I proudly introduced him to all my new friends. He was a huge hit with my friends and at a party he taught us the new college rage dance called the Shag. He liked Luke a lot and I loved having him home. He was the only person with whom I could completely talk about the state of our family.

Home life seemed to have calmed down some, until a lump was discovered in our dad's neck.

It appeared it was a fatty tissue lump, but the doctors wanted to remove it, so a simple surgery was scheduled downtown at Wesley Memorial Hospital. Mom, Sonny, and I were there to kiss Dad before he went into surgery and then waited and waited before the doctor came out and told us he had Hodgkin's Lymphoma, a form of cancer. The tumor was malignant and he would need radiation treatments. Dad had to remain in the hospital for several days. Dr. Clark estimated he had six months to two years to live. Mom was shell-shocked, looking as if she might collapse right there in the surgical waiting room. Together, we sat watching her struggle to hold herself together. There was nothing we could do or say to comfort her. She was locked in her own world of hell. We kept making eye contact with each other, but neither of us spoke until we were told we could all see Dad.

Except for standing in front of the hospital baby nursery window to see our infant brother in the incubator, I had never been in a hospital before. I was not prepared for how dead a person looks after surgery when they haven't fully awakened from the anesthesia. Dad definitely looked dead, like dead, dead. He was white as a ghost and it appeared he wasn't breathing or moving. The reality of dying hit me and honestly, I didn't know what to do with my head and heart full of foreign thoughts and emotions. I didn't cry. I was frozen, stunned, in utter disbelief. I always assumed that with all the bad stuff that kept happening to us since 1957, life was as bad as it would ever get. Somehow, we were protected from anything else bad that could happen. We'd already had our allotment, reached our quota of bad, so to speak. I mean, how much worse could Sonny and I manage? The somber grey dawns that turn into dazzling bright daylights never seemed to come for us, just scary dark nightmare after scarier dark nightmare. What were we supposed to do now and who was going to take care of Johnny? If Dad was going to die and Mom goes further off the deep end, what happens to him? Sonny now lived, went to college, and worked in Missouri. I was almost sixteen. I could probably find somewhere to live, but I never would be able to take care of Johnny too.

Then, deep down, I remembered I was never alone. My faithful guardian angel had my hand and God had this. He knew what was going on and how it would end. He would guide me through whatever happened. It's amazing how reassuring this knowledge was for me. My faith and trust provided *hope* and a life ring to grab onto.

Hours later, we arrived home, physically and emotionally drained. Sonny and I hadn't had any chance to talk alone. Mom was pretty much a total mess. She was overwhelmed at having to simply walk. My wonderful aunt and uncle were already there, lovingly trying to help and console Mom.

I quietly disappeared upstairs so I could call Luke in private. Our conversation was brief, but his warm support and empathy made me feel better. He was coming over the next day. I was so happy that I had that to look forward to.

The sleeping rearrangements were made and I was informed I would sleep with Mom. I hated that I was the chosen one, then felt instantly ashamed of my selfish feelings. She was completely devastated and beside herself. Once I turned the light out and we settled in bed, she curled into a fetal position and sobbed throughout the night. I lay, hearing her talk to God, pleading with Him, "Dear God, how could you do this to me? I need my husband, even if I think I hate him. Please, please heal him. I can't handle life without him. I'm so scared." She also was incredibly mad at God, blaming and blasting Him for all the bad things that had happened to them. "Why have you punished me? I haven't done anything wrong, nothing has been my fault. My life was stolen from me. You took away everything I loved: my home, my friends, my things, my money. I have nothing left and now you are taking away my husband. Why are you doing this? What kind of God are you? Haven't I suffered enough pain? When is enough, enough? I've lost everything. God, where are you? Why won't you help me? Please, God, don't take my husband away too. I can't carry on by myself."

Hearing her most intimate conversations with her Creator stirred a compassion deep within me that I didn't know I possessed. For the first time, I viewed her not as my disconnected, alcoholic, mean mother, but as a frail, helpless child, unable to care for herself, much less anything or anyone else. I never realized how alone, scared, and helpless she felt. It was also clear she felt no responsibility for any part of the horrific last five years. To Mom, it was God's and everyone else's fault. Her little world of denial had become her safe zone. She was not able to initiate any positive changes to help herself move forward. She could only look backward, at the "things" she was convinced had been stolen from her. She was the victim. Her children were her burdens. Her husband was at fault for all her losses, yet she was obsessed with him. She loved him yet despised him while needing and depending on him for her survival. She had trapped herself within herself, as if chained to the wall of a death row prison cell. She was the keeper of that key, yet helplessly unaware how to use it. She was hopelessly delusional and required professional help. I knew that kind of help was not on the way anytime soon. It hurt to see someone, much less my own mother, so sick. Had she always been like this? Even back when I was four?

God chose her to be my mother. He knew her and He loved her. Obviously, I had some role here in His plan. Instinctively, I knew I needed to be less judgmental about her; her demons were too big and powerful for her to overcome. Perhaps I could be more helpful and certainly more compassionate. I would purposefully stay on my path with my plans to get to college, but at least I had a bit more clarity on why she acted and reacted so strangely. I also had a better understanding why she drowned herself in alcohol. It numbed her pain so she wouldn't have to see—moreover, deal with—the truth or rational thoughts about herself and life circumstances.

I loved her so much, even though I detested her weakness and selfishness. I was grateful for the insight that had begun to emerge from within. I was also thankful that my vision for my life goal was clear and I didn't have those demons to distract me. As I began to drift off to sleep, a happy thought occurred: Luke was coming over tomorrow.

The entire summer flew by quickly. Sonny became the family anchor. Twenty hours a week I would go work at the dealership with Sonny. My exciting job consisted of filing a bunch of boring car sales and service record receipts at the whopping "get rich quick" rate of one dollar an hour. Babysitting was my other source of income during those summer months. By the time school started, my secret shoebox of stash for college was almost full. On a positive note, I was excited to realize that I needed to search for a bigger stash box.

Aside from working at the dealership, Sonny drove Dad to his radiation treatments in those early weeks. Sadly, Dad would return home severely nauseated with the skin on his neck raw from radiation burns. Emotionally, his spirits were lower than I had ever seen, but I think Dad was greatly comforted by Sonny's presence. Personally, I loved that my wonderful big brother was home. We continued to be thick as thieves and spent hours and hours talking and enjoying being together again. Our bond remained strong as ever.

Luke represented the best of my summer. He was always supportive as I poured out my concern or complaint over the latest home life crisis. Sadly, he had a few of his own to share. He was my human calmness. He was my dearest friend and confidante. Most importantly, he made me laugh and he made me feel special. The thought of seeing him every day had me excited and anxious for school to start again. Now a junior with only two years left, I was bound and determined to achieve my goals. I needed to do my best and make the most of each day in every way.

As it happened, my junior year was the best high school year ever. A year filled with new experiences, great girlfriends, and good teachers. I was involved in every high school event and club I could be a part of, plus I was president of our local community's Teen Center. College fund money was accruing by babysitting and working as a part-time fill-in at the local florist. On occasion, I would work at the dealership helping them catch up on the dumb filing, which I hated, but loved earning the extra dollars.

The beautiful fall weekends were filled with exciting football games and fun Saturday night dates with Luke. He played varsity and was #80, a tight end. I never missed a game. Somehow, my parents decided that I should babysit Johnny on Saturday afternoons, so I took him to the games with me. He was a good little guy and sat on the bleachers cheering and yelling along with the rest of the crowd, even if the cheering and yelling was for the opposing team. Despite his slow learning disability, he seemed to instinctively know when it was Saturday game day. Secretly, I loved my Saturday afternoon football game dates with him. After the game, Luke would drive us home. To Luke's credit, he was good to Johnny and never acted like Johnny was in the way. Johnny liked Luke a lot. He'd get so excited, clapping his little hands and jumping up and down when I'd tell him Luke was coming over.

Luke and Me, fall 1962

Luke and Me on a summer date, 1963

Luke, 1963

Diana, 1964

Chapter 39
Chicago, IL,
November 1962–Late August 1963

Say It Isn't So
❦

H omecoming was a huge deal at my high school and I was nominated for junior class homecoming queen. I came in second, but was thrilled that I was even nominated. In November, my girlfriends got together with my parents and threw me a big surprise sweet sixteen birthday party. Luke gave me a corsage and a sterling silver charm bracelet. Of course, my special Aunt Lulu was there making sure my party was perfect. I passed my driver's license test on the first try, Dad's Hodgkin's Lymphoma seemed to have miraculously disappeared, and Mom was doing better. All in all, life was better and again, there was Luke. He made everything wonderful.

Fortunately, I was doing well in all my classes and consistently made the honor roll. When you walked in the main door of our school, directly ahead of you was a large glass case, divided into two sections. Posted on the left side was the "A" honor roll students and the other side posted the "B" honor roll students. When the first quarter results were posted, I noticed I was on the "A" honor roll, but Luke's name was nowhere to be seen. One day, I casually mentioned to him that I never thought I would ever date anyone not on the honor roll and I was perplexed why his name wasn't at least on the "B" honor roll. He gave me a strange look, but didn't utter a word.

The next quarter, his name was listed on the honor roll and remained there until he graduated. I was so proud of him. I knew he could do it; he just needed a little encouragement.

Friday night basketball was the entertainment of the winter season and Luke played the varsity forward position. After the game, everyone gathered at the cozy neighborhood pizza place with steamed windows and mouthwatering aromas of pepperoni, cheese, and sausage greeting you as you entered—the perfect post-game Friday night refuge for starving teenagers to gather on the Windy City's freezing cold winter nights.

Life right then did feel normal for this sixteen-year-old girl. To the outside world, Mom and Dad, for the most part, were good. I tried to stick to my goal and fly under their radar screen.

Early spring dawned and my cheerleading girlfriends talked me into trying out for varsity again. I thought, *why not?* I was going to be a senior next year and it was my last shot. The strangest thing happened: I made the squad as an alternate cheerleader. If one of the main cheerleaders couldn't cheer for any reason, I was second in line. This was exciting to me because it was rumored that one, and maybe even two of the current cheerleaders, may have to step down. Suddenly, I had some hope that senior year without Luke would be okay, just in a new and different way.

Again, this year's prom was a special event. Sonny's girlfriend from St. Louis sent me her last year's prom dress, which was my favorite dress ever. Aunt Lulu took the dress in to fit me and I was Cinderella all over again. This year, there was no surprise Thunderbird from Dad waiting for us on the driveway. Luke and I took his family's car to the prom. His Pontiac stayed home again.

Late in May, I threw a surprise eighteenth birthday party for Luke. Like so many times in my life, Aunt Lulu came through and made him a cool birthday cake. Mom had started "celebrating" early and was so excited, she ran to the front door and yelled "surprise" before he even walked in to the house filled with our friends. I'm not sure who was more surprised—Luke, because it was his party, or me, because I couldn't believe Mom did that. Maybe a rough start to the party, but it turned out to be a great night and I was most appreciative of my parents' and Aunt Lulu's generosity to Luke. I forgave Mom for spoiling my surprise. Well, I *almost* forgave her.

As the end of this school year approached, the memory of Sonny's graduation and his leaving for college replayed in my head. Luke and I had been dating a little over a year now and the thought of him not being here next year was depressing to me. Once again, my "best friend" and support buddy was leaving me.

Graduation night arrived, another bittersweet night for me. Luke was ecstatic about graduating and getting away from his unpleasant home life. I understood his excitement, but for me, a huge part of my life was leaving in a couple of months. I wanted the summer to last forever. I wouldn't allow myself to dwell on it ending. To make money for college, Luke got a horrendously dangerous job with the railroad. He was underage, but they hired him anyway. Luke worked hard and long hours all summer as a switchman/night man on the night shift where he caught runaway train cars. He hated the job, but did it because it paid so well. Once, I was whining to Luke that it had been over seven days since we had seen each other and he would be leaving for school in a few weeks. He agreed to come over for a little while after his shift ended. I could tell he was exhausted when he walked through the door. He stayed about an hour, dozing off more than he was awake. On his drive home, he fell asleep at the wheel and hit the school zone sign in front of his old elementary school. Fortunately, the only thing damaged was the sign. Luke and his Pontiac survived, unscathed. I never complained again about not seeing him. The remainder of our summer dates were mostly about going to the drive-in movie where he would fall asleep halfway through the show. We often would take his younger brother Mike, sister Karen, and Johnny with us. They were excited and fun to have along. Neither of our families were a joy to be with, so we created our own little fun nights out. They also were great company for me when Luke fell asleep and then would keep Luke awake while he drove home.

Despite my denial of the inevitable, summer passed too quickly for me. Fortunately my college fund was continually growing. I decided to open a savings account and had to have my mom sign with me since I was a minor. I secretly thought I had more sense and cents than she did, but the bank had its rules. I loved looking at my balance growing every month. It kept me focused. It was my golden ticket to college and freedom from "home."

While I couldn't fathom Luke being away, I also couldn't ignore my senior year approaching. I had registered for some great classes, was involved in lots of school clubs and activities and remained teen president of the Community Teen Center. Also, it was quickly becoming apparent that at least one of the cheerleaders would be stepping down and I could be stepping into the varsity cheerleading squad. My grades were still A's and I began to look at colleges I might be able to get a scholarship to. I had my wonderful circle of girlfriends and my special girlfriends, the twins, Jan and Jen.

In July, Mom and Dad asked me to join them so we could have a talk. Drawing on my past experiences with Mom and Dad meetings, I wished to decline the invitation. I had no choice, so I gave myself a personal pep talk and took my seat at the dining room table. Before they even opened their mouths, I had the ugly feeling that the first three words were: "We are moving!" Bingo, right again, we were moving in a couple of months."

I didn't want to move, but the house I lived in wasn't going to make a big difference. After all, I was leaving in a year anyway, so basically whatever floated their boat was fine with me. That was ...until the second sentence registered in my brain.

"And you'll have to change schools."

My mind silently screamed out at them with every fiber of my being, "Say it isn't so!" My stomach alerted me that I had to leave the table *stat*, or I would be sick right in front of them. I bolted and ran as fast as I could. How could they do this to me, again? I was losing everything, again. They had lied all this time to me, again. They had let me make my plans for my senior year, all while hiding their little secret from me, again. They knew I would not be able to remain in the clubs, activities of my school, or continue as the student president of the Community Teen Center. I had spent the entire summer working on and planning out the teen center events and activities for this upcoming year. I wouldn't get to be a varsity cheerleader and most of all, I wasn't just losing Luke, I was going to leave all my friends, especially Jan and Jen. This was the worst ever! Even Aunt Lulu couldn't fill this void in my life.

Reality with old questions set in quickly. Again, where we were moving? Why had we run for so many years, then—*poof*—it's okay to live in Chicago and reunite with family and old friends? They never bothered to explain this to me, although I posed this question to each of them several times before. They were masters at ignoring and deflecting—or maybe just plain lying and denying.

Back in my room, I immediately dialed Luke. When he answered, I totally lost it and couldn't speak, but hearing his voice calmed me down enough to deliver the unbelievable news, "Luke, my parents are moving and I have to change schools, again! It's my *senior* year and I won't know anyone. Now I can't be a cheerleader and I have to quit all my activities, including Teen Center." I sobbed. "What if it ruins my chances for a scholarship and I won't be able to go to college? I hate them, Luke!"

Luke was as shocked as I had been. I could tell he felt awful for me. Fully aware that there was nothing Luke could do, knowing that he understood and empathized with my pain was comforting. He validated my thoughts. "Diana, I am so sorry for you. It's awful what your parents are doing to you. I would be so hurt and angry too. Hang in there. You have made it this far and you have the grades to earn a scholarship. Don't worry; just keep focusing on what you need to do for you. You'll come down to school and visit me. It'll be okay, just remember that I love you and am always here for you." Luke was my earthly rock.

I allowed myself a few hours to fixate on my problem and feel sorry for myself. You know, the "I-absolutely-hate-my-parents, why-are-they-so-mean" kind of pity party? Deep down, I knew I didn't have a choice and was going to have to move on, so I'd better find out where I was going. Begrudgingly, I made myself be cordial and asked Dad, "Where are we moving? I thought we liked living here, so why do we have to move, now? When we moved here, you promised me that I would never have to change high schools again. I would graduate from here."

Dad took a deep breath and explained, "We have a chance to buy a house. I don't want to rent a house anymore. I want to own a house again. The new house is in Des Plaines and it will be ready before school starts. I did talk with your school but you can't stay there for your senior year unless we pay tuition. The cost is as much as a private school or college and I can't afford it. I'm sorry."

Okay, it was only ten miles away but in a different county and school district. I would at least be able to occasionally get together with my friends. I was upset my current high school wouldn't allow me to remain for my senior year unless my parents paid tuition equivalent to a pricey private school. I knew they didn't have that kind of money or *any* extra money. What they did have in abundance was a stack of bills overflowing with past and ongoing attorney fees and medical expenses. They'd just now added a mortgage the stack.

We moved in August. The new house was a little bigger in a brand-new area. It was three levels and my bedroom was larger. It was nice, but my heart wasn't in it. All I could focus on was how many days I had to live in it until I could leave for college. I continued to work at the dealership each day and tried to see Luke at every possible opportunity. I couldn't bear to think about him living 244 miles away, so I didn't.

I knew owning their own home again was their dream since 1957. It was now mid 1963 and one more child later. I hoped a semblance of my old mom would return. Harmony, maybe even real laughter, would return to our house and both parents would finally look forward to the future instead of lamenting and rehashing their past; pre-, and post-1957. Maybe you can't move forward without resolving your pent-up anger and resentment issues. At least, it was apparent they couldn't.

The drinking started again, subtly at first. The fighting resumed, old issues compounded new issues. Dad went away. Mom retreated. I remember they went to an employee's backyard party shortly after we moved in. When they returned, they were in a fierce fight. They were downstairs but the fight was loud and nasty enough that it woke up Johnny. I brought him into bed with me and languished over this poor little guy. He was only three and had years and years left to live with our parents. It made me sick to think about his life ahead. Strangely though, despite truly feeling hurt and invisible, I never felt deep anger toward my parents on issues affecting me. I was leaving and could take care of myself, but why wouldn't they get over their issues and focus on this precious, innocent, special needs little boy they had brought into this world? He was so dependent, needing security and parents to look out for him—parents not so wrapped up in their greed and selfishness. I hugged him a little tighter and snuggled him to me, asking Heaven to please watch over him.

The next morning, I was driving to work with Dad when I realized he had deep scratches like cat claws up and down his face and his arms. I asked him what had happened. He replied, "Last night I caught Mom a little too cozy sitting on someone's lap at the party. I brought her home against her will. She fought me while we were driving home. So, if anyone at the dealership asks you about my scratches, tell them that we have a kitten and the kitten scratched me during the night."

I turned and looked at him, disgustedly shaking my head. "Dad, do you really think anyone's going to buy the kitten story? What's up with Mom? Is she crazy?" I thought to myself, *am I the sole adult in the house? I'm only sixteen and they are a huge load.*

I can still feel the heartbreaking pangs I felt saying goodbye to Luke as he drove out of our driveway heading off to school. Thankfully, he was going to college, not being deployed to Vietnam. For that, I was grateful. However, I was so worn out by my parents and my circumstances, that at that moment, Luke's leaving for college was the same as him going halfway across the world. He wasn't here with me. I was left behind, feeling alone on this planet, in the war zone, like a prisoner of war being held captive by my own family.

Still not speaking to Dad, Mom took Johnny and left a couple of days before my new school was to start. At first, I was a bit upset with her abandoning me and then I thought better of that emotion. Now I could start my last year of high school focusing on just me for a day or two. Dad didn't come home until around ten at night and I would have the house to myself. I could even vent my sadness and cry openly because I missed Luke so much. Maybe I would call Sonny too.

Johnny and Me, New House under Construction, Summer 1963

Chapter 40
Des Plaines, IL,
September–December 1963

Keeping My Eye on the Prize

"You can have what you want, it just may not be the way you had envisioned it."

My senior year began at the new school. It was not just a new school to me, but new to the entire student body. The first day of school was also the first day for the new high school. Three surrounding high schools each sent one-third of their students to this new high school. Additionally, there were a few of us who were simply new to it all. Our senior class never totally gelled. Everyone hung out with the kids they already knew. I don't think anyone was particularly happy to be there as a senior. The physical property was the ultimate state-of-the-art in September 1963. It was my thirteenth school and third high school, so I didn't care. I was there to get good classes, good grades, hopefully a good college scholarship, ending with a great big "adios" to my present life.

Meanwhile, I had to focus—really focus—on how to secure my scholarship and do whatever I needed to do, here at this new school, to make what had been my biggest dream become a true reality. This began with a serious heart-to-heart meeting with my new counselor where I emphasized, "I have one goal and that's to go to college. My only path to college is a scholarship and I need your best guidance. My parents are not able to help me. I am on my own. I will work as hard as I can to do whatever it takes to achieve this goal. I have been working on this since I was eleven."

Mr. Hill was great. He stated, "First of all, you have already done all the right things to place yourself in the upper tier of kids trying to get a scholarship. Congratulations on your hard work, but there is still work to be done."

Clearly excited, I smiled. "I am one hundred percent committed to do just that."

"Great," he exclaimed. "Let's get started and place you in all top-level college-bound classes. They will be challenging but I think you're up to the task and will enjoy them. Keep in close touch with me and good luck."

The classes I took blew me away. The school itself not only looked amazing, the caliber of courses offered were more than anything I could have imagined. I was challenged, enlightened, motivated with a fire in my belly and thirst for knowledge that I had never encountered before. The teachers had unconventional methods and stimulating subject material. They were interactive with the students as well. These educators were passionate about what they taught and that had a positive effect on their students. Classrooms were alive and everyone was engaged. Not only did we learn, but we had fun learning. They taught with Socratic openness, allowing everyone the freedom to express themselves while not having to worry about the "right" answer in the study materials. We got to think out loud, out of the box, not just regurgitate the rote answer from the textbooks.

During my morning study hall, I was a chemistry lab assistant with two classmates in the same college-bound track as me. We mostly roasted hot dogs and made tea over the Bunsen burners. We also sat around on the station tables talking with the teacher, who treated us more as friends than his students. I thought I would hate chemistry, but I ended up learning and loving it a lot. Criminal Justice and Far Eastern History were not offered at my old high school, but were exhilarating subjects here, taught by exceptional instructors. I ended each day with journalism class where I was a junior editor of the school paper and the yearbook.

In lieu of an afternoon study hall, I took advantage of participating in a newly offered, intense, study skill class. I thought I already was a good studier, but this class honed my skills, taking them to a higher level. Scholastically speaking, this was a special school and I felt lucky to experience this new approach and level of learning. With that said, there was no way I would ever admit to my parents how much I appreciated the educational aspect of my thirteenth school.

On the social scene, I wasn't interested in guys since I already had Luke, the best guy in the world. However, on the second day of school, I literally ran into a girl Luke and I had double dated with several times over the last eighteen months. She did not go to the same high school Luke and I had attended, but her boyfriend had. Kenny was a good friend of Luke's and he also played varsity basketball. On basketball nights, his girlfriend, Ann, would sit with me during the game. So, when I saw her in the hall, I called to her and we started talking. I found out she was new, like me, and had just transferred to this school. Kenny went to a college about a half an hour from Luke. They were still going steady. Our friendship was sealed and we were inseparable best friends from that day forward.

Ann was not going to go to college. She wanted to start on her career right out of high school. She was a hard worker and was all about making money. Our career paths to achieve our goals were different, but we were in sync regarding our motivation to make money now. Together we applied for cashier jobs at the local big box store, Zayres. We worked weekends, nights, and as many after-school hours as we could. We nicknamed Zayres "FABS" because every ten minutes or less, the store manager would announce "another fabulous deal at faaaabulous Zayres." I swear I heard his voice in my dreams. The best reward of working at Zayres was the steady paycheck I got each week. My college savings account was continually growing and I was proud of myself and my hard work.

In late October, I made my first visit to see Luke and check out the university. It was homecoming weekend. I was excited yet anxious about seeing him. During the entire train ride, doubts crept into my mind like, *will Luke still like me when he sees me? Will I seem too young to him now that he's around all those college women? Will he dump me because of my family issues?* I had kept the family secrets and never told him about my name change, the FBI and bad guys issue, or any of the ugly stuff. He thought I had an alcoholic mother and a seriously ill, on-and-off-again, disappearing father, along with two brothers, one three years older and one thirteen years younger.

As the silver train pulled into the station platform, I saw Luke waving and smiling. He looked happy to see me. He ran to help me get off the train and gave me the biggest hug and a wonderful kiss, erasing all my jittery doubts.

Luke had arranged for me to stay with a couple of girls in their dorm room. They were friendly and we hit it off from the start. We even stayed up most of the night talking. I was so excited about college that I could hardly wait for next year when I would be "one of them," a freshman in college, hopefully at this same university.

The weekend was special. Nothing had changed between Luke and me. The awful part was that I knew I would be leaving early on Sunday and have to say goodbye to him until Thanksgiving. I prayed I would get a scholarship to this university so I could be with him. The train ride home gave me time to reflect over my forty-three-hour college experience. I was on fire to go to college more than ever now. My motives had expanded and clarified. It wasn't just about escaping anymore, but about everything in my life—growing, learning, achieving, along with self-sufficiency that included having control of my life. With all these goals almost within my grasp, I was more determined than ever to get that scholarship, work however many jobs necessary to earn enough money, and to do better than my best efforts at school. It was as if my whole future life depended on this timeframe. Along with the help, guidance, and protection from above, I had all the confidence in the world that it would come together and happen. Nothing was going to stop me.

In mid-November, I turned seventeen. It wasn't a big deal. Luke was away, Sonny was away, and in true family tradition, my parents forgot it was my birthday. In fact, they went out to dinner with friends, leaving me home to babysit Johnny and celebrate with a peanut butter and jelly sandwich for dinner. I put a big candle in my sandwich and Johnny and I sang "Happy Birthday" to me seventeen times. I can still see him singing away and blowing out my candle after all seventeen songs. Despite my parents, that little guy made it a very special birthday.

Six days later, on a Friday, John Fitzgerald Kennedy was assassinated. I was at lunch in the school cafeteria when we heard the news. Stunned, everyone froze, as if each student was holding their breath. School was cancelled for the rest of the day. I arrived home to find a note that my dad had disappeared for a few days again and my mother had taken Johnny and gone to stay with friends. Her actions left me home alone and stranded without transportation for the entire weekend. When I called the phone number on the note she had left, whoever answered said she would give my mother the message that I had called and hung up. I spent the weekend glued to the TV and crying into my sandwiches, not certain who I was crying for—JFK, Jackie, or myself.

On a happier note, Luke was coming home on the following Wednesday for Thanksgiving break. I could hardly wait; I had missed him so much. Thanksgiving was okay. We celebrated with my grandmother, my precious—however, visually weakened—beloved grandfather, my Aunt Lulu and her family, and one of Dad's cousins and family. Luke came over early in the evening for dessert. Sonny didn't make it to Chicago since he was coming for Christmas vacation.

Saturday night, Luke and I had a date for a bite to eat at our favorite hamburger place. He was leaving early Sunday morning to head back to college for finals week. He would be back again in about ten days, remaining home until after New Year's. I was excited to have more time to spend with him.

A few hours later, as we pulled onto my street, we noticed a lot of flashing red lights up ahead. As we approached my house, we realized those flashing red lights belonged to the ambulance in my driveway and the police car behind it. Jumping out of the car and running into the house, I couldn't imagine what had happened. When we left, less than three hours ago, everything was normal. My two cousins, Marie and Kevin, were spending the night, and all had seemed well.

An ambulance gurney was stationed by the front door. The doctor and police were asking questions and taking notes while talking to my mother about my father. I noticed my dad didn't look too well and my mother had obviously been spending her evening with her favorite buddies, which had now changed to vodka and Salems. Johnny, Marie, and Kevin were nowhere in sight.

I dashed upstairs to see where and how they were. Johnny was sleeping in his room and Marie and Kevin were huddled together on my parents' bed, looking scared to death. Marie ran to me, crying, "I was hoping you would come home soon because I'm so scared and so is Kevin. Uncle C and Auntie J have been yelling and screaming at each other for a long time and Uncle C told us to go upstairs and stay in this bedroom. I don't know how long we've been in the bedroom but it feels like a long time."

Disgusted and concerned, while hugging them, I suggested, "Let's go climb into my bed. We can all sleep together tonight and stay snug until your mom comes to pick you up in the morning. You are safe and everything is okay, but right now I need to go see what has happened and then I'll come right back."

Poor Luke was waiting for me at the foot of the stairs, not quite sure what to do. He went with me to talk to the authorities. Apparently, someone had called 911 (I think my mother) because my dad had taken an overdose of pills and told her he was just going to end it all. He was tired of fighting the courts and her. He wanted to give up and die. We would all be better off without him. As it all turned out, he was given something that made him throw up the overdosed pills and we were told not to let him go to sleep for a few hours.

And that was it. The ambulance and the police left, leaving me in charge of an overdosed, 210-pound man and his incoherent, inebriated wife. I don't think the police were aware of the three children under eleven upstairs. As they both pulled out of the driveway, I did think to myself, *how was it that I, who had turned seventeen two weeks ago, was now in charge of my parents, two cousins, and my little brother?* Again, what in the world were my parents thinking this evening? They had been entrusted with watching and supposedly offering a safe and fun night for Marie and Kevin. My saving grace was Luke, who saw and heard everything. He jumped right in and made my dad strong coffee to drink. He then proceeded to hold up Dad and keep him walking around and through the living room, dining room, and kitchen for at least for an hour or so until Dad became more lucid and we felt it was safe to let him lie down on the living room couch.

I guided Mom to her bed, where she passed out in about a second. I then checked on Johnny who remained peacefully zonked out and found Marie and Kevin sound asleep in my bed. Luke had to be getting dizzy going around in circles, but he kept on walking and hanging onto Dad. I was so grateful to Luke and loved him so much, I thought my heart would break. He was so kind and honest. He was the absolute best person I had ever met. While Sonny was in an elite category of his own because he was my brother and we shared the same problematic parents, I knew Luke could have said he'd had enough and walked away to find some girl that didn't have all this turmoil, mystery, and drama. To have me for a girlfriend was a heavy load.

The next morning, when Aunt Lulu came to pick up Marie and Kevin, my mother had already packed a suitcase for herself and Johnny. She had decided to leave and go home with Aunt Lulu, again. I don't think Aunt Lulu was particularly happy about this, but felt obligated to watch out for my mother.

Sometime earlier in her life, my grandmother had told her that she, Aunt Lulu, who was nine years younger than my mom, had to watch out for and take care of her older sister, my mother. Personally, I think my grandmother was wrong to place that burden on my aunt. I believe, as grown-ups, each of us should be responsible for ourselves and our own actions. If we screw up, we need to own up and live with the consequences or rewards of our choices. Each day, we get to make new choices, good or bad. Will they bring us joy or sorrow?

The house was so quiet after they left. Dad, too, was leaving for wherever it was he kept leaving to go to. He would be home on Thursday. Today was only Sunday.

Luke had called from a gas station early in the morning to see how everything was going on my end and to say goodbye. Fortunately, Mom had driven with Aunt Lulu so at least there was a car available if I had an emergency. Being alone should have been any seventeen-year-old's dream come true if they weren't afraid of being alone after dark. Sadly, I was terrified of being alone at night. I heard every creak and sound imaginable, always thinking the whole world knew I was alone and something bad was going to happen to me. When I would finally fall asleep, I would suffer dark, terrorizing nightmares. I am sure I could have called my best friend, Ann, and stayed at her house, but I was ashamed of my family's situation. I didn't want to have to lie or explain it. I was also embarrassed that I was such a scaredy cat of the dark at seventeen years old. Fortunately, I knew I still had my guardian angel, who was always hanging with me.

I never spoke with Mom until she returned about a week later. Dad had arrived back on Thursday as he said. I don't know what transpired between the two of them, but they seemed to have reached a temporary detente. I could only guess for how long. Once again, no explanations or apologies were given. Maybe they figured if they didn't talk about anything with me, I would forget it ever happened. I felt it confirmed that I was invisible to them, a nonentity; therefore, I didn't deserve any further communication on the sordid topic. My estimated worth to them amounted to being a built-in babysitter that they conveniently didn't have to pay or drive home at night. I must admit, I felt a little sorry for myself and upset with them. One emotion that remained perplexing to me was why I cared about them and still loved them so much.

On a much brighter note, Luke came home on Saturday for about four weeks and Sonny would be here soon as well. I'd have my full support team back for this Christmas. Reason enough to make me happy and celebrate the season.

Chapter 41
Chicago, IL, January–August 1964

Nothing Is Going to Stop Me Now!

I was on the home stretch! My bank account was building and looking healthy. I still had several months to work at Zayres and I was planning on landing a better-paying, full-time job for the summer. My school counselor told me that my scholarship chances looked excellent and I should hear any week now. Out of our senior class of 430 or so students, I was number seven, my ACT score was high, and my activities were strong. I already knew what state school I wanted to go to. It may not have been the strongest in academics, but it had Luke. I knew having his daily support would be my best motivator for focusing and achieving my future goals.

Mom and Dad were better, but still not the kind of parents I would have chosen for myself. Intermittently, Dad would be "on a business trip" for a few days at a time while Mom vacationed in her drunken world on the living room couch. On the night of my National Honor Society induction, Dad was conveniently out of town and Mom decided it was too cold outside to go anywhere, so she stayed home on the sofa snuggled up to the fireplace with her "old friends." Luckily, I had my driver's license so I drove myself. I was rather disappointed in them, but then I remembered I was never totally alone and this "honor" was something I had worked hard to achieve and only I needed to be proud of me. After all, it selfishly was all about me and my goals. Walking across the stage to receive the recognition and National Honor Society pin served to reinforce my resolve and knowledge that I could achieve my goals. At that moment, I believed I could accomplish and overcome anything. I had a terrific support team above that hung in there, holding my hand through thick and thin. All I ever had to do was believe and be true to myself while faithfully trusting in Him.

A few more bumps on the road occurred that spring. The most embarrassing one was having Ann almost trip over my passed-out mother on the bathroom floor late one night.

I was fed up with arriving home to a drunken woman drinking what she claimed was "water" out of a tall glass with ice and denying it was vodka. One day, when she wasn't home, I collected all the vodka bottles I could find and dumped the contents down the kitchen sink and refilled them with water.

Confession #1: I must admit that I secretly was chuckling about how Jesus changed the water in the wedding water jugs to wine and I was exchanging vodka in the vodka bottles for tap water. Quite obviously not same thing, but I did snicker about it while I was pouring out her beloved elixir. As you may well imagine, Mom found no humor in this vodka-to-water exchange. When she discovered the vodka had mysteriously turned into water, she was furious with me. By then, I was beyond caring whether she would get mad at me or not and smugly replied, "If you had honestly just been drinking ice water out of a glass, how would you know or care what was in the vodka bottles?"

Confession #2: To be truthful, my demeanor was a combo of a sarcastic tone accompanied by a disrespectful smirk defiantly planted on my face. She looked like she was going to kill me, but I held my ground and intentionally stared her down. I had the cheeky Ms. Queen of Righteousness thing going on in my head.

The best of that early spring was a surprise visit from Luke. He hitchhiked all the way home from college one afternoon to ask me to wear his fraternity lavaliere pendant, then immediately turned around and hitchhiked back after I said yes and kissed him. I was blown away. This was a step above going steady and the step just before getting pinned. After being pinned, an engagement ring usually follows and we all know what comes after engagement.

A couple of weeks later, I joyously received my acceptance to Luke's same university. I had been awarded a complete four-year scholarship to any Illinois state college or university of my choice. All I needed to pay was a portion of my room and board. Good news, I'd already saved more than enough money to cover that expense and the money was safely tucked away in my savings account. My long-time goal was achieved. Now I just had to get through the formality of the graduation ceremony and possess that coveted diploma. I was ecstatic; not only was I going *away,* I was going away to college *and* Luke. All my prayers were answered, big time.

My graduation night finally arrived. I was proud of myself as I walked across the stage with my cherished National Honor Society gold tassel swinging from my mortar board. For over six years, I had been extremely focused on my goal and my commitment to hard work had paid off. Not withstanding my home dramas and attending thirteen schools, I graduated number seven in my class. Mom and Dad, my grandparents, and Aunt Lulu and family all attended. Sonny and Luke weren't home from college yet. After the ceremony, the whole family celebrated at our house and ate my special graduation cake made by who else but my loving Aunt Lulu. As elated as I was, I missed sharing and celebrating the biggest moment of my young life with my two best friends.

Mom and Dad never mentioned my accomplishments or scholarship. It seemed to me, my going off to college was a non-event in their eyes. If I could get there by myself, that was fine with them. Anything was fine with them, if it didn't cost them any money or be an inconvenience in their lives. I don't think they realized yet that their free live-in babysitter would be leaving as well.

My parents were absorbed with themselves. It's just who they were, the parents I was given—a simple fact of my life. It wasn't that I wanted a different Mom or Dad, I just wanted them to be like other moms and dads—you know, loving, protective, encouraging, interested, and proud of their kids.

Why did I have the mom and dad I had? Clearly because they were the parents God wanted me to have. Maybe it was for them, maybe it was for me, or maybe it was so I would learn how to become a better parent to my own children. Whatever the reason, my early struggles taught me many skills that have helped me throughout my life. I'll never know the real answer and I am fine with that too.

PART 6
Chicago, 1964–1966
The Great Escape

Chapter 42
Chicago, IL, June–September 1964

Sweatin' for $'s
❧

That summer, my friend Jen and I found jobs at an automotive thermostat manufacturing company with no air-conditioning. It was the biggest motivator to make sure I continued to do my best while in college because it was the worst job I could've imagined.

The first couple of days, they placed Jen and me each on a moving assembly line that welded all the oil slick metal thermostat parts together. Apparently, neither of us were gifted with the talent of picking up the preassembled piece from the moving assembly line and gingerly placing it in the special holder on the machine with your left hand while your right arm reached up to grab a lever and pull down on it to weld the parts permanently together. Didn't sound too hard, boring maybe, but not difficult. Well, apparently it takes great skill and concentration because I would quickly pick up the assembled piece off the fast-moving belt, yet somehow, on the way to the machine, I would continually do something that made the piece in my hand spring apart, sending the tiny metal components all over the floor. That meant the foreman would have to sound a large horn blast, indicating a line was being shut down, then stop the line. Once the line stopped moving, the other workers on the line would watch and wait until I picked up all the parts from the floor. I caused this to happen several times during my shift. Across the factory floor on a different assembly line, Jen had similar issues. After two days, the foreman took us both off the lines and we were given new jobs. This line was easier but nasty.

It was the final inspection thermostat testing line. Jen and I sat on tall stools in front of huge vats of hot steaming water. Please note: it is mid-summer in a factory with no air-conditioning or fans and little air circulation. Trays of welded thermostats would be lowered into the vat of hot steaming water while I hung over the ugly water-filled vat to inspect each thermostat as the valve opened in the hot water or not. The ones that opened got a green wax dot on it and the defective ones got a red wax dot. Work began at seven-thirty and ended at four-thirty. Everyone got a morning and afternoon fifteen-minute break and a thirty-minute lunch hour. I hated it. Luckily, after a few sweltering hot weeks hanging over the steaming vats, they needed clerical help in the air-conditioned office. Jen and I were overjoyed to be moved to the front office to help for the remaining time of our employment.

This job was valuable in a few ways. It was a full forty-hour-a-week job and paid a tad over minimum wage. My savings account was flourishing. I realized, even though I was lucky to have this job, I knew without question that I wanted a college degree. My career aspirations were focused on the teaching and psychology fields. My choice of university was focused on my proximity to Luke.

Speaking of Luke, we didn't see a whole lot of each other that summer. He worked the night shift on an Eden's expressway road construction project while I worked the factory day shift. He didn't have weekends off and I didn't have any weekdays off. Somehow, we managed some kind of date once a week, even if it meant me watching him sleep at the drive-in movie.

After what felt like an eternity, my summer job came to an end. It was time to put my energy and entire focus into getting myself ready to head off to college. My childhood escape to freedom dream, which had seemed altogether impossible six-and-a-half long years ago, was suddenly only a couple of days away from becoming reality. My *life*, controlled by *me*. Oftentimes, when things seemed especially hard, the painful memories of planning my future while sitting on that old, splintered, dirty picnic table in the weed-decorated, dirt backyard of the flea-infested Long Beach house, had motivated me to stay my course. I had just turned eleven years old when I formed my dream plan and I had held onto my dream and worked this plan for more than one third of my entire life. The reality of it rather overwhelmed me.

Now, all I had left to do was say goodbye to my relatives and friends, switch my savings account into a checking account, pick up a few last items, and pack it all up. In a mere two days, I would be a true college freshman on a full scholarship. I had made it! Nothing and no one could stop me now!

As I walked into the bank I was so excited and proud of my accomplishment, I silently thanked God for always being there encouraging me. A sweet lady at the teller window asked, "How can I help you?"

I gushed, "It's time for me to close my savings account and transfer my funds into a brand-new checking account. It's for college. I'm so excited and I've already chosen the check design I want." Eagerly, I passed the lady my driver's license as an ID along with my savings account number. I had memorized my account number on the day my account first was opened.

Smiling, she instructed, "Wait here while I look everything up." As I waited, I pinched myself. This was finally—I mean, for real—happening. In two more days, I would be moving into my new dorm room.

After several minutes, regardless of my euphoria, I noticed this was taking way longer than when I'd come in to make my deposits. I'd also seen the teller go ask a man something and then disappear into another office. It felt like an eternity before she returned to the teller window with a perplexed look on her face. She questioned me, "Are you certain you gave me the correct account number because this account is no longer active. It was closed a couple of weeks ago and the funds have been removed."

"I'm one hundred percent positive," I stammered.

She passed a paper through the little opening in the glass and pointed to the signature of the person who had received the money and terminated the account. It was my mother's signature. The account balance was zero. My entire life's savings was no longer available to me. The money I needed for college was gone.

In that moment, I didn't comprehend the total impact of this devastating news regarding my college situation. I believe I was in disbelief and my mind numbed by shock. I don't think I thanked the lady for her help. I just took the paper and ran out the door to the car. I was so beyond upset that I didn't even cry. Shaking uncontrollably, I got in the car, locked the doors, and tried to make myself calm down and think. *What should I do now? Surely, my mother wouldn't have taken my money.* Regardless of her detachment, I still believed with my whole heart that she loved me and if she loved me, she wouldn't do anything that would crush me and my dreams. Would she? Instinctively I already knew the answer but it was too painful to acknowledge. I was aghast even thinking it to myself, by myself, about myself. It was beyond cruel. I quickly opened the car door and threw up on to the pavement.

I sort of collected myself and out of habit, maybe false bravado or simply self-denial, I told myself that all I needed to do was ...when frankly, reality hit me hard. I didn't have a clue about what I could or needed to do. I was alone in this. I was in serious trouble. I felt utterly hopeless. Then, let's just say my guardian angel and the Holy Spirit within me took over. They miraculously calmed me down enough so I would be capable to drive home. Though still deeply shaken, I prayed for guidance from God and to *please* help me figure out a way to leave for school in two days. Suddenly, my reasons became so much more than merely wanting to go to college and be in control of my life. It was imperative I leave home. I had to fight to save my own life.

I could no longer deal with my sick parents. Not the drinking, fighting, lies, affairs, detachment, my total lack of trust of them, the insults, the verbal abuses, instability—not anything, not anymore. They were drowning me. The enormous weight of their issues and constant problems was pulling me under. It didn't matter what I did, how hard I worked, or what I achieved; if I stayed, I was going to lose myself, my life, my future, my everything. I couldn't breathe. I wouldn't let that happen. In my mind, I'd already paid a lifetime price. I was going to get away no matter what. I lived with, coped with, and survived their dysfunctional messes for seven years. The rest of my life belonged to me and I chose to claim it, protect it, live it, and enjoy it.

Driving back to the house, I realized I had one day left to figure something out. Possibly the two hundred dollars I had stashed on me would carry me through until I could get a job at school. I had to pay eighty-four dollars for room and board when I moved in the dorm. I would still have $116 in my pocket. I wasn't sure how much my books would cost because some the books were covered. Perhaps I could just go to the library or occasionally borrow my roommate's book until I saved up enough money to buy my own. Perchance Luke hadn't sold all his core books from last year and would sell them to me at a much-reduced cost. I knew for certain he would give them to me if he could, but Luke was putting himself through school and needed every penny too.

Regarding me finding a job, I remembered that a girlfriend of one of Luke's fraternity brothers had mentioned she worked in the dorm dining hall. If she worked twelve shifts every week, she had enough to pay her room and board, still having twelve dollars left over at the end of each month. She also mentioned her roommate worked at the student union to earn extra spending money. If these ideas didn't work out, the off-campus stores around town might need extra help. I was going to stick to my plan. I was leaving in two days and I certainly was going to find out why and to where my savings had vanished.

As I pulled into the driveway, my stomach tensed up into a thousand tiny knots. Devastated over my new circumstances, I now had to confront Mom. Her reaction would either validate or negate my seven-year fearful question of whether she loved me or not. Entering the house, I was drawn back to my ten-year-old self on November 4, 1957, who so desperately craved her mother's love. I had felt rejected and abandoned then, and presently would say "ditto" adding betrayed and bitterly disappointed to my emotional wounds list. I also felt heavyhearted, as if I was about to attend the funeral of my relationship with my mother.

She was sitting with her head facing down at the kitchen table. Her glass of "ice water" set in front of her and a Salem cigarette dangling from her fingers. A half-full bottle of some no-name vodka faced her. She didn't look up or acknowledge me as I sat down on the beige kitchen chair across from her. My heart was pounding out of my chest, but I had promised myself that I would approach this in a calm manner, not allowing her to see the struggle to keep my pent-up, devastated emotions in check.

I managed to remain composed as I related the bank incident to her. "Mom, I just came from the bank. They said you closed and withdrew every penny from my account two weeks ago. Here's the bank document the teller gave me. It shows a zero balance and it's your signature confirming the withdrawal and authorizing the closing of my savings account."

Trembling, I placed the bank's document in front of her. She didn't look at it; she just kept her head down, making no sound or movement.

Dying inside, I prayed, "What do I do now, dear Jesus? Please help me stay calm and guide me through this."

"Mom, do you know or remember anything about this?" I softly inquired. Again, my words were met with no response.

Slim on patience, I now point-blankly asked her, "Mom, what have you done with my savings? Where's my money? Why did you take it? You know that money was for college. I've saved it up over the past six-and-a-half years. I earned every single cent of it—none of it was yours or Dad's. Where's my money? Mom, I desperately need it now. Please give it to me."

Silence, dead—deafening—silence. I wanted to scream at her, shake her, make her look at me. "Mom! Did you hear or care about anything I just said? Do you care about the urgency of my situation?" And then I asked her the scariest question ever, "Mom, do you love or even care about me?"

With that, Mom finally raised her head and, like in slow motion, turned to look at me. Her once bright beautiful hazel eyes appeared rather blurry, making me wonder if her eyes may be tearing up because of her feelings for me or just watery from her alcohol-induced state.

Fighting back tears and praying my voice wouldn't break, I pleaded, "Oh, Mom, *please*, why and where do you have my money?"

Slurring her monotoned words, she faintly whispered, "I don't have the money. I withdrew the money and closed the account because I needed the money.

I begged her, "Tell me, what did you need my money for?"

Almost imperceptibly, she shook her head, remaining silent. Then dropped her head back down on the table, ending all further discussions regarding my money or me.

Now frantic, I wanted to shout, "Wait, wait! I'm not finished! You haven't given me any answers. I don't know anything about my money. If you love me or despise me or if you even understand, *you stole my college savings*, my college money. You have put my future in jeopardy. How could you do this to me? How could you be so cruel and merciless? Why can't you be a mom to me? A mom I can trust and rely on to be the number one person I should be able to count on my entire life. A mom who wants good things for her child, not a mom who doesn't care—or worse, steals money and a future from her daughter who, despite everything, remains loyal, protective, and loves you."

Spent and empty, I escaped to my room. Lying on the bed, I vowed that if I ever had a daughter, I would always be there for her no matter what, forever. I would want her to know I would always champion her cause. I would want her to know how loved and cherished she was, how proud I was of her, how blessed I felt to have her. I would not lie to her, abandon her, reject her, or betray her, ever.

Oddly, thinking about my hopefully someday daughter brought a sense of peace and new resolve to me. I quit wallowing in my own pity party. It made me feel more in control of my future. It gave me courage to pursue my goals. It made me get off the bed, finish my to-do list and let go of what I couldn't change today or probably ever. I may not be able to rely on or even trust my parents ever again, but I had God. I trusted God one hundred percent. He had always taken care of me in the past and I absolutely knew, without a doubt, that He would take care of me now. I didn't know how, just that He would. Confident that I safely could go off to school and everything would work out, I was cautiously excited again.

I knew I needed to pray for Mom and Dad. Never could I change them, but I could change the way I looked at them. I would change myself and keep moving forward. Each day of our life boils down to our personal choices and I had just made mine.

Chapter 43
Western Illinois University, IL, September 1964

I'm Possible

෴

"Nothing is impossible.
The word itself says: 'I'm possible!'"
By Audrey Hepburn

J ohnny and I sat in the back seat of Dad's car as we drove down the highway to college. I viewed it as the birth of my new life. I was free, finally in control, leaving all the garbage and baggage of the last seventeen-and-a-half years behind. Mom and Dad would be free of me and I of them. The only person I was concerned over was the innocent four-year-old little guy napping with his head on my lap, holding on to my hand even while he slept. I had no idea how to protect him any longer. I could say farewell to Mom and Dad with only relief and freedom of spirit in my heart, but hugging and kissing Johnny goodbye may undo me. Even though I was euphoric that I was finally getting away, I also felt terribly guilty about leaving Johnny with our unstable parents. And yet, I knew remaining with them would never be an option.

Moving into the dorm was quick and easy. After all, I wasn't one of those students who came with tons of personal effects. I didn't have a whole lot, so I didn't bring a whole lot. Let's call it minimalistic. As I put down the last box, I turned to thank them and say goodbye. They still had a four-hour drive back to Chicago. I hugged and kissed Dad, bear hugged, snuggled, and kissed Johnny, then turned to Mom. As I put my arms around her, she glanced up at me with tears welling up and a look of deep sadness in her eyes. She hugged me tightly, then turned and walked out of my room, leaving me on my own, somewhat confused regarding what had just transpired.

Since I was the first one to move in, I quickly put my things away on one side of the room. My second roommate was a good friend from my second high school and the third girl was from another Chicago area suburb. While they moved in with their stuff, I went to find the dining hall manager in hopes of discussing my immediate employment. The heavenly stars had all lined up for me because I got a job starting the next day working ten to twelve shifts a week. I met up with Luke for an early dinner (his treat) to celebrate this momentous occasion: the first day of my new life.

Later, exhausted, as I laid my head down on my bed in my new dorm room, I became overwhelmed merely thinking of the grace and new chance that I'd been given. My heart felt like it would burst with joy as I closed my eyes in great anticipation of what all the new tomorrows would bring.

I loved every single aspect of university life. It was better than I had ever imagined. I liked all my classes and especially loved two of them. It was so fun living in the dorm with all the girls. And, of course, every day, there was Luke, my rock. Life was the best ever. I felt reborn; I could breathe. I only had to worry about myself. I was in control of myself. Problems—what problems? After my childhood, any "problems" here were minor inconveniences, small blips on my life screen. Every day and night, I was so thankful for the opportunity to live this wonderful college life. Twice a month, early on a Sunday evening when the long-distance rates were the cheapest, I would go to my dorm's pay phone in the basement and call my parents. I'd quickly chat with them because I primarily called to talk with and check on Johnny. I didn't ask questions and tried to ignore any slurred words from Mom. Though the calls went fine, I dreaded going home for Thanksgiving. I wished I could stay right where I was: at school.

November 1964 contained three distinct memorable events.

The first event was significant as a historical marker for our country: the presidential elections in which Lyndon Johnson won by an overwhelming margin.

The second event was significant as a historical marker for the rest of my life: my eighteenth birthday when Luke shocked me by asking me to accept his fraternity pin during a surprise fraternity serenade in front of my whole dorm during a freak November snowstorm.

The third event had no real historical value, just a reminder of how much I disliked being in my parents' presence: Thanksgiving, featuring my first return to my family since I began college.

Selfishness, anger, arguments, and negativity permeated every aspect of Mom and Dad's lives and conversation (the ever-present bottomless vodka bottle didn't help). At times, I felt I couldn't breathe, as if I was being choked. I arrived on Wednesday night and left on Sunday morning. It was the longest Thanksgiving vacation ever. Seriously, I couldn't wait to get out of there. Hurrying to return to campus to study for my first-quarter finals the following week was like winning the Monopoly game's "get out of jail free" card.

With the first quarter of college under my belt, I held a 3.44 GPA. I knew I hadn't done my best because I enjoyed being a bit too social. On the other hand, I cut myself some slack because the special memories of the fun frat parties, crazy antics with my friends compromising the rules of the dorm, the tons of new friends, and even the great staff and students I worked with slinging (serving) food in the dining hall all fed and healed my being. Apart from my "made up" last name, which now felt more like my real name than my real old last name, I wasn't having to lie anymore. I didn't have to cover up for my family. I was just me, Diana, or "Di" as my new friends named me. A freshman here at the university who worked in the co-ed dining hall and pinned to Luke at Theta Xi fraternity. What you see is what you get, just the same as anyone else.

I felt I had left that happy college freshman Di back at school, as I stepped off the train in Chicago for the long four-week Christmas break. My dad was there to pick me up. After pecking my cheek and hugging me, he informed me that I had to be at my new three-week job before eight-thirty tomorrow morning.

I was a tad confused since I hadn't begun to look for a Christmas vacation job, but now I was happy that I already had one, especially when I found out I was working at the Fannie May candy store in the Golf Mill shopping plaza. An old neighbor was regional manager for many Chicago-area Fannie May stores and she had graciously offered me the Christmas season job. This was fantastic. I would make money, be away from the house, and eat all the Fannie May candy I wanted. It was like Christmas had just arrived early for me. Thank you Dad! Secretly, I was elated. This was a lot more money and a much more fun job than I could've imagined. Sorority rush week began the end of January and I wanted to be part of it. I knew I would need at least one new outfit and some extra money to participate in rush and become a sorority pledge. With this early Christmas "gift," my new job, I knew I would be able to swing it financially. Someone upstairs was certainly looking out for me. Thank you!

I loved working at Fannie May. I was the only seasonal worker and the full-time ladies were exceptionally nice to me. I stayed in at lunch because I didn't want to spend the money and I was enjoying all the Fannie May candy. One perk of the job was I could eat as much candy as I wanted while I was working. Since I was skinny, having eluded the usual "freshman fifteen" weight gain, I overindulged myself with Fannie May chocolate mint meltaways and assorted dark chocolate creams, thereby effectively managing to keep any lunchtime hunger pains at bay. It was perfect! The month flew by; I loved it and I loved the money more. It became apparent that after three sweet weeks of devouring my favorite Fannie May chocolate, I didn't crave chocolate as much as I had when I first began selling candy. In view of my working twenty-one consecutive days including all weekends, the store manager offered me Christmas Eve off. The twenty-third would be my final day. She also invited me to work the week before Easter. I thanked her and said I would let her know. I would love to work if I could.

Sonny finally made it home for Christmas late in the afternoon of December 23. Mom had taken a part-time job at a major department store in the new all-enclosed Randhurst mall. She was scheduled to work Christmas Eve day. Sonny and I would be in charge of Johnny. We were thrilled to spend the day with our cute little brother. Sonny came up with great ideas so we could make it magical for Johnny. Later that evening, Sonny and I mapped out the fun day with our special guy. The plan was to play games and help him make his list for Santa in the morning, take him to his number one favorite kiddie lunch at the local hamburger joint, then cap it off with a visit to Santa for a picture and candy cane. After that, we would bring him home for a nap since our grandparents, Aunt Lulu, Uncle S., Marie, and Kevin all would be coming to celebrate Christmas with us. Add Santa's surprise evening visit along with a few presents he could open on Christmas Eve meant it would be a late night for Johnny. I was going with Luke and his family to their church's early Christmas Eve service. Following church, Luke would bring me home and share in our family festivities for a while. So far, it was promising to be a merry Christmas. More like the Christmases that Sonny and I remembered pre-1957.

Our plans all set, Sonny and I went together to inform Mom. "Hey Mom, we have tomorrow with Johnny all planned out. You told us you have the nine-to-five shift, so how about Sonny drives you to work around eight-thirty? That way we can use your car while you're at work. We want to teach Johnny some fun Christmas songs and help him make a Santa list in the morning. Then around eleven, we'll take Johnny and do some last-minute shopping, take him to his favorite burger spot, and a surprise picture with Santa and a candy cane. We'll come home, put him down for a nap, and get ready for tonight. One of us will pick you up at five when you get off. We can do any last-minute errands you need done too."

After explaining our thoughtfully planned itinerary to her, she adamantly responded, "*No*, you cannot use my car."

We were astounded by her harsh demeanor and negative response because she had told us she had to work the whole day at the mall. So, we patronizingly stated, "Why not? Logic would tell us you only need the car for transportation to and from work."

Wow, did that set her off! She got angry and then downright nasty to us when we challenged her about why we couldn't use the car. Her staunch refusal told us that she was up to something in addition to work. We eventually gave up on her, exclaiming, "Okay, okay, don't worry about it. We'll work something out with Dad."

Immediately, she got more agitated then stormed out of the room. About fifteen minutes later, she returned, still miffed. She coldly informed us, "If you drive me to work, you may use my car. I'll let you know when to come and pick me up." With that, she left, leaving Sonny and I delighted that our plan was now going to work.

The next morning, Sonny drove Mom to the mall while I fed Johnny and straightened up the house. We took turns playing Simon Says, teaching Johnny simple Christmas songs, and helping him make his Santa list to pass the time until we would leave for lunch. Around eleven, after dressing him in his Christmas clothes, we merrily headed out for our fun afternoon. Along the way, we decided to stop by Mom's store and see if Mom was free for lunch. We planned to ask her to join us, our Christmas Eve treat, with hopes that some of our holly jolly Christmas spirit would rub off on her. She'd been acting as if she didn't have any.

With Johnny joyfully perched on Sonny's shoulders, we rode up the escalator and found Mom's department. When we didn't see her, we asked a coworker, "Would you please go in the back and ask Mrs. S. to come out? Please tell her that her children are here." We were quite excited to surprise her. The nice lady went to find Mom.

However, when the lady returned, she informed us, "It's only eleven-thirty. I don't expect her for at least a couple of hours."

Puzzled, I asked, "Are you sure you have the right lady?" *Sonny had dropped her off this morning around eight-thirty*, I thought.

She assured us, "Absolutely. Your mother is the only lady by that name who works in this department."

With a "thank you for your help and have a Merry Christmas," we three headed out to get lunch and then find Santa for a photo and visit with Johnny. The promised kiddie hamburger lunch and a little last-minute shopping for Dad's gift and one for Mom completed our afternoon outing. Both Sonny and I were rather confused and apprehensive regarding Mom's disappearance and the real story of her whereabouts. Once back at home, we put one tuckered out, drowsy, but happy adorable little brother down for a nap.

Presents all wrapped, list of chores and tasks accomplished, Sonny and I sat down to discuss the mystery of our missing mom. Neither of us had a good feeling. We had both lived out this kind of scenario many times previously and it had never, ever ended well. And it was Christmas Eve; surely, neither parent would do something to spoil it for the entire family, including grandparents and other special relatives. This magical evening was about enjoying family— love, togetherness, and excitement for our baby brother and sweet younger cousins, including extra special time to spend with our beloved grandfather, who became frailer every time we saw him. He no longer carried his old movie camera around with him capturing his excited grandchildren's early Christmas morning awe and exuberance over the gifts left under the tree by Santa during the night. With a pang of sadness, Sonny and I both realized we were the lucky ones to have had him so healthy and engaged when we were little. We knew we were blessed and now cherished all those memories. Perhaps tonight and tomorrow morning, we could help create some other special memories for Johnny, Marie, and Kevin.

Around four o'clock, Dad arrived home from work, full of Christmas spirit and looking forward to tonight. He was interested to know how our day with Johnny and Santa had gone. Apparently, he had bought Mom something special for Christmas that he needed to pick up at the same mall where she worked so he said he would pick her up this afternoon. We told him we didn't exactly know the time she would get off and brought him up to speed about the whole day.

Dad's face instantly turned ashen; however, within seconds, had become purple with rage. Our father flew upstairs, retrieved an object that we saw him tuck into his pocket as he raced out of the house. We heard him pealing out of the driveway like a deranged mad man. It was alarming and downright chilling to witness. I looked at Sonny wide-eyed. Frightened that tonight would turn into a night we would always remember—another Christmas Eve nightmare to add to our collection. I felt it deep inside me. I also felt sick to my stomach.

Sonny spoke first. "What was that all about?"

I had just begun to answer when we heard Johnny awaken from his nap. Our conversation was put on hold. As I went upstairs to get Johnny, I thought about all the past Christmases and how Mom and Dad had usually taken the merry out of "Merry Christmas." This Christmas might be the least merry to date.

After giving Johnny an after-nap snack, I broached Sonny with my thoughts. "I've been thinking I probably should cancel going to church with Luke's family. We haven't heard from or seen Mom and Dad and this isn't a good omen. Grandpa, Grandma, and Aunt Lulu are gonna be here soon. The kids will all be excited and ready for this special night. Maybe it would be better if the three of us are here to entertain them and hopefully avoid ruining the entire evening for everyone."

Sonny insisted, "No, you should go to church and pray while you are there; then come back here with Luke. I'll fill Aunt Lulu in. Besides, you wouldn't be able to avert whatever is going to happen by staying home."

I reluctantly agreed and went to change into my Christmas party clothes. Our parents had not yet returned when Luke arrived.

The church service was lovely. Luke's parents were welcoming and warm. Mike and Karen were adorable with their eyes all Christmas sparkly. Luke was my rock and looked exceptionally handsome. I had filled him in on the day's events during the drive to his church.

Throughout the service, I was moved by the beautiful music, Christmas program, and the sanctuary all aglow with the lit candles everyone held while singing "Silent Night" at the close of the evening. For a few moments, I was lost in the magic and miracle of baby Jesus' birth. The true meaning of Christmas captivated my heart, filling me with peace and joy. For just that little while, I felt the closeness of God and my ever-present guardian angel. I forgot about the unsettling mess awaiting me back at my house.

Immediately, reality set in when Luke and I walked through my front door. Instead of Christmas Eve bright lights, singing, games, and laughter, it was dark and somber. We found my aunt and Sonny deep in serious discussion at the kitchen table. According to Sonny, our parents returned not too long after I left. Both were furious with each other; Mom cried and looked devastated. Dad was almost violently angry, struggling to stay in control. They were not speaking to each other and the evening was tense for everyone.

Aunt Lulu, Sonny, Uncle S., and Grandma and Grandpa did their best to make Christmas Eve normal and fun for Johnny, Kevin, and Marie. However, there was one major issue. In the middle of the festivities, no one noticed Mom's absence. I don't know who went to find her, but when they found her, she was unresponsive with empty prescription bottles lying next to her on the bed. She had tried, unsuccessfully, to overdose herself on pills and alcohol. Grandma was now tending to her.

As for me, I could only wonder how all this could've occurred in the three hours I was gone. I felt guilty about having had a moving Christmas Eve while all this drama and chaos played out at home. Deep inside, I knew it would have happened regardless of where I was.

Aunt Lulu went to bed and Sonny talked with Luke and me. I suggested Luke go home and have a better Christmas Eve with his family and we would talk the next afternoon. Sonny and I sat on the living room couch, reliving a few of our past memorable Christmases, once more reminding us of how much love we had for each other. We talked about our strong bond as kids, now even more appreciated and stronger as we approached adulthood, and how neither of us could have made it without the other.

Sonny quietly asked me, "How is college? Are you loving it? Uhhh, how are you affording it after Mom's little stunt?"

A smile came to my face as I told him, "I love it. It's better than I had imagined. Sometimes I pinch myself. It's been seven years since you and I sat on that dirty awful picnic bench in Long Beach and made up our *dream for freedom* plans. Can you believe we both achieved our big dreams? We are living them right now! As for Mom stealing my money? I was hurt, crushed. I had worked so hard to get to that day I'd be free and with only one more day to go, I decided, no matter what, neither Mom nor Dad was going to stop me. However many hours I would have to work at school, I was prepared to do it. I would find a way, because I was leaving on schedule. I was going to live my dream and now I am!"

Tears of overwhelming love flowed down my face as Sonny gently took my hand and gazing right into my soul, told me, "Do you know how proud I am of you? I want you to know I have money saved and I will be in Air Force flight training as soon as I graduate in May. If you need help with money for college, you let me know. I can and will help you."

Then lightening the moment, he laughed, "I love you, even though when you were little, I thought you were a brat!"

I hugged him, saying, "So far so good. Things have worked out okay. I'm good, but thank you. You are still the best brother ever!" In my heart of hearts, I knew there was no way I would ever take or borrow money from him. I would never jeopardize his future by accepting his hard-earned funds.

Christmas morning was a déjà vu experience. Mom had her and Johnny's things packed up in a suitcase. She was leaving as soon as she possibly could. Grandma and Grandpa were packed and probably anxious to get back to the tranquility of their house. Aunt Lulu gathered the opened Christmas Eve presents and the still-unopened Christmas morning gifts to take and open at home under their own tree. Johnny, Marie, and Kevin played with their presents they opened last night. Uncle S. packed up the car. Dad had not returned and Sonny and I had no clue where he was or when he would show up.

By ten o'clock on the cold, dreary Christmas morning in 1964, Sonny and I had kissed all our beloved relatives goodbye. We gave Johnny extra hugs, but Mom refused to look at us, much less accept our hugs. I'm sure she was furious with Sonny and me for blowing her cover. We found ourselves celebrating Christmas Day alone, just the two of us. Everyone else had left. I liked it. Sonny had bought a car from Dad and was picking it up the next day. Then he would leave to drive back to school. I would head back January 2 with Luke. At least today, the two of us could spend time together without any interruptions. We made breakfast, cleaned up the house, and played the rest of the day by ear. There was plenty of food so we didn't need to venture out. Time to just stay cozy, while we rehashed and tried to make sense of the unmerry events of yesterday. I had yet to find out where Mom had been, what Dad did when he streaked out of here in such a rage, where he finally found her, and what occurred when he did. Also, what was everyone's reaction when they arrived home? Their neurotic drama overshadowed what should have been a joyous family celebration.

I believed our parents truly needed professional help. Their toxic relationship with each other not only brought out the darkest side of them, it negatively affected the entire family. Their irrational behaviors and overwhelming narcissism had driven both Sonny and I away. We stayed connected to them out of a sense of duty because they were our parents. For reasons I didn't comprehend, we both continued to love them. The dilemma of how much responsibility we had for them nagged at us. Is a child responsible for their crazy parents and their mistakes? Are we to stop moving forward in our own life because we need to help them fix theirs? Do we allow our past to define our future or are we allowed to define our own future? We spent most of the day pondering these challenges and choices. It was impossible to come up with any clear-cut solutions, just more uncertainties.

Sonny gave me the rundown as to the fiasco of events on Christmas Eve. Mom had called Aunt Babs to pick her up at the mall and drive her to meet the same guy with whom she had been too friendly with at last summer's company party. Apparently, Dad had an inkling since that summer party that something was going on between the two of them and her mysterious Christmas Eve caper was proof enough for him. When he furiously raced out of the house, he found her at work and created a horrific, messy scene on the sales floor and dragged her home. I already knew how the rest of Merry Christmas Eve had played out.

Dad returned about around five, greeting us with a, "Hey you two! Where's Mom and Johnny?"

He didn't act surprised when we gave him the scoop: "Mom has left, taking Johnny with her to Aunt Lulu's."

He just said, "Go get dressed up and be ready to leave in forty-five minutes. We are going to Uncle Val's annual Christmas night party," Secretly I always thought of it as the annual command performance, a stuffy, awkward Christmas family soirée.

Dad's uncle lived in a huge house complete with full-time help in Kenilworth, one of Chicago's wealthiest suburbs. The evenings were always stiff, boring, and precisely timed. I felt this was an obligatory Christmas mercy invite for the poor relatives, namely us. We were served coffee and cookies for about an hour and then hastily bid adieu until next year. Definitely a "here's your hat, what's your hurry, thank goodness you are leaving, goodnight, and goodbye" kind of evening. Other than that, we had a rip-roaring great time and could hardly wait to repeat it again next year. I must admit we would always have a good laugh about the "great time we didn't have" during the forty-minute ride home.

Tonight's gathering was odd. No one mentioned Mom's nor Johnny's absence, nor asked how Johnny was doing. They acted like Mom and Johnny didn't exist. In fact, I also realized these relatives never inquired about Sonny's plans after graduation in May or how I liked college. They didn't talk to Sonny or me, so we sat with fixed smiles on our faces throughout the evening's conversations. The silver lining here was we never stayed more than seventy-five minutes.

Sadly, this year we didn't laugh on the forty-minute return ride to our house. I guess none of us were in a humorous mood. In addition to the lack of merriment, there was no discussion regarding anything related to the happenings of the past thirty-six hours. Obviously, this was another taboo subject. The same old premise prevailed: if a parent didn't discuss it with us, we had no right to know. Sonny and I were expected to act as if nothing irregular had happened. Later, when Sonny and I talked about this, we realized within this household that we had grown up in, daily neurotic drama was simply regular life.

Sonny left a couple of days later. We were uncertain when we would see each other again. He wasn't planning any trips back to Chicago prior to graduation and then he would be off to Air Force flight training. The war in Vietnam was escalating. This time, it was a tearful goodbye. We both knew we would be headed in different directions with real adult responsibilities. Our bond of love and partnership would forever remain, but now it took on a new dimension. As traumatic as our childhood was, we always had each other. I believed, together, we could make it through anything our parents threw at us. However, now the real threat of Sonny being sent to fight in the Vietnam War felt way too adult for me to handle. It was too dangerous, too horrific. I wasn't ready for Sonny to be a full adult. I wanted him to be my amazing big brother, best friend, and partner. I was so proud of him and admired him for all his accomplishments. I did not want to turn him loose. Sadly, I hugged him one last time and waved till he was out of sight. Never had I felt this alone. This was truly my worst Christmas ever.

As I stepped back into the cold empty house, I heard the phone ringing. It was adorable Luke. Hearing his voice made me feel better, even though I cried and hiccuped while he patiently listened to my mournful tale. Luke instructed me to hang up and get ready. He was on his way over. We were going to go out. Once again, Luke was there for me—solid, calm Luke. The old proverb about when one door closes, another door opens came to my mind. It dawned on me: I wasn't alone on this earth—I had Luke. Sweet, wonderful, movie star handsome Luke.

The whole week flew by. Ann took me to the store where I bought material to create and sew two new dressy outfits and a pair of shoes. (I had put money aside from my Fannie May candy job for these exact purchases.) I spent the rest of the days sewing my new ensembles. Dad worked long hours and I never heard from Mom. Dad and I got along just fine until New Year's Eve when he caught a glimpse of the dress I had chosen to wear. It happened to be one of the dresses I had made for the upcoming sorority rush formal parties and the Greek Winter Princess Formal. Luke's fraternity had nominated me for Winter Princess and I wanted a sexy but classy cocktail dress. This two-piece sheath dress was of emerald green brocade featuring a somewhat low, but not plunging, neckline.

As I came down the stairs, Dad voiced his complete disapproval of my choice of evening attire by demanding, "Diana, you are not going to leave this house wearing that dress!"

Believe me, my green dress may have been a little sexy, but well within conservative taste. Besides, I'm thinking, *I'm eighteen, engaged to be engaged, in college, and self-supporting. I bought, paid, and made this dress entirely on my own and Dad is not going to tell me what I can or can't wear, nor what I can or can't do anymore.*

I respectfully informed him, "Luke will be here any second and this is what I am wearing." With that, I kissed him goodnight, wished him Happy New Year, put on my coat, and walked out the door. Thankfully, Luke had just pulled in the driveway.

I think this was the first time I had ever openly defied Dad and honestly, it didn't feel so good. I was taught God wanted us to honor our parents, presumably despite their faults, by obedience to them. I figured I had tapped my toe across the obedience line but assumed that since I was eighteen, the line was somewhat subjective.

Chapter 44
Western Illinois University, IL, Spring 1965

Having a Smoking
Good Time

❧

U pon my happy arrival back at college, I found that one of my roommates had decided not to return, so it was only two of us sharing the room now. Liz and I had become good friends and were happy to have the extra space. She was serious about her studies, plus dating one of Luke's fraternity brothers. We got along exceptionally well and became close friends.

Sorority rush started the last Sunday in January. I had decided I would participate. I knew a lot of girls in the various sororities from the fraternity parties I had gone to with Luke. I was excited about this new adventure. On the Saturday before Sunday rush, Liz and I were discussing how most of the sorority's girls smoked cigarettes. We both did not. However, we thought we should learn how to smoke for the rush season. We purchased a pack of Newport menthol filtered cigarettes for twenty-five cents from the vending machine in our dorm's basement. Upon returning to our room, where smoking was prohibited, we opened the smaller, eighteen-by-eighteen-inch window within our big, fixed, picture window so we could exhale the cigarette smoke through the little opening, hoping the RA wouldn't get a whiff of the smoke.

Liz and I sat on our desks facing each other while we took turns pretending to master the look of inhaling and exhaling. She would critique my technique and then I would do the same for her. After a few dry runs, we lit one. The person lighting the cigarette would put her hand holding the cigarette along with her head out the open window so our room or the hall wouldn't smell like smoke. We needed to learn how to get over our choking fits every time we inhaled the awful-tasting cigarette. Neither of us liked it, but we thought we would look more like sorority material—you know, cool and sophisticated—if we could master the art. We were probably turning green from our smoking lessons but were committed to look like pros by the end of the afternoon.

Around thirty minutes into our smoking trials, while Liz had her head hanging out the window, literally, there was a knock on our door. It was the RA. "Girls, girls, are you okay? May I please come in? I smell smoke in this area of the hall. I need to check each room."

I cheerily responded, "Just a minute," hoping we had enough time to hide the Newport pack and open our books to make it look like we were deep into studying. Unfortunately, as Liz tried to back her head out of the window, her head got stuck and she couldn't get it unstuck.

Meanwhile, the RA was rapidly losing her patience. "Girls, open the door and let me in now."

I had no choice but to let her in, hoping we had destroyed all our incriminating evidence.

As she walked in, I watched her sniff around while she gave our little room the once-over, but missed the fact that Liz's head was "stuck" in the window. Perhaps she thought Liz was simply taking a mini-break from our hard-core studying. Maybe even trying to wake up with a blast of cold air. I mean, that could be feasible, couldn't it? I sensed this wary RA knew we were up to something, but she couldn't spot any damaging evidence.

Frankly, I don't think she believed our little charade, but had no proof. Having exploited the innocent-until-proven-guilty rule, Liz and I laughed and thought we were ever so clever. However, we were smart enough to realize what could be at stake if we had gotten caught; therefore, we decided not to push our luck again.

Smoking goal achieved, dressed in my only suit and new heels, I headed to my first sorority rush meet and greet. A little anxious yet delighted at the prospect of becoming a member of a sorority, I hoped I would make a good impression and the girls would like me.

At the first house, all the wannabe pledges were instructed to enter by the rear door and take the back stairway up to the second and third floors for a tour of the bedrooms and baths. Following the tour's completion, we were to come, one girl at a time, down the main staircase that flowed right into the living room. As each girl reached the bottom step, she would introduce herself. The "active" sorority members would then have a "get to know you" chat with each prospective pledge.

When my turn came to descend the grand staircase, I was confident. I made friends easily and people usually seemed to like me. I thought I could make a good impression if I treated this like I did every time I had moved and changed schools. In case anyone has forgotten, that would be thirteen changes of schools, not including college. I told myself I was prepared. I had this.

What I wasn't prepared for was the soles of my new black leather heels being extremely slick, causing me to slip and thump, down every hardwood stair tread, landing on my posterior, legs askew, at the bottom of the stately staircase. Finding myself deposited smack-dab in the middle of the living room filled with the sorority women that I was trying to impress, all I could think to do was smile and introduce myself.

Mortified, yet smiling my perfected new girl in school smile, I introduced myself. "Hi, I'm Diana. I was hoping to make a stand-out impression, however, clumsy was not quite the trait I had in mind."

At first concerned, they asked, "Are you okay? Does anything hurt?"

Then we all laughed as I retorted, "Just my pride!"

I got up and found a seat, thankful the "meet" part was now over. Fortunately, they began the "greet" part as if nothing had happened. I decided not to pull out my ace-in-the-hole pack of Newports.

I was afraid I would have a choking fit upon my first drag, wisely surmising that would not be sophisticated "sorority woman" cool.

The rest of the visits at various other sorority houses went more like I had envisioned. I was too gun-shy to try any attempt at smoking and decided to save that treat for the next round; that is, if I was invited back to any house for a second "look."

It was already cold and dark as I walked back to my dorm. I was also tired. These sorority rush events were much more intense than I had imagined. On the other hand, I knew I wanted to be part of campus Greek life and live in a sorority house next year. I had been told that the room and board fees in a sorority house were less that the university dorm room and board costs. Rush week ended and sorority bids went out. I was excited when I received bids to all of them. My first-choice sorority was not the sorority where I had made such a memorable entry. Despite my less-than-graceful entrance, the Alpha Sigma Alpha sisters had kindly offered me a bid to join. I liked them lot; they were a real close second choice. However, I felt I fit better with the Alpha Sigma Tau sorority that I selected as my number one.

Though thrilled to be an official sorority pledge, I didn't tell my parents right away. I wanted to keep my college life separate from life with my family. So far I had not talked at all about my family with anyone at college, not even my dear roommate Liz. Years before, I had learned to compartmentalize my life. Home life was in a compartment I kept locked away when I wasn't at home. I did not want to merge it into any other part of my life and tried to ignore it as much as I possibly could. So far that had worked well for me and I enjoyed my freedom from home problems and drama. Information about Johnny was the only exception I allowed myself.

Some other girl won the Winter Princess title, but I was chosen to be one of four Winter Princess Court attendants, aka, runner ups. I wore my green brocade dress. Luke loved it and that's all that mattered to me.

Classes were good and I was on track for a 3.8 GPA this quarter. Classroom time, library, studying, two shifts a day working in the dining hall, sorority pledging, and Luke kept me busy and out of trouble. Well, not completely out of trouble. My pledge sisters and I got in tons of trouble over some of the ingenious pranks we pulled on the actives. Sorority punishment notwithstanding, we plebes were impressed with our creativity to keep the actives on alert and dreading what scheme we might dream up next to inject more chaos into their lives.

In late February, I was summoned to come home. I learned that Johnny needed hernia surgery and Dad also needed surgery, both at the same time. Mom needed my help. Johnny's and Dad's surgeries were the same day at the same hospital. I said I would be there. As it turned out, the surgeries were scheduled during my second quarter break so I didn't have to miss any classes; fortunate timing for me.

I felt a little compassion for Mom, as she was overwhelmed. I chose to disregard that most nights for the last seven or eight years, she would sit in her favorite chair with her liquor and cigarettes by her side. The evening would end with her nasty drunken slurs about how much she despised and hated Dad. Two minutes later, she'd be crying that she loved him so much and couldn't live without him. Right now, she was in her "loved him" phase, which was better than her other choice. As for Johnny, that had her pretty worried and I was happy to be there with him and for her.

It was a huge relief when both "boys" came through their respective surgeries. Mom stayed with Dad, I stayed with Johnny. He was a trooper. I had missed cuddling with him, so I treasured having the time to read him his favorite stories and snuggle him. More than that, I felt good about the time I had with Mom. Our roles had reversed way back when I was eleven, and I still felt protective of her in a weird, twisted kind of way. I couldn't explain why she had changed so drastically, but I did remember the wonderful loving mother she once had been. Maybe that's why I continued loving her no matter what. Kind of like how the nuns taught me about how Jesus loves us unconditionally, despite our sins.

One funny incident at the hospital occurred the day Dad was released. Mom and I were in the cafeteria where Dad was going to meet us. Mom knew I smoked but Dad didn't. Both of us were enjoying our cigarettes, when out of the blue, Dad came into the cafeteria. My back was to him so only Mom saw him approach. She grabbed the cigarette out of my hand and sat with a lit cigarette in each of her hands. Dad looked at her, then gaped at me. He must have realized one of the cigarettes belonged to me.

Dad shook his head and uttered these classic words, "I hope you choke on the damn thing," turned, and walked away.

Mom and I looked at each other and burst out laughing. We connected for the first time in several years. I saw a tiny glimpse of the wonderful mother I had once adored. I so wished that this precious old mom would stay a little longer. Dad never spoke about the incident or my nasty smoking habit again.

The week flew by and Luke and I drove his car back to school for the last quarter. When I say "his car", it was not his old dream car, the green and white 1955 Pontiac Catalina with rolled and pleated interior that had been my arch rival for his affection. Instead it was an old green and white Opel station wagon, which his father had purchased with the insurance money from his unfortunate car crash while using Luke's car to drive to work. This was a major bone of contention between Luke and his dad, as his dad had forbidden Luke to ever take his beloved vehicle to school. Instead, his dad would use it as his work car in order that Luke's mom could keep the family car at home for her use.

On a more positive note, he now had "wheels" on campus. This meant we had transportation to the infamous Spring Laker beer parties and the means to return home when the school year ended.

Chapter 45
Chicago, IL, April 1965

Paying the Piper

S ometime in April, my mother phoned me at the sorority house. It was a pledge housecleaning workday and I had pulled the house favorite torture chore of cleaning the yucky bathrooms. I was taken aback when I was called to the telephone and informed my mother was on the line. In truth, I didn't even think she knew what sorority I had pledged nor had a clue about the phone number. This was the first and only call from home I had received since I arrived last September. Instinctively, I knew it was not good news.

Mom was hysterical, almost incoherent, severely slurring her words, "Diana, you have to come home. Dad's been convicted of income tax evasion and taken to Joliet State Prison. How could this happen? I can't believe this. I don't deserve this. What am I going to do? When are you coming home? You should be here, at home with me, not at some college. You need to help me, now. When will you be here?"

She went on and on, sounding if this was somehow on me. I had to be quiet and calm; after all, I was right next to the sorority house formal living room with other sisters within earshot. There were no portable phones or cell phones in 1965, just hardwired-into-the-wall, big, plastic telephones with rotary dials and no privacy.

Though caught off guard by her call, I told her, "Mom, calm down and I will call you back shortly. I can't stay on this phone any longer."

I explained to my sorority sisters, "That was my mom. There's been a family emergency and I'm sorry, but I have to leave." I was pretty sure they had already figured that one out themselves. They all hugged me and wished me well and then I raced out the door to find a quiet private place to call home.

It was a chilly spring afternoon walk through the early budding, tree-lined campus back to my dorm. The fresh air helped me assess the multitude of concerns and emotions running rampant throughout my whole being. In truth, my thoughts were more like, *whoa, Mom! Stop the drama. Let's take a moment to revisit the years of reprehensible scandalous life events and crises that have plagued our family up to this day. How could you honestly be surprised about this? What about all those years we ran, hiding from the FBI and the infamous bad guys, had to lie to everyone about everything, slip out at times in the dark of night and isolate ourselves from our relatives and friends? In your heart of hearts, did you think all of this would go away because you wanted it to? Did you hope these problems would merely evaporate into your booze bottles?*

Years ago, Grandpa explained to me that if you make bad decisions, you will have to pay for them, one way or another, at some point in your life. I believe Grandpa spoke truth and now it was pay up time. Grandpa called it justice.

While sincerely attempting to conjure up some empathy and compassion for Mom and Dad, my mind took off on its own chaotic rant, reminding me that Sonny and I didn't even know the whys and causes of our tumultuous childhood. I needed an adding machine to count the numerous traumatic trials and tribulations that comprised our life.

How come they abandoned us, mentally and physically?

Why did Dad do whatever it was he did? How could he be charged with this offense? This was the first I'd ever heard of income tax evasion. We had been living paycheck to paycheck since 1957. What money could they possibly owe taxes on? What in the world did they do that was the grounds for all of this? Sonny and I were never provided with knowledge or explanations regarding the causes of the dysfunction and destruction of our family. Long ago, I determined that Sonny and

I had already paid a huge price. I was not willing to pay anything more. I was empty with nothing left to give. Why then, I searched within myself, did I feel truly sorry and terribly guilty about my reaction?

With my hardhearted Diana hat on, I couldn't dredge up any real compassion. Love and concern loaded with contempt for Mom and Dad, combined with lots of love with worry and distress over Johnny's fate, I was at a loss how there was anything at all that I could do about this new bombshell. I prayed for Mom and Dad and asked for a lot of help and guidance. Alone in my room, I picked up the phone to make the call, relieved that Liz was out and I had the phone privacy I needed.

I placed the call. It rang several times before Mom answered and acknowledged me. She sounded inconsolable, still slurring her words interspersed with moments of silence or hysterical crying.

"Mom, it's me. I can talk now. First, try to calm down. Let's talk this through. I know you're upset. I get it, but we need to think about today first, then we can talk about tomorrow, and so on. Wondering why, isn't going to change what has just happened or help with what you need to do right now. Okay? Mom? Mom! Can you hear me? Are you listening? Do you understand me?"

There was dead silence followed by a sob and a hiccup. "I hear you," she whispered.

I begged God for inspiration to find the right words. I needed them *now*. As I opened my mouth to speak again, I was still at a loss. It was crucial that I held my ground and didn't cave, but offered the emotional support she needed at this second.

I continued, "Mom, I love you and this isn't the end of the world. I'm sure it feels like it and I know it is a bad time for you. But think, at least the past eight years of running, hiding, and constantly looking over your shoulder or in the rear-view mirror has now ended. The full story has been revealed; the worst is over and you know the result. Now, you can start anew and begin to build a safe solid life plan. Have you called Aunt Lulu, Grandma, or Aunt Babs? And most of all, Mom, have you asked God for help? Strength? Comfort? Clarity? He's there for you. He'll help you, but Mom, you have to ask Him for help. Promise me right after we hang up that you'll say a prayer to Jesus and ask Him to hold your hand and guide you right now. Then call Aunt Lulu; she will be there for you and help you. Mom, please promise me that you'll do that for Johnny and you and for me, too. I'm going to hang up now, but I'll call you back in one hour and you can tell me your plan. I love you and Johnny. You can do this. Remember to talk to God."

She was somewhat calmer when I called her an hour later as she explained, "I am packing up some things because Johnny and I are going to spend a few days with Aunt Lulu. She'll be picking us up shortly."

I told her, "Excellent idea. I'll call you in a couple of days at Aunt Lulu's. Remember, I love you and please hug Johnny real tight and tell him that I love him so much." I hung up feeling sad for her and Dad, but comfortable with the position I had taken. I hoped God agreed with my decision.

Chapter 46
Des Plaines, IL, May 1965

Enchiladas and the Milkman

❧

S pring quarter was whizzing by and all was good. Sonny called me. "Hey sis, Ella, my girlfriend, and I are going to be in Chicago for a weekend in early May and I'm hoping you can come and meet her."

Delighted, I immediately shouted, "Of course I'll be there. No way I'd miss an opportunity to see you. Besides, I am dying to meet this girlfriend. For you to bring home a girl from college sounds pretty serious to me."

Sonny laughed, "We'll see. Can't wait. Love you!"

Excited, I thought, *in addition to seeing Sonny and Ella, going home gives me an opportunity to determine how Johnny was faring and how Mom was dealing with her new circumstance.*

I arrived late Friday afternoon. Sonny and Ella were arriving after midnight and presumably staying until Monday or Tuesday. My heart was overjoyed to find Johnny looking recovered from his surgery and acting like his same old cute self. It was a total surprise to find Mom sober, wearing full makeup, and sporting a new hairstyle. The house was spotless and mouthwatering aromas of Mom's enchiladas and Spanish rice emanated from the kitchen. However, it was a rather unpleasant surprise when Jack, a milkman (not ours), showed up for dinner shortly after I arrived. Apparently Mom had cooked most of the day for Jack, not as I had first foolishly assumed for Sonny, his girlfriend, and me. The astonishing revelation of Mom's boyfriend, Jack, caused me to quickly scrub my initial plan of staying home to share an evening with Mom and waiting up for Sonny. My new altered plan became spending the evening with Ann, thereby leaving Mom and her milkman friend alone. Believe me, I had nothing but respect for the milkman trade and nothing against Jack. They get up in the middle of the night to provide a great service, but where did she meet him and wasn't this romance a little quick? How conveniently she could forget that she and Dad were still married. Dad hadn't died; he was in prison. He'd been gone only about three weeks. Mom certainly worked fast.

Returning home around eleven from Ann's, I walked into a suspiciously dark house complete with a big-time make out session in full progress on the living room couch. I felt embarrassed, awkward, and disgusted. I mean, really? I knew both of my parents had not exactly kept their marriage vows, but to bear witness to it was another story. Having no idea how to gracefully handle this situation, I said goodnight while I hastily headed up to my old room. I wished I could warn Sonny about Mom's lover boy downstairs.

Hopefully Jack would be gone before Sonny and Ella arrived. It would be oh-so-offensive and embarrassing for Sonny. What was Mom thinking? Her choices were alarming and continued to worry me, a lot. Sonny and his girlfriend cruised in around two-thirty in the morning. We all hugged and went to bed; we would get to know each other later. Sonny was already up, making coffee and toast by the time I surfaced the next morning. Johnny was busy eating his cereal and grinning as he happily sat glued next to Sonny. We discussed our plans for the day which included visiting Grandma and Grandpa at their lake house then stopping by to see Aunt Lulu, Marie, and Kevin. We took Johnny along with us. Ella came down to join us and we had a great time getting to know each other. We were the exact same age, only one week apart, and had tons in common. She was nice, pretty, and wore her killer yellow polka dot bikini exceptionally well. I liked her and was happy for Sonny. He gave off the impression that he more than just liked her.

It was a delightful day with no drama. I decided not to burden Sonny with the news regarding Mom's new boyfriend. There was nothing either of us could do about the situation and who knew how long this would last. Unless it became serious, I saw no reason to cause him concern. Our casual dinner and the rest of the evening went quite well. Everyone's plans remained on track. I was heading off back to school early in the morning while Sonny and Mom would head out to the prison to visit Dad for the first time since he was arrested.

The remaining few weeks of the spring quarter were filled with finals, Sorority Hell Week, induction into the sorority, year-end parties, and graduation farewells. My sorority "mom" was graduating and I was going to miss her a lot next year. We had bonded and become close. I found out that there weren't any room vacancies in the house for next year so Liz and I would be roomies again but in the brand-new dorm across campus. Our corner room was on a high floor, much more spacious and nicer than the one we had in the old dorm. It also had a smoking room on every floor, so our blowing-smoke-out-our-window days were over.

I had already been hired to work in the new dorm's dining hall. My scholarship would handle the rest. Along with the money I would make working this summer, there should be enough to get me through next year if I remained frugal.

All in all, I was terribly sad to see my freshman year come to an end. I loved every single solitary minute of college life. I couldn't wait to come back in the fall.

Luke and I packed up the Opel wagon with all our stuff and bid our final year-end farewells to our friends. He had been hired for a major highway construction job, which held the potential for him to make a nice bundle of money this summer. I had the opportunity to work at Fannie May, but was hoping I could find something that paid more money and offered a chance for overtime pay. There were a few good leads—nothing solid—but I was hopeful.

The drive back to Chicago zoomed by too fast for me. I cherished every moment I spent with Luke, especially in the car when it was just the two of us with no distractions or interruptions. We could talk about our hopes and dreams, summer plans, our dysfunctional families, what we expected to find when we reached home, and how many days until we could return to college.

Chapter 47
Des Plaines, IL,
June 1965–June 1966

Homeless with $1.27 in Change
❧

Luke pulled into my driveway and proceeded to get my two suitcases out of the car while I dug out my house key and opened the front door. Whoa, was I ever in for a surprise. I hadn't necessarily expected to find anyone home, but I was shocked to find no furniture or anything else left in what I thought was still my home. The house was void of everything except my bed in my old room. There was a note on the bed that said I needed to get rid of it by the end of the weekend. There was no other note anywhere. I had absolutely no clue where anyone was, where any of our things were, or what in heaven's name had happened. Even the refrigerator was empty, clean, and turned off. Mom and Johnny had moved out—lock, stock, and barrel—and Mom hadn't bothered to tell me.

Checking everything out, I found that the phone still worked so I started calling my grandparents, Aunt Lulu, Aunt Babs, a couple of my dad's cousins—virtually everyone I could think of. The result was either no one answered their phone or if answered, had no idea where she'd gone. I was dumbfounded; this was unbelievable. How could my entire family be MIA?

Luke was aghast that even my mom was capable of such neglect. He felt so sorry for me and was furious with her. However, we both knew there was nothing he could do about it. I told him to go home; his folks, Mike and Karen, were waiting for him. I would keep trying to figure this out and call him in a little while. I was sure there was a good explanation and I would find it.

After he pulled out of the driveway, I sat down on the stairs in the middle of the empty house. Just me and my two unpacked suitcases, trying to hold myself together and think. I knew I couldn't stay there alone. I would be paralyzed with fear for several reasons, like being afraid of the dark and alone at night in an empty dark house with no electricity. It hit me that there was no food or even a glass to drink water. My wallet held exactly $1.27 in change and I had no means of transportation.

I couldn't believe how my mother could have done this to me. Through the years, she'd pulled some nasty tricks, but this time she'd left me stranded out in the proverbial cold. Did she care even a little bit about me? Since I was eleven, I had known she was undependable and mostly unavailable to me, but this went way beyond. In the past, I had told myself that it no longer mattered what she did. I didn't care; therefore, she couldn't hurt me anymore. So most of the time, the things she did or didn't do wouldn't faze me because I had convinced myself that I was beyond expecting anything from her. But leaving me utterly homeless, penniless, and abandoned was a new low, even for her. I wanted to hate her, curse her, and tell her she was the worst possible mother anybody could ever have, but deep down I still loved her and craved to feel loved by her.

I sat on the stairway completely numb. Questions with no answers plagued me. *What am I going to do? How am I going to survive? I need to do something and do it now, but what? Oh my gosh, I only have me to rely on; there's no one else. Whatever I chose to do right now is important, but I have no idea what that is.*

Out of nowhere, it occurred to me that I once read, "We are free to choose, but we are not free from the consequences of our choices." I believed that this was true; just look back at my life. I had been paying the price of my parents' bad choices since I was ten. Now, I had to be especially prudent in making my next choices, the most important of my life so far.

In my panic-filled state, all I could think to do was pray, in between my pity party fits of hysteria and tears, to the one who had never, ever let me down. He had been unceasingly faithful to this eighteen-year-old girl who had called upon Him countless of times before to save her.

Miraculously, once again, a calm from deep inside enveloped me and a plan began to emerge. I called Ann and tearfully explained my state of emergency. "Hi Ann, it's Diana, I just got home. My mom took Johnny and cleared out the house. The only piece of furniture left is my bed and I gotta have it out of here by Sunday night. There's no electricity, food, or even a glass for water. I've called everyone I can think of, but no one knows what happened or where She and Johnny are."

Before I could ask her if I could spend the night, she interrupted me exclaiming she'd just gotten off work and would be right over. Within thirty minutes, Ann walked through the front door with her mother right behind her.

Immediately, her mom came over and gave me a huge hug informing me, "Diana, don't you worry, honey. Ann and I are here to take you and your belongings to our house. You can stay with us while we figure this out together. In fact, you can live with us as long as you need or want. It will all work out and we'll find out where your mom and brother are. So come on honey, let's get this party started!"

I was overwhelmed by their show of compassion and love. I mean, Ann and I were best friends and though I had never discussed my home life with Ann's mom, I had spent enough hours at their house that I am certain they had surmised my home life didn't resemble Beaver Cleaver's. Ann had noticed my embarrassment over many difficult situations when she would come over. Per chance she had shared her observations with her mom, who had always been exceptionally warm and kind to me. This was a blessing without a doubt, reminding me once more that I was never all alone. I quickly called Luke and informed him of my good fortune and new address.

Ironically, again, I found myself in the role of an abandoned, homeless orphan. The difference was this time I knew I had some control of my future and my parents did not. Confident in the architect above, I had great hopes and could hardly wait to see what His plan would bring.

Finding a job was first and foremost on my to-do list. Second was figuring out the mode of transportation to whatever job I landed. Late Tuesday, I finally reached Mom at Aunt Lulu's house. "Mom, why are you with Aunt Lulu? Is Johnny with you? What happened? Why did you move out and not tell me? How could you let me come home from college with no idea of where you went or what had happened? I called everyone I could think of and no one knew anything. I was worried sick. I can't believe you did that to me, Mom."

In true ugly Mom form, she disregarded all my questions, never acknowledged she did anything wrong, nor showed any concern for my situation. She, matter-of-factly responded, "Johnny and I are living with Aunt Lulu now, but there is no room for you."

Hurt by her callous lack of caring, I explained, "I am temporarily living with Ann's wonderful family; however, I would appreciate it very much if you would drive me to the Illinois state employment office because I am in desperate need of a job."

Mom was surprisingly agreeable and we set a time for the next day. Thankfully, this time she came through and on time.

We had to wait about fifteen minutes for my interview. Our conversation was rather strained. I learned that everyone in the family had been at Sonny's college graduation and his commissioning into the Air Force. He was now officially a second lieutenant, heading off to flight school. I was thrilled that my brother had the full support of the family and his well-deserved achievements were recognized and honored. However, even though I knew I would not have been able to attend, I was incredibly hurt that I was not informed of the date of his graduation and commissioning ceremony. We had survived our childhood misfortunes together, and in my mind, only I could comprehend and appreciate the sheer determination and hard work he had needed to accomplish these goals. I wished to have been there to celebrate his success with him. He was my hero in all things. Even today, I am sad I hadn't been able to show Sonny, in person, my joy and admiration for him.

Mom finally did shed some light regarding why she had moved out of the house. She simply couldn't afford the mortgage, leaving her no choices other than to rent or sell the house quickly. I didn't bother to state the obvious question regarding letting me know in advance where she was or if she even once thought about my surprise abandonment dilemma of no family, shelter, food, or money when I returned home from school. I figured it was all water under the bridge at this point. Just another lesson learned for me to note in my book of life study. I had to continually remind myself, *Diana, keep moving forward; looking back won't change anything.*

With that self-to-self conversation now put to rest, my interview went great and I walked away with another interview scheduled for the next day at one of the big three car rental companies at O'Hare airport. The job was manning a car rental kiosk in one of the three terminals.

Ann graciously took the morning off from her job and drove me to my interview at O'Hare. I wasn't sure what to expect, but whatever I said worked, because I came away gainfully employed, with a training class starting in a few days. The job included uniforms like those of an airline stewardess. For me, that was a big bonus. I didn't have to worry about buying business clothes.

After the elation and realization of having secured a full-time fun job and wonderful home calmed down, the depressing reality that I might now have to withdraw from college set in. Even with my scholarship, there was no way I could make—much less save—enough money for school while paying this summer's rent, a car payment, insurance, gas, and personal necessities. For me to also afford college books, room and board, and sorority dues, not including any surprise miscellaneous extras, wasn't going to work right now. The catch-22 was that I had to work. To get to work, I needed to own a car. To own a car, I had to work. It was a vicious circle regardless of how I spun it. Even if I was somehow able to afford the college expenses, I remained obligated to pay my monthly car payment and all the other car expenses associated with that responsibility. I didn't see any other choice but to completely withdraw from school and hope I would find a way to afford a local college a few months later. I fervently hoped withdrawing would not mean I would lose my scholarship that I had worked so hard to earn and keep.

The cause of all these disappointments, I, justly or unjustly, blamed on my parents' irresponsible and neglectful ways. I felt they had forced me into a box. Number one, I needed to secure a decent-paying job so I could have shelter, food, and you know, basic living requirements. Number two, I had to figure out some mode of transportation to and from work. There were no buses or trains to O'Hare available to me. After much deliberation, I concluded that I had no alternative. I must purchase a car and pay all the associated car costs. Meals during working hours, dry cleaning of my uniform ...the total of these expenses were staggering to me. In addition, I was aware that other surprise expenses crop up. Comparing my total monthly funds earned versus funds owed each month was going to be a tight rope balancing act. I would have to find a second job if I wanted to save any money. It also became depressingly evident that for now, continuing my college education was clearly out of the question. This money-managing exercise, including the reality of withdrawing from college, exhausted and overwhelmed me.

For the first time in my eighteen years, I felt utterly defeated. I mean, for the last eight years, every accomplishment and goal I had worked so hard to achieve was unfairly undermined, cutting off my path to reaching my lifetime goals. Why was it that practically everything I aspired to, dreamed, hoped, or wished to accomplish kept hitting brick walls created by my parents?

The myriad of emotions that shot through me rocked me to my core. The feelings of anger, abandonment, astonishment, mortification, betrayal, and total mistrust I directed toward both parents. Frustration, disappointment, disbelief, fears of failure, and my now-crushed college dreams threatened to shatter me. Yet, I felt motivated by the generosity of Ann's family and recognized that I somehow must embrace my new situation for me to succeed. I needed to get over myself, suck it up, be ever-thankful for my good fortune to live with such a loving family, trust in God, and move forward. Time to try to make lemonade out of this sack of lemons—my current life.

Over the weekend, Ann and I decided to go car shopping. I vaguely remembered a car guy who used to come into Dad's dealership when I was working there. He had a used car lot nearby. Perhaps he would remember me and be able to help me out. I had no down payment and knew less than zero about cars. Nevertheless, I felt confident that this was the day I would own my first set of wheels. It had to be; I had no other solution. Not knowing if he knew about my dad being in jail left me on the fence whether I should mention I was his daughter or not. I decided not to mention it unless that was my last shot at getting a car.

Wanting to look older than eighteen, I borrowed the wig Ann had recently bought. We felt that the fake hair color and style made me look more mature, like I was twenty, with a professional flair. Dressed for success in my only suit and heels, complimented by Ann's frosted blonde wig, we set out on my mission of the day. I was going to purchase a car.

We found the used car lot without any trouble. It was exactly where I had remembered it to be and the same guy was there. I introduced myself, but didn't mention we had met a couple of years before. Explaining that I was looking for the cheapest car that wouldn't give me any problems, he directed us over to a blue 1961 Chevrolet Corvair Monza. It looked passable to me. He encouraged us to get in and drive it around the lot. After getting the seat set right and starting the engine, I had trouble locating the gearshift. It wasn't on the steering wheel column and there was no center console. He noticed we were not moving, so he came back and informed us that the gearshift lever was on the dashboard. I am certain he got big laughs relating the two ditzy girls who couldn't find the gearshift story. Anyway, it drove like a car. The total was $635.00 and he would finance the whole thing. The payments were sixty dollars a month. The only glitch in the whole transaction happened while I was filling out the paperwork and accidentally dropped the pen on the floor. As I bent down to retrieve the pen, the whole wig shifted forward over my eyes and I had to reposition it in front of the guy as I sat back up to complete the paperwork. It was a tad embarrassing, but I chose to pretend it didn't happen. I remember how ecstatic I was that I owned a car and was in control of my transportation to my new job. I proudly drove off the lot, following Ann back to her house. Unfortunately, Ann hit the side of her parents' garage while pulling their car in. For some demented unexplainable reason, we both thought it was hilariously funny and couldn't stop laughing. Her usually calm Dad did not share our humor and was more than a little ticked.

The car rental job was a cool job. Everyone thought we "ladies" were airline stewardesses, which made me feel grown up. I'm sure it was due to our uniform, complete with an upside-down opened-envelope hat. My job was to smile continuously in all situations, regardless if the customer was rude or obnoxious. The ultimate goal was to send the happy traveler off with a car, map and directions to their destination, creating a fast, competent, enjoyable experience and a repeat patron.

My favorite customer was a young salesman who worked for a famous Chicago chocolate candy maker. He did not realize he would need to have an air-conditioned car so his chocolate candy samples wouldn't melt in Chicago's hot and humid July heat. He was so impressed that I alerted him about his potential candy fiasco, thus saving a heat-induced melted chocolate disaster, that he wrote a glowing letter to the big boss about me.

My worst was a famous singer/entertainer who insisted he needed a better car and demanded I take him to the lot so he could personally choose his car. He made such a fuss at the counter that I decided it was better for me to smile and humor him before he created a bigger scene. He followed me across the road to the row of our best cars available. They were the most expensive; however, he was demanding the smaller car rate. After making his choice, he followed me back across the street into the terminal. Suddenly, I feel his big fat hand squeezing my derriere. Training had not mentioned this as part of the job, so I turned around to confront him. A smile was not pasted on my face as I turned to him. "Mr. Smith, please take your hand off me. I am not included in the rental of any car for anyone."

He took his time staring me up and down then with a sarcastic smirk on his face, he belligerently quipped, "Ditch the girdle, girlie, and let your fanny wiggle free. What's up with girls like you, so standoffish and uppity? Think you're too good for me? Don't you know who I am?"

I did know and that made him even more disgusting.

Back at the counter I quickly excused myself and asked another girl to complete the transaction. Sadly, this wasn't the only harassing incident.

The scariest was with one of my coworkers. The rental car employees carpooled from the airport property car rental office, where the car maintenance bays were located, to the actual terminal and rental car lots. This was their way of transferring cars. One evening, I was carpooling from the terminal back to the office with one of the maintenance guys after the three-to-eleven-o'clock shift. He was a nice guy and I frequently worked with him. His lovely wife was employed by a competitive rental car company in the same terminal. At the end of one shift, while supposedly returning to the office where our personal cars were parked, Benny didn't take the normal turnoff back to the office. Instead, he drove to some remote dark lot on airport property.

I asked him, "Hey Benny, why are we going this way? Where are we going?"

Benny replied, "I've got to first pick up something in this other lot."

I was on alert but not alarmed until Benny stopped the car, turned the motor off, and moved toward me. My antenna skyrocketed and I was terrified. In a flash, he had me pinned and trapped between him and the locked passenger side door.

He whispered, "C'mon Diana, how about one little kiss? That's all I want."

It was the dangerous, scared-for-my-life kind of scared that I hadn't ever experienced in the past. I might have only been eighteen, but I instinctively knew this wasn't just a one-and-done little kiss kind of trap. All I could think to do was calmly remind him, "I love Luke, and I'm not the kind of girl that cheats on my almost fiancée. Luke trusts me and I will never betray his trust. Benny, you have a beautiful wife and I see her every day, so let's just forget this incident, call it a night, and go back to the office. I promise not to mention it to anyone. I'm sure you don't want your wife to know about this and neither do I."

At first Benny didn't move, but a few seconds later, he backed off and sat with his arms crossed, silent. It felt like forever. I hoped he was having second thoughts. I would have jumped out of the car, but I had no idea where I was. It was late, somewhere out in a pitch-black area off a runway service road with no lights and no road noise. It was without a doubt my worst nightmare—only this time, it was my reality.

Suddenly, I was aware of a protective presence, almost as if a shield was around me. I felt calmer and braver as I once more suggested, "Benny, let's just head back to the office." Ben turned and stared at me. I don't know what he was thinking, but thankfully he started the car and took me back to the office. I ran to my car, instantly locked the door, and sped home.

The impact of what could have occurred hit me. I couldn't stop crying or shaking all the way to Ann's house. Before I went in, I sat in my car, trying to calm down. I didn't want anyone to know what had almost happened. Although nothing horrific had taken place, I felt ashamed and violated, an innocent victim guilty by association. I couldn't report it; I had promised. If I did report it to my manager, what if Benny came after me and attacked me? I wondered if I could continue to work there. Maybe I could request all day shifts, citing I would be going back to college by way of night classes. I decided to take a day and think about it. I was thankful I had the next day off.

The following week, two unsuspecting incidents took place as I was leaving the rental car office parking lot after my daytime shift.

First, one of Benny's friends came up to my car, making lewd comments regarding my "special evening" with his friend on the dark airport road. Then he brazenly ran his hand over my breast stating that he may have not gotten what Benny got, but at least he had touched me. I was furious and pulled my car right in front of the glass doors of the main office. I was going to barge in on my manager and report exactly what just happened. As I approached the door, my manager's big boss, the regional vice president, came outside and asked, "Diana, can I speak with you for a moment?

"Yes, of course," I answered, instantly on alert and wondering if he'd heard rumors or lies about what happened with Benny.

As we moved to the side, Mr. Big VP boss quietly inquired, "Tell me, Diana, have you ever gone out to dinner with an older man?"

I was confused, and in my innocence, I responded, "Sure, with my dad." He looked taken aback and had a funny look on his face. I think my naïve, honest answer took him by surprise and it took me a second or two before I "got" the true meaning of his strange question. Totally disgusted, I couldn't believe what had just occurred. I thought, *who are these dirty old men? Even this big executive boss is obnoxious. I'm going to get into my car, drive away, and I am never coming back.*

I locked myself in my car and quickly headed for the safety of home. I decided I was finished with this job. If my direct manager asked me why I was quitting, I would tell him; however, I now knew this was the way it was if you worked there. If you wanted to keep your job, either go with it or try to avoid it, but under all circumstances, keep your mouth shut. Once home and calmer, I called my direct manager and told him, "I quit. Right now, today."

He commented, "I am so sorry to lose you. You did a great job and we will all miss you." However, Mr. Direct Manager never asked me why, so I didn't explain. I'm betting he knew.

I have never shared with anyone the frightful Benny incident. At the time, my dad was in prison. Mom would have probably accused me of causing it. Luke was at college and I didn't want him to leave school, driving four hours to avenge my honor. That wouldn't serve anyone well, especially Luke. I did not want to involve Ann or her family, and best of all, it was over. I had handled it. Nothing bad had occurred and I was now a little smarter and wiser about this dangerous adult working world. So far, I was not impressed and disappointed, but a valuable life lesson was learned.

My new personal business motto: always keep my Lecher-o-Meter on high alert and never let my guard down. Dirty old men lurked everywhere.

I got a new job as a receptionist for a famous national cosmetic company the next week. My boss, Merriam, was an exacting taskmaster but fair. Her boss was a kind older gentleman who was nice to work for. The other secretary was cool. I liked Cathy a lot. Her boss, who traveled extensively, rarely spent any time in the office. After a few days, I found the job somewhat unchallenging and monotonous unless you displeased Merriam, who then would instantly fly into a tirade. My ultimate daily goal was to not displease her.

Life with Ann's family was great. Her parents were exceptionally loving. They always made me feel part of their family, including me in all family events. On Saturday mornings, when the written list of chores was assigned, I had a list with my name on it as well. If the family was having a movie night or going to an extended relative's home for dinner or a party, I was automatically invited and expected. Ann, her sister Jean, and even young Allen treated me like I was their sibling. We all got along well. I loved this whole family.

Mom lived at Aunt Lulu's with Johnny, continued to date Jack the milkman, and had a new job as office manager for a one-man independent insurance office. Dad remained in Joliet Prison where I would visit him every other Saturday and put ten dollars in a prison account that he could use for commissary items.

I immensely disliked going to Joliet to see him. Some of it was about having to visit my father in a state prison communicating through an opening in the glass partition that separated us. Who in their right mind would want to do that? The other part, I was frightened by other inmates chained together that I had to pass on my way to and from the visiting room. They would whistle, call me disgusting names, and yell out some terrible things detailing what they wanted to do with me. On "prison Saturdays" I would return home to find Ann's mom waiting with hugs and comforting words. She and I would sit down to "talk." But she'd do most of the talking. "How was your visit with your dad? How long do you get to be with him? What's it like? Does it look like it does on TV or in the movies?"

Sometimes, I'd choke up, explaining, "It's awful! I have to be body-searched by a guard before I can go into the prison, then searched again at a checkpoint in the hall where the visiting room is. I get to kiss Dad, but we both have to open our mouths to be checked, before and after we kiss hello or goodbye. It's pretty degrading. Dad talks about Mom, then he tears up. I don't tell him that she wants a divorce or has a boyfriend. He gets sad when I have to leave. I hate it. It makes me feel dirty. There's no privacy and always a lot of visitors for other inmates. Dad tells me I'm the only person that comes to visit him. He's taken up smoking since he's been there. Then when I leave I run to my car and lock all the doors. I don't feel safe until I'm on the highway."

Ann's mom would always grab my hand, comforting me. "Honey, you are so courageous and such a good daughter. In my mind, no daughter your age should have to deal with the all demands and situations your parents continually burden you with. I am so proud of you and love having you here. I think of you like another daughter."

Every day during that time, she was my encouraging angel on Earth. Humble and small in stature, yet endowed with the most gigantic, loving heart. Who knew a carpenter and a handicap children's school bus driver would be so impactful on my life.

Luke was in his junior year of college. On the weekends that I didn't go visit Dad, I drove down to school to be with Luke and my sorority sisters. For the most part, my life had settled into a comfortable rhythm that I enjoyed for the first time since I was ten.

I loved my happy, no-drama life—well, almost no drama. Mom had begun to have epileptic seizures, mostly occurring when she was at work. An ambulance would be called and then the hospital would call me to come and get her when she was released. I'd check her out of the ER, then drive her the thirty or so minutes to Aunt Lulu's house, staying with her until Aunt Lulu returned home from work. I don't know why Mom had these epileptic seizures. To the best of my knowledge, there was no family history. My self-diagnosis concerning the cause of Mom's seizures was that her years of excessive drinking and stress had brought them on.

The other drama source involved my dad. One miserable, dreary, rainy early November afternoon, while typing away at my desk, I heard the glass office door open. I looked up and there stood my father. To say I was shocked would be a gross understatement. I thought he was a couple of hours away tucked behind bars in Joliet. I sat frozen and speechless.

He asked, "Aren't you going to come over and give me a kiss and hug? Aren't you happy to see me?"

I was shaking as I got out of my chair, wondering, *how did he get here? Was he released from Joliet?* He'd only served six months of his sentence. All the while, I was mindful of Merriam behind the glass wall overseeing me and my warm encounter with a strange man in the reception area during office hours. No one knew anything about my family, only about Luke.

I quickly ushered Dad into the hall. "Dad, wait right here. I'll be back."

Hurrying into Merriam's office, I explained, "I have a serious family situation that I have to take care of right now. Could I please leave and take the rest of the afternoon off? I promise to be at my desk bright and early tomorrow morning."

I think she recognized the panicked look on my face and told me, "Just go."

As we left the building, Dad explained, "I took a bus to your office but I need you to drive me to Aunt V's apartment. I'll be staying there for a little while."

As he continued talking, it dawned on me that I never told Dad where I worked. Mom didn't even know where I worked. Dad didn't know anything about Ann's family or where they lived, so how in the world did he know where to find me? I was rather creeped out about this. I wasn't trying to hide anything from him or anyone else. In fact, I had already experienced enough hiding and secrecy to last me my entire life. It was just that where I lived and worked had never been a topic of our conversations. While I wanted some answers, I thought better of the timing.

As soon as we got into my old Corvair, Dad began insisting "You need to take me to see Mom after we go to Aunt V's. Do not give Mom a head's up about us coming. I want my visit to be a total surprise for her."

The way he spoke and looked at me made me uncomfortable. I had a warning bell going off in my head, but was too afraid to try to dissuade him. I felt trapped. Regardless that I was one hundred percent self-sufficient, my erratic, irresponsible parents continued to use me by imposing their problems into my life. Right now, my father's callous demeanor and the spiteful look in his eyes unnerved me, just short of feeling threatened.

I decided to drive him to Aunt V's and perhaps while there, I'd figure out a way to give Aunt Lulu a call. I would not arrive ambushing them with my uninvited passenger. I knew no good was going to come from Dad's bad idea. Mom didn't want to see him or have anything to do with him. She didn't want to be married to him any longer. What if her boyfriend was over for dinner? After all, Jack was also my uncle's friend and I knew he dropped by their house often, regularly staying for dinner.

This situation I found myself in was surreal, like a bad movie, and I had a supporting role. If everything blew up tonight, I would feel responsible because I provided the transportation knowing this meeting was a dreadful mistake. It was imperative I warn Lulu who could prepare my mom. I wasn't taking any side; I merely wanted to prevent another catastrophic hurtful evening.

Arriving at Aunt V's warm and charming antique and family-memorabilia-filled vintage apartment, Dad announced he needed a shower and clean clothes. Instantly, I knew this was my only chance to alert Lulu. While he was showering, I asked, "Aunt V., may I please use your phone? I really need to call my office. I won't be long."

"Of course you may, dear. Let me take you to my room where you can have some privacy."

Closing the door behind me so no one would hear my conversation, I immediately called Aunt Lulu at work and hastily whispered what had occurred and Dad's unwavering plan. She understood my no-win situation and assured me she would give Mom a head's up. We hung up quickly, but I proceeded to carry on a loud conversation with the dial tone pretending I was talking with Merriam.

The drive to Aunt Lulu's took about an hour. I used this time trying to convince Dad that this wasn't his best idea "Dad, maybe we should just turn this car around and find someplace to eat first. Together we can talk and work on a better game plan, one which offers more success. Honestly Dad, other than Mom being shocked and likely angry, I am certain you're not going to have the reaction, much less the reunion with her, that you are hoping for or imagining."

I ticked off my reasons. "First, no one expects you to return for at least another year. Therefore, your mere presence is bound to be a major shock to her even under the best of situations. Second: When I recently drove her home after one of her seizure episodes, Mom informed me that she was not planning on living with you when you were released."

In fact, she was seriously contemplating a divorce before his time was up, but I decided to keep that information to myself.

I further cautioned, "Dad, she may not be too welcoming—or worse, downright nasty. And third: just this morning, you left a depressing and stressful incarceration situation. Consequently, I don't want you to be so demoralized and heartsick over your and Mom's current relationship status that it'll cause you to do something irrational, perhaps inadvertently impacting your parole or impeding you getting back on your feet. Please Dad, take a step back and give yourself a few days to get grounded and more settled."

He replied with stony deafening silence. I kept driving and never mentioned Jack, her job, or any other commentary about her state of affairs, literally or figuratively.

It was cold, dark, and raining as we pulled up to Aunt Lulu's house. From the curb, her home looked so warm, safe, and inviting. For the first time in my life, I was filled with dread as I knocked on her front door. I purposely did not let myself in like I normally would because I wanted to let them know we were here. This evening was only going to go in one direction and it wasn't upward.

Chapter 48
Chicago, IL, November—December 1965

I Can't Make This Stuff Up
∽

A unt Lulu greeted us by giving me a warm hug but only nodded to Dad. He immediately strode into the kitchen where Mom was standing against the back wall. She looked both defiant and terrified. Johnny was at the table eating his dinner, but Dad didn't bother to acknowledge him. Out from nowhere, eleven-year-old Marie came for Johnny, promising him a cookie that he could eat right now in her room before he finished his dinner. He eagerly followed her and the enticing chocolate chip cookie down the hall.

A chainsaw could not have cut through the thick atmosphere in the room. It was so quiet no one moved, as though we were all stone statues cemented in place. I felt like the oxygen had been sucked from the air. Everything and everyone were suspended in time, holding their breath, waiting for the storm to begin. I know it was only a matter of seconds, but it felt like an eternity when finally, Dad took a hold of Mom's arm and tersely asked, "Can we go in the other room and talk ...privately?"

Mom jerked her arm away, making it apparent she wasn't keen on the arm holding nor the private conversation. She reminded me of a deer in headlights as she followed him into the living room. They talked quietly. After twenty minutes or so, Dad returned to the kitchen, barking, "Diana, it's time to leave, right now!" He looked devastated. I immediately grabbed my coat and car keys while nodding to Aunt Lulu and guided Dad out the door and into the car. He was deathly quiet, almost despondent, as we pulled away from the curb. Then, out of nowhere, he turned to me and in a condemning voice demanded, "Why, just tell me why, if you knew she didn't want me anymore, did you force me into seeing her tonight?"

His irrational words and chilling accusation stunned me. Was he serious? Did he not hear anything I said to him while driving there? His behavior gave me the feeling that Dad was delusional, acting like he was the victim and I was his kidnapper. He had it all twisted. My gosh, he arrived with no warning at my office, sort of hijacked me, then forced me to take him to see Mom all the way up in Lake County. I'd told him this wasn't his best idea. Mom used to fault Dad with being delusional, irrational, and always blaming everyone else for his misfortunes or mistakes. I had tuned her out long ago, attributing those demeaning insults to her alcohol and cigarette abuse. Perhaps there were threads of truth between her drunken slurs.

This pressure-filled day had left me with a roaring headache. All I wanted to do right now was take this sobbing broken man sitting next to me back to Aunt V's. Then I could go home to Ann's house, take a shower, and hope the stress of this day would swirl down the drain with the soap.

Shortly after that unforgettable evening, the hospital called me at work to come and pick up Mom, again. She'd suffered another seizure, but was released. On the drive to Aunt Lulu's, Mom updated me, "I've filed the divorce papers against Dad. I want full custody of Johnny, but Dad can have visitation rights."

Sadly, it didn't matter to me what Mom and Dad did about their sham of a marriage. I sincerely believed Johnny would be better if he didn't live in a house infused with their toxic, unstable relationship. Living in Ann's house drove home just how appalling life had been growing up with Mom and Dad. I did not want Johnny trying to cope with the bizarre challenges of living with both of them in addition to his handicaps. How could he be encouraged and thrive if he was parented by the two perfect examples of how to best create an irresponsible, unstable, and unloving home environment? The poor little guy wouldn't stand a chance. The worst part was our parents had never acknowledged Johnny needed special help. They were too selfish and always wrapped up in themselves. I was worried about him and furious with them. This was their one child that they could not ignore and abandon. Treating him as invisible and not getting him the appropriate help would thwart any chances he would ever have at being self-sufficient. I was frustrated beyond words. They were impossible to understand.

Mom called me at work the next morning claiming, "I left my purse behind the front seat of your car when you picked me up at the hospital yesterday. I'm hoping you can bring it to our new insurance office during your lunch hour."

"Okay, Mom, but I'll just have enough time to run it in and leave because my boss, Merriam, will have a fit if I return even a minute late from lunch." Inwardly I was not thrilled because of the twenty-five-minute drive to her office and the twenty-five-minute ride back. Now I had to skip lunch if I didn't want to catch Merriam's wrath for being tardy.

When I entered the small wood-paneled office to deliver Mom's purse, I found there was no one at the front desk. I knew the staff only consisted of her boss, who was the insurance agent, and Mom, so I called out her name. There were muffled sounds of laughter coming from the other office toward the back. Then I heard Mom say, "I'll be with you in a minute." Impatient, I waited, keeping my eye on the time. A few minutes ticked by when Mom and her boss finally came out of his office. Her deep coral lipstick was all smeared and he was oblivious to remnants of the same shade on his lips and face. I noticed Mom's blouse buttons were not quite buttoned right and his shirt tail was hanging out on the left side. I suspected they weren't just filing customer claims folders in his office.

He put out his hand, "Hi, I'm Ed. Sorry. We were in the middle of composing a letter when you arrived. It's so nice to finally meet you."

I nodded and smiled back, thinking, *good grief, I'm almost nineteen years old. Surely you don't think I am that naïve.*

I handed Mom her handbag, replying, "Nice to meet you too. Sorry, but I've got to run or I'll suffer a ticked-off office manager if I am late. Bye Mom." I turned and hastily fled to the serenity my car. The scene I had just witnessed was disconcerting. I was under the impression Mom had a boyfriend—Jack—and oh yeah, the other minor fact that at this moment she remained legally married to Dad.

Mentally putting Mom and Dad back in my brain's "parent compartment," I was excited to celebrate the weekend before my nineteenth birthday visiting Luke and my sorority sisters down at school. It was a great birthday weekend with them and then a surprise "family" birthday celebration when I arrived back at Ann's house early Sunday evening. As for my own family, Aunt Lulu, Sonny, and my grandparents remembered; my parents did not.

Leaving Luke wasn't at all stressful this time because I knew he would be home for Thanksgiving in a few more days. This year, I decided I would not have Thanksgiving with any of my family. I didn't want to have to make a choice between Mom or Dad. I needed a break from all the drama they created and unfortunately dragged me into.

Luke and I jointly decided we would dine with his family for Thanksgiving dinner then spend the evening enjoying Ann's family and their hilarious relatives who knew how to have fun together.

Thanksgiving dinner at Luke's was not like any Thanksgiving I had experienced in the past. We took our assigned seats at the Thanksgiving table, thanked God for all our blessings, and hungrily anticipated the delicious dinner we were about to be served. I was aware Luke's mom wasn't the best cook. She tried hard and served all the traditional foods; they just weren't tasty or cooked well.

The turkey, which everyone knows is the meal's main event, was more like medium rare, obviously not thoroughly cooked. When Luke's dad started to carve the big bird, pink turkey blood oozed all over the platter. Luke's sister and brother were silent, as were Luke and I. Taking turns, we dutifully passed our plates around so his parents could fill each one. Try as I might, I could not make myself take a bite of the majorly undercooked bird. All I could imagine was the soggy turkey dressing that also had not been cooked enough while being stuffed inside the raw bird. I tried to hide my sudden lack of appetite by moving the other food choices around my plate to cover up the bloody bird and undercooked dressing. I was anxious that Karen or Mike might notice me gag as I pretended to be enjoying my dinner by putting empty forkful after empty forkful into my mouth. I refused to look at Luke seated across the table from me in that he would certainly gaze over at my plate, make a face, and cause me to nervously laugh. I did not want to insult his parents. What if they eventually became my in-laws?

To add to the meal's enjoyment, no one talked during dinner—no conversation, no bantering, just focused eating. It was like the rule Sonny and I were taught so many years ago when we were included in our parents' business dinners: "Do *not* speak unless you are spoken to." I surmised if Luke's parents were not engaging in dinner conversation today, none of us "kids" should either. During this awkward silent feast fiasco, I kept thinking dinner here was almost as agonizing as I thought having Thanksgiving with my family would be. The agony was simply of a different sort.

Thankfully the Thanksgiving "feast" was in full celebration party mode when we arrived at Ann's house where Luke and I helped our starving selves to their leftovers. In reality, what I ate or didn't eat on Thanksgiving was of no real consequence. This year, my Thanksgiving was all about being thankful for Luke, Aunt Lulu, Sonny, my Grandparents, and this wonderful family—an entire family who treated me like one of their own. Without them, I could have found myself this Thanksgiving standing in line at a crowded food kitchen while living in a homeless shelter. All I could think was, *"Oh, but for the grace of God, go I."*

Christmas arrived in a flash. My brother was being sent to Southeast Asia. This was the only thing that dampened my holiday spirit. I didn't know exactly where he was going, but the TV news reports were terrorizing. All I could do was pray for his safety. The rest of my family was status quo, final divorce papers pending.

I continued to happily live with Ann's family, looking forward to a great Christmas and the many fun Christmas duties that her mom gave us three girls. Ann's mom and dad were so wonderful and loving to me that I would have done anything they asked. Ann, Jean, and I made each other laugh whenever we did stuff together, including when it was our turn for kitchen duty. We thoroughly enjoyed completing "Mom's" Christmas task list of making cookies, wrapping presents, decorating the tree, and even the cleaning up was fun. The house looked magical despite the fact we had no idea what we were doing, especially when it came to the lights outside. Their dad, a carpenter, had been injured on a job site and was not in condition to do any of the outside decorating. We were the chosen three, with a little help from their eight-year-old brother, Allen, to complete all of "dad's" prior Christmas tasks. I am sure the house didn't look anything like the previous Christmases, but I am also confident their dad never had the fun we did decorating, snowball fighting, and of course, the snow angel contests.

Work continued to be boring, but I was grateful for having a job. Cathy, one of the secretaries, had secretly informed me that she was looking for other employment due to the erratic disposition of Merriam. I most definitely could concur with her reasoning and thought I, too, might poke around to see what opportunities may be out there after the new year. Merriam had become hard to read and even more difficult to satisfy. She would yell at either of us at any given moment for no reason. Oftentimes, we weren't certain what her rant was about. On the other hand, the regional manager was easy to work for and easy to please. Rumor had it—and I secretly believed it to be true—that the regional manager and Merriam, his office manager, were having an affair. I kept my thoughts to myself, choosing to not share with Cathy. I was happy that I felt safe in this office with no unwanted overtures to fend off.

Chapter 49
Chicago, IL, December 1965–January 1966

All Wrapped Up in Luke
❧

J ust before Christmas, Luke arrived home from fall quarter with all his belongings jammed packed into his station wagon. Apparently the pre-law program that he had been enrolled in for the past two-and-a half years had been terminated. He had just been notified. This program was the major reason Luke went to the smaller university in the first place. Someone, somewhere in high authority decided to scrub this program, now leaving him with several minors but no major in the middle of his junior year. It was unfair and left Luke hanging out on a limb, so to speak. Therefore, he decided he would move back home for the remainder of the year. His plan was to take a couple of second-semester courses toward a major at a renowned Chicago college and work. In the summer, he would take an additional major's course or two while continuing to work, then finally enroll full-time in the fall. A counselor at the college had assured him that he would have enough credits to graduate with a major at the end of his senior year in June 1967. I was elated. Luke would not be leaving again; he would be working and finishing college in Chicago. This was the best Christmas gift I could have ever received.

On December 23, Luke picked me up from work and we went downtown with Ann and her boyfriend, Ken, for a date at a fancy restaurant followed by the theater to see the new James Bond movie,

From Russia with Love. It was a blustery cold evening in downtown Chicago. We were frozen after walking from the restaurant to the show. The theater was toasty warm and the movie was good, but apparently not quite exciting enough to keep me from dozing off on Luke's shoulder. Luke was exceptionally quiet on the car ride back to Ann's house. I didn't think too much about it, feeling extremely tired and looking forward to getting home and retiring to my warm comfy bed. Fortunately, our office was closed for Christmas Eve so I planned on sleeping in.

As it turned out, sleeping in had to be saved for another time. This Christmas Eve day happened to be filled with special to do's for Ann's mom. In addition, I was going to the early Christmas Eve service with Luke's family. After church we would exchange gifts with his family before heading up to Aunt Lulu's for a few hours, then cap it off at Ann's house where I knew their large merry family party would be in full swing.

After another awe-inspiring candlelight service, we returned to Luke's house. I'd hardly gotten my coat off when his dad pulled me toward a chair, telling me, "Diana, sit down so we can start to open a Christmas Eve present." He then handed me a huge gift box to open first.

Unknown to me, he had taken several boxes of graduated sizes, placing the smallest box inside a slightly larger box and that box inside a bigger box and so forth until all the brightly wrapped boxes were nested in one large package. Luke's family laughed as they watched me carefully open each empty box.

As I undid the smallest box and again found it empty, Luke said, "Diana, come over here. Maybe the last box is under the tree. Come on, help me look for it."

Laughing and sort of embarrassed, I sauntered over to him. He gently grabbed me, then planted a huge luscious kiss on my lips. Now I was totally embarrassed with his family watching us.

He encircled me with his arms as he said to me, "Diana, I love you. Will you be my wife?"

I threw my arms around him and stammered, "Yes, yes, *yes!*" as he opened another tiny box hiding the sparkling diamond engagement ring that he now slipped on my finger.

Of course we had talked about someday getting married, but never did I expect to get engaged tonight. His family all hugged us and I don't remember anything else until we were in the car driving to Aunt Lulu's. I couldn't wait to show off my Christmas surprise. Luke informed me that he had the ring in his pocket the previous night. He was planning on proposing then, but since I had fallen asleep during the movie, he decided to wait. I was happy he had waited; it would give every future Christmas Eve an extra special reason to celebrate.

Everyone at Aunt Lulu's Christmas Eve family party was excited for us. Luke had been considered a member of our family for a few years now and they were thrilled he was about to gain permanent status. Everyone toasted us several times. What a happy difference this Christmas Eve was from last Christmas Eve. For me the only sad points were that Sonny wasn't there and a part of me felt bad for Dad, whom Luke and I would see tomorrow afternoon. Most upsetting was seeing my beloved grandfather not looking well. I had a sick feeling he wouldn't be celebrating Christmas with us next year. Giving him extra kisses and hugs before we left for Ann's house, I prayed he'd be able to make it to my wedding. I knew his fate was in God's loving hands.

Showing off my new piece of jewelry at Ann's house caused pure pandemonium! They were whooping and hollering, singing crazy songs, and making toasts for what felt like hours. Hugs, kisses, and more toasts rendered Luke unable to safely drive back to his house. Ann's parents insisted he spend the night. He could sleep on the rollaway bed down in their half-finished basement. I was grateful for their kind and caring invitation. He accepted, then asked me if he could look at the ring on my hand again. A second after taking a hold of my left hand, he abruptly barfed all over my engagement ring and me. Of course, the room exploded in laughter. I, the new bride-to-be, wasn't overly thrilled with the fate of my brand-new ring or the condition of my now fiancée. In fairness to Luke, it wasn't his fault. I am certain Ann's uncles had purposely celebrated Luke into his current state, knowing the outcome. They thought they were hilarious. I had to admit they made it a night I would always remember in more ways than one.

Later that night, I fell asleep, offering intimate prayers of thankfulness. The most precious dream of my entire life had miraculously come true. It wasn't just the best Christmas Eve ever—it was the absolute best night of my entire life. Our God is full of beautiful blessings and perfect surprises.

Around dusk after an incredible Christmas Day, Dad came to pick Luke and me up at Luke's house. It was the annual Christmas night coffee and cookie soiree for us poor relatives at his wealthy uncle's home. This year Sonny wouldn't attend, but Luke was with us. I was beyond excited to show off the ring. Dad arrived right on time, but was altogether dumbfounded when I ran up to him, shoving my marquis-cut diamond ring in his face while gushing the words, "Look, Luke and I are engaged!" The wave of expressions that rippled across his face were disappointing. I was taken aback when it was clear none of them included a smile. After a couple of seconds, he recovered his composure and half-heartedly murmured, "Oh, congratulations! You sure caught me by surprise." He added, muttering under his breath, "Are you sure? Isn't this a bit impulsive? What about waiting for another year or two? After all, marriage is a huge commitment."

I wanted to mutter right back, *you have got to be joking. Luke and I've been each other's solace and best friend for almost five years—about a quarter of my life. Luke is the one always there for me every traumatic day, supporting and encouraging me throughout all the roadblocks and trauma Mom and you have caused me. As for marriage being a huge commitment—you two aren't exactly stellar role models on that topic. Why can't you be happy for us?*

I didn't need his blessing, but I would have liked to think he was supportive. Suddenly, my brain lit up like the lights on the Christmas tree in the corner. Dad was selfish and controlling. This was all about him regarding me and my soon-to-be husband, Luke. Dad would no longer be able to pull my strings. I would no longer have to acquiesce to his demands. The mere fact that we did not ask him for his permission revealed that I was already distancing myself.

Mom's and his divorce would be finalized in a matter of weeks. She had been hinting about marrying Jack. Sonny was in flight school and engaged to Ella; the wedding date was already set for this coming June. And now I, too, was abandoning Dad, forging a new family of my own, exempting myself from his manipulation or domination. Without warning, he now found himself standing alone at his command post facing the consequences of his past transgressions. His once-beautiful family was moving on and away. I'm sure he felt completely forsaken. The extreme high price he suddenly had to pay for his past poor judgments and follies was colossal and tragic. He had a bitter pill to swallow. Despite the havoc he had caused, I felt great empathy for him. I would always love this man; he was my father.

Despite Dad's lukewarm response, I was in a euphoric state during the entire Christmas week. I couldn't absorb that I was truly going to become Luke's wife, spending the rest of our lives together forever. Anything and everything, good or bad, that had ever happened in my entire life didn't matter anymore. My wildest dream, my most fervent wish, the fairytale of my life was coming true. God had blessed me beyond my comprehension. He had blessed me for the rest of my life. I positively knew He had chosen Luke for me; He designed us to be together. I felt God's amazing love deep in my soul. Surely no one could possibly be as joyful as me. One moment, I would feel chills wash over me, and the next second I felt as if I couldn't breathe. My heart would start racing every time I glanced down at my left hand. *Could this honestly be real and happening to me?* I would find myself having moments of disbelief and pray for this dream come true to be the reality of the next part of my story. I presume this sense of uneasiness was rooted in my life's numerous disappointments relating to trust. For whenever I felt my life circumstances were about to embark on a more conducive path toward achieving my goals, negative events occurred, popping my dreams, leaving me to watch my once-soaring hopes flutter to the ground, airless and lifeless.

Suddenly, my mind flashed back to the time when I was eleven. I could still remember looking out the rental house's filthy windows at dusk in my childlike attempt to mentally escape, if only for a few moments, the fearful realities of my current life. I would intently watch the glorious colors of the fading sunset sky while fantasizing they were heaven's glimmers of hope assuring me there would be better tomorrows. I desperately wanted to believe when the sun rose again it would bring in a fresh bright morning, erasing the scary darkness of the night. I would envision the beams of the sunrise were God's way of offering me more hope that today might be the day. The day our "old" parents would return to love and take care of Sonny and me.

The wait was painfully longer than I had wished for, but now I knew I'd been blessed with my bright sunbeams of hope. I had Luke and a joyful lifetime ahead filled with an overflowing basket of sunbeams. God has His perfect timing for each of us to be blessed with our own bright beams of light.

By New Year's Day 1966, I had no doubt that this truly was the start of my new life. Luke and I had spent the entire week talking about the more practical matters. For example, when did we want to get married? My personal preference was yesterday. Luke, the more level-headed one in our partnership, preferred September, explaining that would allow him to have nine months of earnings at a high hourly wage from his construction job plus lots of overtime pay during the summer months. As usual, he made an excellent case and I had to agree with his logic. We were going to need a considerable amount of money to pay for our wedding, much less set up our apartment and then, there was the cost of his senior year of college. We knew the total sum of either parents' participation in any or all of this would amount to zero. It was no surprise that we were completely on our own, and honestly, we were perfectly fine with that. Together, we were more than willing to work hard and work as many hours as necessary. We would do whatever it took. Our future belonged to us. It was ours to shape.

Chapter 50
Chicago, IL, Winter 1966

The Priest, the Pastor, and Uncle Les

❧

O ur list of to-do's kept growing longer. Luke and I had to decide what we wanted our wedding to look like. How much could we realistically afford to spend on our wedding? Where and how we wanted to get married was a major discussion as I was raised Catholic and he was raised Methodist. I went regularly to Mass, but for all practical purposes, my parents had left the church in 1957. His parents attended the community church, but Luke didn't feel any special connection to it. We met with the priest from the parish where I had been attending Mass. He was irritatingly old school at a time when some of the old rules and saints of the church had already been altered. Apparently many of the new rule applications were determined by each individual parish priest. This old-rule parish priest made impossible demands on Luke, insisting he become a Catholic and we join his church before he would even consider marrying us.

I was heartbroken when we crossed the Catholic church wedding off the list before we ever drove out of the church parking lot. I had never encountered such a rigid and uncaring priest like this man. Now I would be the first woman in at least five generations from both sides of my family to not be married in the Catholic church. I knew the godly lessons that those loving nuns had taught me had kept me grounded and safe throughout my life. I had truly wanted to honor God and be married in the Catholic church. It was a disappointing and an intensely sad moment for me.

Luke was understanding while trying to reassure me, "Diana, we are going to honor God in our wedding and throughout our marriage. A minister of God will perform our ceremony. Jesus is in every Christian church, even if it isn't a Catholic one. Haven't you told me a thousand times that Jesus was always with you, everywhere? Do you think Jesus would skip being beside you when we get married just because it isn't a Catholic ceremony?"

Good old logical Luke had me there, so we proceeded on our quest to find the perfect minister of God who'd be focused on Luke and me joining our hearts and lives together to create the best *us*. I also insisted this perfect minister would allow the beautiful song "Ave Maria" to be played as one of our wedding songs. It was my family's wedding song tradition for every bride from my great-grandmother through Aunt Lulu's wedding. It was a non-negotiable item on my side of our checklist.

After interviewing—or rather, being interviewed by—several ministers, we finally met the one. His time with us was full of questions about us: how we felt about God, each other, our finances, each of our expectations and dreams. Did we want a family? How soon? He was perfect. It was a small Lutheran church not far from Aunt Lulu's. Neither of us knew much about Lutherans and this pastor didn't dwell on that. However, by the end of our lengthy intimate interview, he knew a whole lot about who we were, our hopes, and our dreams. This kind pastor handed us the list of open September wedding dates, then asked, "So Diana and Luke, which day will I have the honor of uniting you two before God in Holy Matrimony?" We chose Saturday, September 10 at one o'clock. We were so excited, not just about our official date being set, but by the amazing minister God had chosen for us.

Holidays and engagement celebrations over, life returned to ...well, life. Luke registered for two night classes at his new college while he worked on a huge road construction project during the day. Often I did the research and helped him study at night and weekends. He was eternally exhausted but determined. I was overwhelmed that this guy was going to be my husband. I would gladly go without sleep for days if it meant I could make his studying, homework, or life easier. We were partners and going to be partners for the rest of our lives.

Meanwhile, back at work, Cathy had moved on. Merriam had become impossible and irrational. I decided to start checking around for other jobs that might be available—hopefully one with higher pay.

Christmas night, during my dad's uncle's soiree, the husband of one of my dad's cousins had mentioned his office was across the courtyard from where I worked. He suggested, "Hey Diana, since our offices are in the same complex, we should have lunch one day. In fact, I know of a job that may be coming available. How about I contact you when I know more?"

I eagerly responded, "That would be great. I am not positive how long I'm going to stay at my current gig."

He called me a couple of weeks later suggesting we get together. We agreed on a day and time. I would meet him at his office. The morning of my lunch meeting, I arrived thirty minutes early at my office. I explained to Merriam that I had a doctor's appointment and would need to take a ninety-minute lunch hour to cover it. She nodded and shooed me away. Phew, that went better than I imagined. Merriam had been exceptionally difficult since the holidays. I never knew what rollercoaster mood I'd find her in. Hence, I was especially curious about my lunch meeting and what future employment news Uncle Les had to offer.

Arriving about five minutes early, I found Uncle Les waiting for me in the reception area of his office. He explained, "We aren't going out to lunch, but I've ordered lunch to be delivered here. My secretary recently quit and I don't want to leave the office unattended."

"Okay," I answered and sat down on the sofa in the reception area, assuming he would sit down across from me in the big leather armchair facing the sofa. Wrong assumption—he sat down next to me, so close that our thighs were touching. I subtly moved away so I could turn and look directly at him. Smiling, I recounted, "My boss, who is the office manager, is crazy and driving me nuts. I really need to find something else. What do you know about this job opportunity you mentioned?"

As he answered, he again shifted closer to me, revealing, "Actually I am looking for someone for this office and thought of you. I think you are a perfect fit. I've known you your entire life and I'm confident you are more than qualified to handle any type of issue that may arise in this office. I'm really not interviewing anyone else. The job is yours if you want it." He then suggested, "There will be some after-hours duties, but you'll be well-compensated for your after-hours time.

My good old Lecher-o-Meter alert sent loud and clear signals to my brain.

Once more, Uncle Les edged closer, now placing his hand on my thigh. I stood up, asking, "Um, how much longer do you think it will be before lunch is delivered?"

He answered, "Soon, very soon." I thought, *never*. I seriously doubted he'd ordered any lunch and now I was in an awkward, sticky situation. This man was married to a close cousin of my dad's. Dad and his younger brother had grown up with his wife. His children were my cousins and he was taking advantage of his chauvinistic misconceived notion that I was incredibly naïve and trusting of him.

Still standing, I asked him, "What are my benefits options and what kind of the salary are you offering?"

He stammered, "Just get back to me with your thoughts on salary and we'll work something out." As I headed for the door, he got up and put his arm around me, stating, "I have time to discuss your options right now."

I reiterated, "Thanks Uncle Les, but I'd better get back to work, before my boss has a heart attack."

I left his office wondering, *what is he thinking? I'm his niece by marriage. His wife is Dad's first cousin! What Uncle Les is looking for isn't in any job description I'm interested in. His insinuated proposal is insulting and demeaning. The irony of all this is that I have to invite him to my wedding. His youngest daughter is my flower girl. He's disgusting.*

I never responded to Uncle Les about anything. However, I was offered a job in the credit department of a giant building supply company in the same office complex. I was one of many "ladies" who sat in rows of desks with typewriters punching out monthly invoices. It sort of reminded me of the turn-of-the-century pictures of women's sewing sweatshops. The difference in our 1966 sweatshop was our electric typewriters replaced the treadle sewing machines and we had air conditioning. It was beyond boring, to say the least, and the boss was a man who hadn't heard of the suffragettes or women's rights. Why did I take the job? It paid sixty cents an hour more and offered health insurance. A ninety-six dollar per month bump in wages was a big help with our upcoming expenses. Luke was working so hard for us, I wanted to do the same.

Chapter 51
Spring 1966

Mom, the Mustang and Grandpa

℘

Late winter, Mom called me. "I just want to let you know that Jack and I are getting married this Saturday at six. I hope you'll come to the wedding and join us along with Aunt Lulu and Uncle Steve for a celebration dinner afterward. Also, everyone is paying for their own meal."

I responded, "Of course I'll be there. If Jack makes you happy, then I'm happy for you. Don't worry. I can pay for my own dinner."

On the appointed time on Saturday afternoon, I arrived at the church and took a seat with Johnny, Marie, and Kevin. It was a short and simple ceremony, not longer than thirty minutes. In the vestibule, Mom pulled me aside and informed me, "Diana, you need to take Johnny, Marie, and Kevin back to Aunt Lulu's, make them a snack, and stay overnight with them. Johnny will be spending the night there and you can sleep with Marie in her room."

What! I was dumbfounded and furious; this was not at all what I had been told when she invited me. If she had, I would have declined. Once again, I was blindsided, lied to, and boxed into a corner. I wouldn't leave Aunt Lulu in the lurch nor did I want to create a scene, so I gathered my three charges and off we headed to Aunt Lulu's house.

The evening with the kids was a lot of fun. We entertained ourselves by playing games, being silly, and laughing a lot. I fell asleep hurt and angry, vowing Mom's disrespectful surprise tonight was the last straw. She'd crossed the line. I was over turning my other cheek to keep the peace with her.

By early April, Luke and I had spent hours going over our wedding plans and costs. We'd nailed down the church and invited the people we wanted to be in our wedding party. One outstanding issue we'd yet to decide involved the reception venue. Not having attended any weddings since we were small children left us rather clueless concerning what all was involved after the ceremony ended. The couple of places we had looked at were way over our budget. In addition, we had begun to look at apartments. Last but certainly not least, we had to be sure our budget allowed for Luke's senior year's tuition, a key factor for our future. Who knew there was so much to consider when two people simply were in love and wanted to share their life together? I knew we would figure it all out and right then, my world was all good. My heart overflowed with real joy.

There are times, however, when the reality and fragility of life blindsides you, interrupting your moments of jubilation. On April 19, my most beloved grandfather passed away after a sudden stroke. He was seventy-five. In 1966, that was a considered a long life. He died peacefully in his sleep. I adored him. I respected him. I trusted him more than I ever trusted anyone. I loved him fiercely. I knew he would leave a huge hole in my heart. He has; I still feel it today. However, my memories of times spent with him—his accent, his arms holding me to his heart that terrible morning in 1957—keep him alive in me. I am grateful God chose me to be his granddaughter.

Within the last five years of Grandpa's life, he had become close with Luke. They connected at their first introduction, finding they had a lot in common. Often Luke would suggest we drive out to the lake house so he could spend time with him. He was honored to be one of the pallbearers for Grandpa's funeral. Sadly, for Luke, his paternal grandfather passed seven days later in Kansas. Luke was a pallbearer for his own grandfather as well.

My dad did well acclimating himself back into his new "not running and hiding from the FBI" life. However, I wasn't convinced that he'd lost his overzealous "you're gonna love the big life" drive. He'd acquired a girlfriend who joined us for dinner a few times. She was nice but I thought she was more enamored with Dad than Dad was with her. I don't think he'd gotten over Mom remarrying so quickly. In my humble opinion, Dad was either the most optimistic or the most delusional man on the planet (I vacillated, depending on the situation). I believed he believed Mom would come back to him one day. I thought what he possessed was wishful belief. As far as I knew, she never wanted to see or speak to him again. Mom purposely had Dad pick up Johnny from Aunt Lulu's house on his visitation days. She arranged it so she wouldn't have to interface with him. She clearly didn't want to have anything to do with him. I stayed out of it. If his fantasy made him happy, so be it.

Dad had found full-time employment at a large Ford dealership. One day, he called. "Hey, can you meet me for dinner tonight?" This wasn't unusual, as we got together for dinner every two weeks or so. When I arrived and walked into the showroom, he told me, "Go check out the new burgundy Mustang on the showroom floor. Climb in it cause it's really sharp."

I went over to look at it. As I opened the driver's side door to peek inside, I noticed an envelope with my name lying on the seat. I reached in and opened it. It was a bill of sale in my name, a sheet of dealership letterhead paper with "paid in full" written across the balance owed on my less-than-fabulous 1961 Corvair and a car payment booklet for this brand-new 1966 Mustang 289.

By now, Dad had sauntered over, sporting his "you're gonna love this new big life" smile plastered on his face. I was confused as I looked up, waving the papers in front of him. Dad was the consummate car salesman. He had been in the business for most of his entire life. It was his biggest asset and his worst liability.

I was aware of this as he explained, "I don't want you driving around in that unsafe rattle trap piece of shit you have."

I looked at him, "I agree, Dad. I don't love it either but it's all I can afford and it gets me to work."

Putting his arm around me, he went on, "Nnnooo, You can afford this, I made sure. Look honey, I have the opportunity to do something nice for you that will also benefit Luke. I helped Sonny get a car a couple of years ago and I want to do the same for you."

Now, he claimed, "I made a deal with the dealership's owner; he also owns the finance company. This is how the transaction works: you trade in the Corvair, we give you the dealer price on the Mustang, then we finance it at a one-percent interest rate. I checked and the car payments on this brand-new Mustang will cost you eighteen dollars more per month than you're currently shelling out for your unsafe piece of junk."

I'll admit I was a bit dubious, however, Dad had done right by my brother. Sonny had told me how Dad had helped him. Luke and I needed a newer car, and we wouldn't have money for something like this in our budget anytime soon. We didn't have a car repair budget either and according to Luke, the Corvair was on the village of the doomed short list. It never occurred to me that a car needed other juice than just gas. Luke and his dad had mentioned something about cars needing oil. I didn't listen. When Luke's dad asked, "When was the last time you put oil in the car?" I'd replied, "When I last got gas." I didn't think my car's oil was any of his business.

Luke had checked the Corvair's oil a couple of days before and found it had none. "Dry as a bone" were the words he used. He may have suggested the car was on borrowed time.

After running all this through my muddled brain, I decided this was the smart move. Eighteen extra dollars a month was a big budget hit, but doable. It was a good opportunity and I couldn't fathom Dad orchestrating such an elaborate plan to hurt me. I knew he loved me in his own special warped kind of way. Thanking him for this fabulous and generous gift, I gave him a huge hug, then hurried to clean out the oil-less doomed blue piece of junk and follow Dad to dinner in my brand-new 1966 Mustang 289!

I'd like to add a couple of points:

1. I couldn't wait to call Luke and tell him about our new hot wheels.
2. I would never tell my dad I didn't like the color burgundy on any car, nor did I know what the "289" after "Mustang" meant.

And, in case you are wondering, Luke loved everything about the car and took over all future "car maintenance responsibility issues."

A couple of nights later, Ann and I found the perfect wedding dress. It was exactly the style and color I preferred, required zero alterations, and most importantly, it was a summer sample dress marked seventy percent off, making it one-hundred-percent affordable. I also found the perfect veil and floated out of the shop. One more bridal shop stop and we had found our bridesmaids' dresses. My wedding day was becoming more real by the moment.

I was so excited that I called Aunt Lulu the next day and described the dress in explicit detail, right down to and including every bead on it. I continued to bless her with the entire story on the veil made with Grandma's same type of wedding veil lace. This wonderful lady displayed saintly patience with me and did not remind me that I had called her at work.

I then called Grandma, who was at home, and gave her a slightly shortened version of my wedding ensemble description. She quietly listened to my excitement then declared in her somewhat broken accented English, "It sound *bery* nice, but tell me how much *everyting coss?*" After disclosing the total, Grandma revealed, "I buy you your *weddin* dress *an beil.* Is my *gif* to you because you are my *granddaughder.*"

I was speechless. Grandma didn't do stuff like this, ever. Her unexpected generosity gave me chills. This was the greatest present Grandma could ever bestow upon me. It touched me deep within, meaning so much more than I could explain or express to her. For in my heart, her precious gift of my wedding dress and veil symbolized her love for me and her blessing on my marriage to Luke; even though her disapproval that we were not being married by a priest in a Catholic church was well known.

Chapter 52
Chicago, IL, Early Summer 1966

What Could Possibly Go Wrong?
✿

O ne late June morning driving to work, an old pickup truck traveling approximately fifty miles-per-hour slammed into the rear end of my Mustang while I was stopped at a red light. A young guy with an expired driver's license and no insurance was the driver. The crash happened in front of an all-night lounge. Several witnesses ran out of the bar to check if I was okay. I thought I was, but I wasn't too certain about the early all-night lounge patrons' conditions. Within seconds, the police arrived. More furious about my damaged car than assessing how I felt, I waved off any offers about going to the hospital to get checked out. I was also upset that now I would be late for work. So I quickly handed over my driver's license, car insurance card, and registration to the police, gave them my statement, signed their report, and dashed off. I was relieved the car was in safe drivable condition but beside myself that the rear of the car was noticeably dented and slightly squished in. As I drove off, I felt my neck becoming stiff and a headache coming on. In 1966, there were no seatbelts, headrests, or air bags.

Morning commuter traffic was heavy and the longer the drive took, the more my neck and head hurt. By the time I was a few miles from work, I was miserable and concerned about my ability to drive. I found I couldn't turn my head from side to side and when I moved my head, it was immensely painful. One of my bridesmaids, Connie, a close girlfriend from my rental car days, lived a couple of blocks away from where I was. I decided my best alternative was to get myself to her house. Those last two blocks took forever to drive. Connie saw me pull up and came running out. She helped me inside and pronounced she was taking me to her doctor right now. I called work and informed them I had been in an accident and would be late. The office manager didn't respond as if she believed me. At that moment, I didn't care.

Connie's doctor saw me right away. He insisted, "You need to get to the hospital sooner than later. There's obvious swelling and limited mobility. I can't assess the problem here in the office." I agreed as my head felt like it was split open with an axe and I could no longer move my neck. Connie drove me to the hospital emergency room.

After a couple of long hours and a multitude of X-rays and tests, the results were delivered by a no-nonsense resident at the hospital. "Here's a neck brace that you'll need to wear twenty-four hours a day. You can take it off to shower. There's absolutely no driving and no working for at least six weeks. Also I've scheduled your daily physical therapy here at the hospital. You will need someone to drive to and from your appointment. I've set your appointments for one-thirty every afternoon starting next Monday through Friday."

The disastrous no working, no driving limitations meant I had no means to get to the hospital for daily physical therapy. Clearly, I needed to move out of Ann's house. There was no way I was going to be a temporary invalid/burden on that caring family. I had no money coming in for six weeks and I wouldn't live with them rent-free. I may be forced to live with Mom and Jack. Jack had offered me that option several times, but then Mom would have to drive me forty-five minutes each way to my daily treatments. She was no longer working but wasn't reliable and still drinking, a lot. Jack drank almost as much. Sometimes they were fun, but most times they were not.

Connie insisted I stay with her and her husband for the first night while we sorted out all my options. I agreed, as all I wanted to do right then was lay my head down and close my eyes. Once back at Connie's, she called Luke and brought him up-to-date.

Luke rushed over to Connie's and explained, "I spoke with my parents and they insist you stay with us. My mom will take you to your treatments. I'll drive your car to work so mom can use the Opel. The kids are home on summer vacation and thrilled that you may live with them. This way, in the evenings, you can help me with my classes more, plus we'll get to see each other every day. Also, it makes it easier for us to complete our wedding plans and start shopping for our apartment. Can you believe our wedding is less than ninety days away?"

I thought that was unbelievably sweet and generous of Luke's family. It was sort of a great solution, although their home was rather small. Me moving in would be a total inconvenience for them. Karen and Mike would have to share their room with me, causing Luke to sleep on the living room couch—not too comfortable for my six-foot, four-inch fiancée. Five people living in a two-bedroom, one-bath house was difficult; six people crammed in their house was insanity. In the end, for lack of an alternative solution, I acquiesced, just until I could drive again. My hope was that I'd heal quickly and be driving in half the time quoted. I had to work. I had bills and a meager savings.

I did, however, have one added deep concern about this proposed living arrangement. I knew Luke's parents had serious problems. On occasion, he'd mentioned a violent temper and domestic abuse. Luke had confidentially related stories of when he was a young boy how his dad would sometimes beat him with a belt when Luke came home from playing football with his friends after school. Numerous times Luke had been frantically summoned back home from my house because of an ugly domestic situation. He was seriously concerned for his mother's, brother's, and sister's safety. Luke felt he had to protect them from his dad.

I wasn't afraid for myself. I merely didn't want to add more stress to an already stressed household. That wouldn't be fair to any of them. Luke countered my reluctance with the assurance that my living there would help the situation. His dad would never act out in front of me. If I was living in the house, peace would reign and everyone would be safe.

The next day, Luke collected my things from Ann's. I'd already called her and her mom and explained my situation. They insisted I should continue to live with them; it would be no problem. I thanked them profusely, but explained I needed to live with Luke and his family. Once I could drive, I would come and spent a night or two. I was so grateful and loved them as if they were my own family. Everything I told Ann's mom was true. They were amazing.

My neck injury was the first medical challenge I had ever had. Until now, my collection of illnesses had consisted of the chicken pox, German measles, tonsillitis, one ear infection, and an occasional cold. I had never had a sprain, break, or even a stubbed toe that I could remember. This whiplashed neck was painful and severely limited my independence. I hated the do's and don'ts list the hospital gave me. The do's hurt and the don'ts severely cramped my style. Outwardly, I was a calm compliant patient; inwardly, I was driving myself crazy. I failed at being a patient patient and stressed about paying my car payment. If I didn't work, I didn't get paid. The silver lining about the typing sweatshop job was the excellent health insurance plan that was covering my medical expenses; however, it didn't cover my car payments.

Luke and his family could not have been more loving. Each afternoon, his mom religiously drove me to and from the hospital for my neck treatment. The rest of the day I would spend talking with her or playing games with Karen and Mike. It was great bonding time with them. I was excited that they would soon be my sister and brother too. Finally, I would have the little sister I had always wanted.

As soon as my neck therapy ended, I needed to earn money. My almost-mother-in-law drove me to my office so I could have them sign some insurance papers. While waiting, the big corporate boss asked me to step into his office. "Nice to see you, Diana. I was very surprised that your injuries from a simple rear-ender were this serious. Exactly how much longer will you be in therapy and when are you planning on being back at your desk?"

I answered as honestly as I could based on what the doctor told me. "Unfortunately it may be a few more weeks. I go to therapy every day and will have X-rays again in about three weeks."

Mr. Big Boss immediately fired me, stating, "Well, I need someone at your typewriter yesterday, not in a few weeks. You have taken too much time off already and then you have requested another week off when you get married. That just isn't going to fly around here. You may wait right here in my office while Helen prepares your final check. This will only take a few minutes."

I never imagined that scenario when I walked in this office to have a simple insurance form signed, the result would be me walking out unemployed. I was blindsided and it felt like punishment without committing any crime. I wanted to confront him, "Hey, I'm the victim here." But, my smarter judgment took over and I thought better of it. It wouldn't have made a difference anyway. I couldn't work; therefore, I was fired. They needed someone to sit and type past-due invoices today, and it couldn't be me. I was worried about no paychecks but relieved about not having to work there any longer. I'd never liked it. I would immediately begin searching for something more exciting, a job with a little challenge and variety, and hopefully a larger paycheck.

Chapter 53
Chicago, IL, Late June–July 1966

Gotta Get a Job

❧

Our wedding day would be upon us before we knew it. We had
plenty of to-do's left on our list, especially the reception details,
including finding a venue for our reception. Nor had we rented an
apartment yet. Luke and I decided we needed to talk with my mother
about how she may be able to help us. We met up with her at Aunt
Lulu's late one Friday afternoon. I shared where we were regarding our
completed plans, but mentioned we would appreciate some help on
the reception. If I had asked her in plain terms, my question would
have looked like, "How much were you planning on contributing
to my, your one and only daughter's, wedding?" I full well knew she
didn't have a lot of money, but I was her only daughter and I hopefully
assumed she would help me in some way.

Mom "got" the question but was insulted. In no uncertain words,
we were told, "It's *not my* problem. It's *your* problem. Just tell me
when and where."

Obviously, she had no intention of helping. She'd show up, period.
With that, she got up and stormed out of Aunt Lulu's kitchen, letting
the door slam loudly behind her. Obviously not the reaction I expected.
Again, I wondered, did she care anything at all about me or my life?

Luke looked at me while shaking his head. "You know," he confessed,
"late last summer I drove to Lulu's to confront your mom and ask her

why she had moved out of your house and never told you. I was going to question her regarding how she could have abandoned you, leaving you penniless and homeless ...why she treats you the way she does. It turned out, she wasn't home so I spent an hour asking Lulu about your mom's behavior. She was appalled and unaware that your mom has been so cruel. I left without ever speaking to your mom, but the way she acted just now doesn't surprise me. Don't be sad. We'll handle our wedding ourselves."

His body language showed his disappointment in Mom, yet compassion and love for me. Was I a little hurt by Mom's reactions? Yeah, I was, but I instantly realized whatever she did couldn't hurt me anymore. I had Luke right here on this planet and I was always surrounded by the same heavenly love that had sustained and protected me through the years. Add Aunt Lulu and Sonny to the list and all was perfect in my world.

Aunt Lulu perked up the mood after Mom's startling outburst and exit by suggesting we go have some fun. We'd go to the bowling alley where Uncle Steve was and wait for his league to finish their games. She would help us with our questions regarding the reception and other loose ends. When Uncle Steve finished, we'd get a pizza and do some celebrating.

We three brain trusts came up with great ideas and a few solutions that night, all because Aunt Lulu came to the rescue. I remember thinking how being with her had brought me joy my entire life. I hoped someday I could repay her.

As for Dad, I didn't see him as much. He was working a lot and I couldn't drive yet. Thankfully, Dad took care of the car repairs for me. Occasionally, Luke and I met him and his new girlfriend for dinner. She was very nice and quite attractive, a mother of three children all around my age. I could tell Dad was in to her. I was interested to see if anything would come of it.

Sonny and Ella got married that June. Luke and I drove to St. Louis for the lovely military wedding held in a magnificent cathedral. I loved the pomp and circumstance of the ceremony, complete with an arch of swords for them to walk through while they were pelted with rice. Sonny looked so handsome and grown up in his Air Force dress blues. His beautiful Ella was a beaming regal bride as her father escorted her down the aisle. I was happy for them.

As they recited their vows, I realized in a few short weeks, I would be walking down a church aisle to marry my own handsome groom, Luke. Glancing around the church, I smiled at Aunt Lulu and her family, my recently widowed grandmother, and a few old family friends. Johnny, Luke, and I were seated behind Mom and Jack. Suddenly, I noticed I didn't see Dad. He wasn't anywhere in this church, yet I knew he would never miss Sonny's wedding. Where in the world was he? Had he had a car accident? I was disturbed that something may have happened to him and there was no way we would know.

The lovely cocktail and hors d'oeuvres reception was held in a posh St. Louis hotel; however, my enjoyment was tempered because Dad had yet to arrive. He finally showed up as Sonny and Ella drove away in their Mustang adorned with a "Just Married" sign. Sonny and Ella waved at him as they drove off. I was relieved that he'd finally made it, but he never explained why he was late.

Upon returning from the wedding, Luke and I relentlessly searched for somewhere to host our own reception. Something simple that we could afford. Connie and her husband, Ron, mentioned a possible wedding reception venue they had recently seen that might fit our needs. It was the party room of a motel restaurant rather far from the church, but near where most of our guests lived. The four of us went to check it out. Luke and I thought it looked okay. It was a private room with a bar and enough space to accommodate our invited guests. The fee we were able to negotiate fit within our budget and included extras like linens, liquor, and bartender. Our date was available. We signed up, excited to have finally secured a space. It wasn't our dream spot by any means, but our budget wasn't dreamy either. It served our purpose and a big item could be checked off our to-do list.

Unfortunately, the wedding invitations had to have a do-over. Dad's girlfriend, Linda, called to enlighten me that my dad was hurt over his name not being on our wedding invitations. Luke and I had discussed this and decided since none of the families were "participating" in our wedding, we would only have our names on the engraved invitations—less script, less cost. It was apparent that their choice to not help us with our wedding did not diminish their right to interfere with our choices. At this point, we didn't want to cause any animosity with any of our parents. We explained our plight to the stationary store owner and asked her to reprint them to include all parents. The owner of the store, who knew we were on a slim budget, reprinted them at no cost. She made it clear that she felt our family was being inconsiderate to us, therefore this was her wedding gift to Luke and me. We thanked her profusely.

Serious apartment hunting was the major item up next on our combined to-do list. For me, getting another job was number one, way ahead of anything else.

Four weeks had passed since my car accident. I hadn't been released to drive, but I decided that one little item wasn't going to stop me. I needed to work and I needed to work *now*. Luke's family had been great, but it was important to me that I move out as soon as possible.

I scoured the *Chicago Tribune* and found a couple of interesting job opportunities. The first job was at a national conglomerate that had many diverse divisions. It was an after-hours interview, which I thought was a little abnormal. The office was empty except for one older woman who conducted my interview. She asked the normal interview questions, then requested, "I would like to have an additional meeting with you on Saturday evening at my place downtown. Here's the address. Come alone around seven-thirty."

I thanked her and left as quickly and politely as I could. She weirded me out with that request. There was no way I would go alone to an unfamiliar downtown address to meet up with this questionable woman for a second unconventional interview. My inner voice suggested the interview I just left was not a legitimate sanctioned interview for the world-famous company; rather, it smelled like an after-hours interview for this bizarre woman's personal reasons. Whatever the true story was, I wasn't interested, didn't go, and did not RSVP.

My second interview was for a glass manufacturing company in one of the old stately Chicago office buildings on famous Wacker Drive. While taking the train downtown to work daily was costly, it eliminated driving so I could start working immediately. Besides, taking the train with all the business commuters might be a fun experience.

My interview was with the Regional Manager, Mr. Parks. His office manager/personal secretary, who would normally do my interview, was on vacation. There were two salesmen and one secretary whom they shared. My potential job involved learning the teletype machine, normal receptionist duties, and any overload work from the office manager or sales secretary. Mr. Parks also mentioned he occasionally had a special project that I may have to work on. The benefits were good, the pay my best yet, and he was amenable regarding the week off for our wedding. In August, the office was moving to North Lake, a suburb about twenty minutes from where Luke and I planned on living. Furthermore, I could start as soon as I wanted. Hooray! I'd hit the jackpot. Since Mr. Parks, himself, hired me, I felt safe in my job. All I had to do was convince the doctor that I was ready to roll.

My doctor agreed to the early work release, but no driving for another week. Since my transportation was by train, I got the "good to go" nod. My game plan was to move out of Luke's house the day I got my car keys back.

With our wedding day less than six weeks away, I broke my own vow by asking my mom if I could stay with her and Jack in the interim. Basically, I stored my personal stuff in their house but rarely slept there. For most nights, I camped out at Ann's or Connie's. They lived closer to Luke's and it was easier to catch the train than from Mom's.

Both she and Jack were receptive to my request and it turned out okay. She never asked about my dress, any wedding plans, or where Luke and I planned to live. It was fine with me. The last thing I needed was another of Mom's alcohol-induced blowups regarding anything to do with my wedding. So far, the only wedding event she had participated in was showing up for the lovely bridal shower that Ann's family had given for me. Aunt Lulu took charge of transporting Mom, Grandma, and Marie. I believe everyone should be blessed with an Aunt Lulu of their own. She was and is the best.

With all the elements for interim living and the actual wedding under control, Luke and I focused on a place to live. The apartment needed to be fairly near his college and preferably on my way to work. With my office relocated to the suburbs, I wanted no more than a twenty to thirty-minute commute between work and Luke's school. If I could drop him off in the morning before work and pick him up on my way home from work, we could save gas and maintenance on the ugly old Opal station wagon.

Chapter 54
Late July–August 1966

The White Hen, Ruby, and the Beast

❦

W e looked at several apartments in various locations and finally settled on the apartment we wanted. It definitely wasn't the best location for a drive by the college route to work but we compromised because we fell in love with the new apartment complex. It was an upscale one-bedroom apartment with a balcony and elevators and at the top of our budget. Okay, it was well over the top of our budget, but we signed on the dotted line and the apartment was ours beginning September 1. We were over the moon for about a day or two, then the reality of our meager budget brought us back to Earth. Our solution was to make additional money by finding ancillary jobs on nights and weekends.

God takes delight in surprising you when you least expect it. I've noticed He's often extraordinarily cunning in His own fatherly way. Shortly before we took possession of our apartment, Luke and I stopped to buy a coke from the new White Hen Pantry (like an upscale 7-11store) that was next to our new apartment. While there, we chatted with the kindly gentleman at the checkout, mentioning Luke and I were soon-to-be married. For some unknown reason we told him our whole story including Luke's college, my job, and our tight budget situation.

Right away, the gentleman, who turned out to be the owner, asked, "Hey, would both of you be interested in working four evenings a week from six to eleven for me? Luke, you'd be the night manager; and Diana, you would be the assistant manager. The pay's a bit more than minimum wage but you could eat anything including all the expensive gourmet stuff straight from the imported meat and cheese deli department case. Absolutely anything edible in the whole store, you can eat for free. The only conditions are you must consume it within the store and you can't take anything home. The nights would be Monday through Thursday. If the store's not too busy, Luke can do his homework while Diana waits on the customers."

Holy cow. Instantly, we knew this was a blessing wrapped in deli paper from God. We accepted the generous offer on the spot. We'd meet him on Sunday, the week after our wedding, for training and begin the following Monday night. Life was looking good.

My new daytime office job was bewildering and uncomfortable at first. Mr. Parks was out of town and I was met by the disapproving office manager, Ruby. As soon as I walked in the door of the office my first morning, she informed me, "I have reviewed your employment application, In no way are you qualified for this job."

Obviously, Ruby was furious that Mr. Parks had impulsively hired me and for now, she was stuck with me. Showing me to my desk, she laid down her laws, "Any mess-ups of any kind and you will be terminated. You are on probation until I say otherwise." After handing me my job description manual, she turned on her heel and marched back into her office, slamming her door closed behind her. No one else in the office came out to meet me, much less welcome me into the fold.

I spent the first part of the morning figuring out the phones, then delved deep into the job's manual. The tasks looked fine except for the teletype machine. A huge iron beast roosted behind my desk ...best guess, the beast is the teletype machine. It looked intimidating to say the least. The good news: I recognized the electric typewriter and adding machine on my desk. I knew how to navigate my way around both of those quite well.

Ruby, via the intercom, informed me, "Miss Rosemary Wurst from the teletype machine company will be arriving after lunch to give you teletype lessons. A proficiency test this afternoon and another test tomorrow morning will complete the training. I hope you pay attention; your continuing employment depends on it."

Politely, I responded, "Thank you, Ruby. I am a diligent student and a quick learner. I will give Miss Wurst my complete attention."

At lunchtime, I found the ladies' room one floor up and rested my head against the art deco inspired chipped tile wall. I wondered what was up with Ruby, who I'd already dubbed the office dragon. She wore old fashioned wire-rimmed glasses, a short puffed-sleeved purple pansy flowered shirtwaist dress. Her hairdo was a plastered down finger waved style reminding me of the iconic secretarial look back from the old 1930s and 1940s movies that I sometimes had watched with Grandma. Ruby's demeanor was so daunting, I pictured fire spewing out of her nostrils at my first mistake. Convincing myself to shake it off, I returned my attention to the paper pile on my desk, thinking, *Ruby obviously has issues; I've got to learn how to work around them. I need this job and I can do it well. I've dealt with difficult, irrational people my whole life, and hey, my life is perfect. I'm marrying Luke in about forty days.*

The lady from the big beast machine company, Rosemary, arrived promptly at one o'clock. In her large flowing olive green and brown leaf patterned dress, she resembled the beast machine but she seemed to be nice—almost too nice to me. The antithesis to my dragon lady boss spying on me from her office behind the closed door.

The teletype beast teacher pulled up a chair next to me as we began our lesson. The machine made logical sense and wasn't difficult. However, Rosemary was being overly complimentary to me. After a couple of hours, she prattled on, "Diana, you are catching on to this faster than anyone I have ever taught before. I am incredibly impressed. This machine is difficult. Often I have to spend an extra day teaching a new hire. You'll be more than ready to take and pass the test tomorrow."

As she showered me with her overstated compliments, I noticed she kept scooting her chair closer and closer to mine. After two hours of lessons and chair scooting, Rosemary's huge thigh was touching my left thigh and I was trapped against the wall. I excused myself and again ran up to the ladies' room. Not quite sure of what to make of this lady, I made sure I did not take the elevator. I wanted to be able to be free to escape all untoward situations. When I returned to my desk, I found a note from her stating she had left for today but would see me bright and early tomorrow morning.

Rosemary didn't disappoint; she did indeed arrive bright and early the next morning. After a minor review of yesterday's skills, Rosemary showed me a few more mechanical tricks requiring both of my hands to perform the tasks. While both of my hands were busy with the big beast machine, I felt the beast lady's hand lightly on my left thigh then slightly edging up ever so slowly under my dress as if testing out my reaction. I immediately removed her hand by standing up for a moment to stretch. Then sat back down, informing her, "Rosemary, you are an incredible teacher. I am confident I understand all these lessons and think I am ready to take the final test."

She hesitated but concurred, "Well you've been speedy catching on. Let's go ahead have you take the test."

I passed the test with flying colors. With nothing left to teach, Rosemary stood as if to leave, but stopped and asked me, "One more thing before I leave, Diana. Would you please show me to the ladies' restroom?"

I replied, "It's easy, just go one flight up. You can either take the stairs right around the corner or use the elevator across the hall. You can't miss it."

She pushed back, "Why don't you simply show me?"

Repeating, I encouraged, "It's simple. I guarantee you'll have no problem locating it."

She pressed me a third time. "Really, Diana, I would appreciate it if you would accompany me to the ladies' room."

This time, I looked up at her, and politely yet firmly responded, "Rosemary, thank you so much for being a wonderful teacher. You don't need me to help you find the ladies' room. It was nice to meet you. Goodbye and have a nice day." I turned back to the paper pile on my desk and didn't look up again.

I was so confused. All I wanted was to do was the job I was hired to do. It wasn't my fault that Ruby found me deficient for the job.

How could she know? She had only spoken to me for a total of ten minutes at most. If she disagreed with Mr. Parks, she should call him, complain, and explain her reasons. So far I thought I'd done a great job of deflecting the dragon lady's abuse and the big beast machine lady's unsolicited unwanted overtures. I knew that new jobs differed in-office procedures, but these past two days certainly didn't speak of normal office policy or conduct. Then, as I reflected on my past fourteen months of interviews and employment, I thought, *ah ha, maybe I'm mistaken.* Thinking back on my encounters, most did seem to share a disturbing common thread: #metoo.

The following week at work went fine; Mr. Parks had returned. I never knew if, when, or what conversation he and Ruby may have had concerning me. When he was around, Ruby was not exactly friendly, but office cordial. The other secretary and the two salesmen had come around, which I rated pre-business friendly.

My third week, the office moved out to the suburbs. It was a gigantic mess. To Ruby's surprise, I proved I was an accomplished location "specialist." I had organized and packed up the front office, then unpacked my work space in the new office within record time. At the same time, they were chaotically unpacking their boxes, I was teletyping away and preforming my given duties as if there had been no office move interruptions. Secretly, I think I climbed up a notch or two in Ruby's assessment of me. Of course, she had no clue who she was dealing with. I mean, seriously, how many nineteen-year-olds could Ruby know who had been homeless several times and have a Master's degree in relocation skills? Believe me, God has a unique plan for each of us. He'll surprise and bless you with a beautiful medley of gifts that you never realized you held. I say thank Him, then put those gifts to good use.

Chapter 55
Chicago, IL, August–September 9, 1966

Thirty-five Days
and Counting
❧

M arie's thirteenth birthday party was about a month before our wedding. Aunt Lulu was having everyone from both families over to celebrate Marie's special day. My whole life I had grown up with Uncle Steve's side of the family. In a way, I counted them as my relatives too. Looking forward to spending Marie's memorable fun party with everyone, Luke and I scheduled our final premarital session with our caring wedding pastor on the same day. Conveniently, Aunt Lulu's house was just a few blocks from the church. We planned to quietly sneak out to our one-hour meeting and return before dinner; no one would ever notice.

Our meeting with the marvelous Pastor W. was emotionally moving. He was an inspiring, kind, and gentle man. On the short drive back to Aunt Lulu's, Luke and I discussed how prepared we felt about our life together and how thankful we were to have this godly man for our premarital counselor.

Returning to Marie's party, we found the merriment in full swing. Uncle Ted loved to sing and would direct everyone in song. Marie and her cousins on her dad's side had been taught several songs in three-part harmony and the big show was about to begin. With everyone enjoying their beverage of choice, Luke and I assumed no one had noted our absence. We were wrong. Eagle-eyed Mom had.

She grabbed my arm, practically dragging me into the bathroom where she denounced me for going off with Luke to have sex. She hissed, "What in the world were you thinking? How could you embarrass me by acting like a slut in front of Uncle Steve's family?"

I stared at her in disbelief concerning her outrageous allegation. First, why this sudden interest in me or what I was doing? It was a little too late to start now. Secondly, her X-rated thoughts and condemning imagination lived in her mind, but not in my life.

Instead of being furious, I surprised myself by feeling so sad that her broken self always led her down that ugly path. How depressing to always accuse and imagine the worst about someone. She'd feel so much better if she would consider their positive attributes first. I'd never done anything in my life to embarrass her and I never planned to in the future. What repeatedly made her assume the worst possible behavior mode when it involved me? Though confused and hurt, I was not going to make a scene and ruin Marie's party. Mom was absurd, drunk, and frankly, wasn't worth the effort at this moment to argue my defense. I reminded her, "Mom, Luke and I will be married in thirty-five days; we were completing our final pre-marriage consultations with the pastor. Feel free to call and verify the truth with him." I took her hand and guided her back to the party. The show had begun.

After working at the new office location for a couple of weeks, Ruby invited me to lunch. On the ride to the restaurant, I silently steeled myself for the possibility that Ruby would fire me. Though I hadn't made any major mistakes, she'd never accepted me. I presumed she merely tolerated me because Mr. Parks daily complimented me on the great job I was doing. In fact, he invited Luke and me to join him for an after-work celebration cocktail the week prior to our wedding.

Once Ruby and I were seated at a quiet table in the corner, she ordered herself a strong cocktail. She began, "Diana, I want you to know how pleasantly surprised I am at how well you perform your tasks. So far things are progressing well and I expect you will continue to keep improving. Also, would you please go over your wedding agenda plans? I need to know what the exact date is and how many days you will be out of the office." She failed to specify what skill I needed to improve.

As the server returned to take our lunch order, Ruby handed the waitress her empty cocktail glass and ordered a second. About halfway through lunch, Ruby ordered her third strong cocktail. I got the drift; Ruby had personal issues. As she sipped this cocktail, she had relaxed and began to share some personal items. For one, she was a single mother with a daughter the same age as me. The difference was her daughter was severely handicapped, mentally and physically. She had home care during the work week, but Ruby cared for her nights and weekends. Her daughter would always live in a wheelchair and need constant care.

Not quite certain what to say without sounding condescending, I responded by sharing, "Ruby, I know it's not the same, but I have a sweet mentally challenged six-year-old brother whom I dearly love. I realize I cannot possibly comprehend nor appreciate all the demands made on you to satisfy your daughter's needs. I truly am sorry for your situation. If I can help either of you in any way once I am married, please just ask me."

I was uncomfortable with this line of sharing. I certainly was not going to unpack any of my past with her and I couldn't be exuberant about my dream-come-true soon-to-be husband and our joyous life plans. Luckily the bill came, she paid, and we left, heading back to the office to resume our professional roles. Once there, I thanked her again for the lovely lunch and conversation.

We never became confidants, but she warmed up to me. I felt sympathy for her and understood her three Manhattan lunches. I also thought I gained insight as to why she originally treated me as she did. Perhaps she had wanted to hire someone older who would not be a daily reminder of what her beloved daughter couldn't be and the life she'd have. I was that daily, in her face, living proof that the normal, happy life dreams she may have imagined for her daughter were dreams that could never come true.

Thereafter, I'd ask Ruby about her lovely daughter and tried to remember when Ruby would be a bit short with me or even downright unreasonable, that she'd probably experienced something unpleasant or even worse. I vowed to make an extra effort to be patient and purposely extra nice to her.

The week preceding our big day was crazy and wonderful. We got the keys to our apartment, our new furniture was delivered, and all our shower and wedding gifts had been transferred from Luke's parents' house. Our clothes, momentos, anything and everything either of us owned was brought into our new home. It was so exciting putting our stuff away, our clothes sharing the same closet, hanging curtains and towels, and organizing our new life together. Even having our telephone connected and the electricity turned on in my soon-to-be-married new last name was thrilling. I'd stand in the middle of the rooms and twirl around, hugging and pinching myself just to prove these sunbeams were real ...and for me!

As promised, Mr. Parks had Luke and me meet him at his favorite lounge for cocktails to toast our upcoming marriage. He was extremely gracious as he handed us an envelope suggesting we open it right then. We were shocked to find a paid certificate for a downtown hotel suite on September tenth, our wedding night. Mr. Parks was aware that we couldn't afford to take a honeymoon for two reasons: Luke's first day of senior year classes began on Thursday, September fifteenth. The other consequential factor: Luke and I had zero money. We were counting on wedding gift cash to help cover Luke's college bill due five days after our wedding day. Mr. Parks' special gift allowed our wedding night plan to change from spending it in our new apartment to celebrating in grand style at a downtown Chicago hotel suite. Excited, we now would have a real mini-honeymoon.

I sat, stunned at the generosity of my boss, thinking what a wonderful man Mr. Parks was. He was the best and kindest boss anyone could have. Around a half an hour later, Luke excused himself for a moment, leaving me alone with my forever-favorite employer. As all these thoughts were processing through my mind, Mr. Parks leaned in, put his arm around me and kissed me. For a moment, I thought he was being fatherly friendly until he whispered, "Diana, I'd like to go out with you for cocktails, take you to dinner or a play after you and Luke are married. You could tell Luke you had to work late on a project with me." Then he quickly removed his arm and changed the subject. Thankfully, before I could react or respond, Luke slid in next to me.

Completely unaware of what had just transpired during in his brief absence, Luke returned and shaking hands with Mr. Parks, explained, "Mr. Parks, your thoughtful gift is special. Thank you so much. Also thank you for the drinks. We are going to have to run now. We are meeting our best man and maid of honor for dinner."

I smiled and thanked my now Mr. Dirty Old Man Boss, Mr. Parks, proclaiming, "The next time you see me I will be happily married to Luke." I decided to wait to tell Luke about the real disgusting Mr. Parks until after we were married. Why spoil one single second of our unforgettable, once-in-a lifetime, glorious pre-wedding week?

All our plans moved along splendidly. Luke and I were proud of what we were able to accomplish on our own. He was the master budgeter of our combined funds, earning and contributing way more money than me. However, despite our detailed to-do lists and planning, there was one item we never thought about: the after-rehearsal dinner party the night before the wedding. We both knew Luke's parents didn't have much extra money, but they'd never mentioned not hosting the rehearsal dinner. At least they'd never told us that they weren't planning to host the dinner until a few days before the rehearsal.

If you are wondering why Luke and I hadn't thought about this before, I can explain. Neither of us had been in a wedding party since Luke was five and I was two. We were the first in our immediate circle of friends to get married, therefore, Luke and I had never really attended a wedding. We were clueless. We had focused on the things my parents were not doing, never realizing Luke's parents weren't "doing" anything either.

So now we found ourselves hanging out there with no more money and no resolution to our significant immediate problem. Here again, remember when I told you that I thought everyone should have an Aunt Lulu? Well, Aunt Lulu rescued us again, choosing to host our after-rehearsal dinner at her house.

Chapter 56
Chicago, IL, September 9–10, 1966

Two Weddings, Baloney Sandwiches, and a Fire

❧

F inally, it was our wedding rehearsal day. Luke and I had everything moved in to our apartment. Earlier in the day, we'd completed our final touches. The apartment was perfect, ready and waiting to become our first home. Deciding to drive to our rehearsal together, we left the Opel station wagon parked at the apartment. We arrived at the church thirty minutes early. Luke's family, Aunt Lulu, Uncle Steve, and the bridal party arrived with time to spare. Five minutes prior to the start of the rehearsal, we realized Johnny, our ring bearer, hadn't shown up. That meant that Mom hadn't shown up either. Come to think about it, my dad was MIA as well. Luke hopped in our car and drove to Mom's to see what the problem was.

The issue? Mom and her drinking buddies were in the midst of their own partying. Slurring, she informed Luke that she wasn't planning on attending the rehearsal, but she'd be at the rehearsal dinner party. Furious with her, Luke grabbed a confused Johnny and brought him back to the church so the rehearsal could begin. We never heard from Dad.

I guessed the rehearsal went like all wedding rehearsals go, the highlight being Aunt Lulu's fantastic after-rehearsal party. Everyone, including me, had a wonderful time. She created a beautiful evening and lifelong memory for Luke and me.

Ann, my maid of honor, and Laura, my best friend from St. Louis, also one of my bridesmaids, spent the night at Mom's with me. The next morning, the girls and I got up, showered, and headed out for breakfast, a couple of quick stops, and then on to the church. We decided to get ready there because it was too difficult to get ready at Mom's with only one bathroom. I was concerned about Mom and Johnny arriving for photos at the church by noon because Laura's parents, Jack, and Mom had begun drinking mimosas way before the girls and I left.

Fortunately, everyone made it with time to spare. Mom looked beautiful in her long pink mother-of-the-bride dress. Johnny, missing his two front teeth, looked adorable in his little tux, as did Marie and Karen in their long green dresses. My sweet little flower girl, the daughter of my lecherous Uncle Les, charmed us all. Even Grandma, in her mourning dress of black, was radiant, whispering, "Diana, I *tink* you make a beautiful bride. I love the lace on your head. It *remind* me of mine. Your dress with *dese* beads is *bery* pretty. I love you and wish you a *bery* happy life *wit* Luke. You deserve it."

As we all gathered in the church vestibule, I noticed Luke's parents and both his grandmothers had arrived. His mother was radiant and Luke's maternal grandmother looked stunning in her ice blue gown and ever-so-slightly tinted blue gray hair (perhaps a touch bluer than gray). His dad's mom had come in from Kansas dressed in black having recently lost her husband, as well. With everyone assembled and waiting for the music to begin, I realized I'd yet to see Dad.

Now you may think I'd have been in a panic about him missing in action for my wedding. However, as his daughter for the past nineteen years, nine months, and twenty-four days, nothing he did or didn't do rattled me. In secrecy, I'd already gone over the scenario of him not attending my wedding. I had no false illusions and no expectations. Dad had already missed Ella's and Sonny's wedding, so why should I be alarmed if he didn't show up to mine? I'd already done much of my life without him.

During the 1960s, society expected the father of the bride to ceremoniously walk his beloved little girl down the aisle, then give his precious daughter to the groom. Her new husband was to love and cherish her till death do they part. Of course, I loved the idea that

Dad would escort me down the aisle and place my hand in Luke's, but nothing was going to tarnish the first day of my life with Luke. I didn't need Dad's presence to make this momentous day become more meaningful and beautiful. Besides, I wasn't going to be alone walking down the aisle toward Luke—I'd be accompanied by my other Father. The Father who loved me and had always been there, protecting me every second of my life. The Father who had chosen Luke for me and me for Luke long before we were even twinkles in our earthly parents' eyes. The Father who would walk beside Luke and me every day for the rest of our lives and then forevermore. He would be there holding my hand as I glided down the aisle toward Luke, thanking God every step of the way. Naturally, the memory I would cherish the most would be to have both Fathers take these important steps with me.

At 12:55 pm, I heard the church doors behind me open. I turned to see my dad and his girlfriend Linda come through the door. Linda looked like a bride dressed in her exquisitely tailored white silk suit with a huge white corsage adorning her lapel. The way she was beaming and smiling at Dad, she looked as if she was the one about to be wed. Dad escorted Linda over to all of us. Mom gave me a quizzical look. I returned her look with an "I know nothing" shrug.

Dad announced to everyone. "I'd like to introduce my wife, Linda. We were married last night."

I now knew why Dad hadn't shown up for my rehearsal. He then proceeded to parade Linda down the main aisle, thus being viewed by all our waiting guests. Gallantly depositing her in the front pew on the left, Linda was now sitting in the same pew and occupying the exact seat reserved for Mom. Poor Mom. How awkward for her, as she was seconds away from being escorted down the aisle herself. This new arrangement meant Mom would be situated next to Linda, who was sitting next to Jack. The irony was, once Dad walked me down the aisle, he would sit in that same pew next to Mom, leaving Mom stuck between Dad and Linda. The four of them intermingled together on the reserved pew. How cozy!

My fleeting thought focused on how selfish and conniving Dad was. *Would he stop at nothing to embarrass and get back at Mom, even if it meant grandstanding Luke's and my wedding ceremony? Poor Linda. I hoped she knew what she had signed up for.*

The Big Life

The organist began to play my song. At last, it was time for me to take the first step into the rest of my life. I only had eyes for Luke as I practically raced up the aisle to him. Everything else faded away. I was laser-focused on the man I wanted to spend all eternity with.

The ceremony was perfect. Our caring wedding pastor made it intimately personal for us. I was so overjoyed at the beauty of this very moment that tears streamed down my face as I choked out my vows. This was the most glorious day of my life. Clinging to Luke's arm as we stepped down from the altar, now officially man and wife, I wondered how many people in this world are blessed enough to truly live their dream. How did I deserve to be one of the fortunate chosen? I have never understood why, but I am so thankful that I was.

Dad's little game had no lasting effect on our wedding service. I had to give Mom five stars. If anyone was observing her, they'd never guess how upset and embarrassed she was. Instead she acted cordial to Dad and gracious toward Linda. Whatever Dad hoped to accomplish with his dramatic entrance and astonishing announcement antics didn't appear to have the impact that I'm certain he'd been going for. He'd played a dirty sneaky game of hardball, not caring how a disastrous result could have decimated Luke's and my wedding day.

As Luke and I entered the room we chose for our reception, everything was as we requested, right down to the tablecloths and stocked bar with a bartender. Our three-tiered square wedding cake was set and ready on a separate round table waiting to be cut, then smashed in Luke's mouth. I thought the room looked way tackier than I had remembered.

About forty-five minutes into the reception, Mom came up to me, inquiring, "When are the hors d'oeuvres being served?"

I gave her a blank look and responded, "What hors d'oeuvres?"

She looked back in horror telling me, "You can't possibly serve liquor and not serve food!"

I smugly replied, "Apparently we can because we never discussed food with the management and this is all we can afford."

At that point, she must have gone and found Dad. They both approached Luke and me, inquiring again about food. Luke's and my answer remained the same: "There is no food. Just drinks. We had no idea that food was even necessary and with our small, already-stretched budget, food was not an option for us."

Dad jumped in, "I'll pay for the food."

We found the manager and explained our last-minute dilemma. He shook his head while informing us, "The kitchen doesn't have anything ready and there's nothing we can make on short notice. The best we can do is prepare some baloney sandwiches on white bread without the crust."

We said, "Fine; please hurry."

About twenty minutes later, two servers arrived with baloney sandwiches sans crusts artfully displayed on aluminum foil covered baking sheets. Obviously, we were fifty some years ahead of our time by serving cutting edge, minimalistic wedding reception fare. Throughout the years, the picture of our baloney sandwiches on white bread have brought us fits of laughter and wonderful memories of our exceedingly tacky wedding reception. Sometimes you have to remember it's the simple and silly things that get you through life.

As soon as the cake was cut and smashed, the garter and bouquet tossed, and our thank you hugs, kisses, and goodbyes all said, Luke and I hightailed it out of the reception venue. With a "Just Married" sign attached to the trunk of our Mustang, our bags for the night already stowed on the backseat and streamers on the radio antenna, we left the parking lot. Our plans included changing into our dinner clothes and leaving my wedding dress and Luke's tux at Connie's house, then full speed ahead to downtown. Our surprise hotel suite and dinner for two at the fancy Top of the Rock restaurant awaited us.

We quickly parked our car in the covered parking lot and grabbed our bags, eager to check into a hotel together for the first time. In the excitement of recounting our unusual wedding events, I failed to explain that the bags we grabbed to take into the hotel were just that: brown paper grocery bags. We each had one stuffed with our needs for the night. Luke nor I owned a suitcase. Just before we left the new apartment for our rehearsal the previous night, we'd gathered up the items we needed for our wedding night stay. It was at that moment when we realized we owned no luggage and had no time to buy any. Buying a suitcase was a moot point. We had no money to pay for any kind of luggage. Therefore, we solved the problem by grabbing two brown paper bags, packed them with our items, and were good to go. It amazes me today how easily we got by with nothing.

BEST KISS EVER!

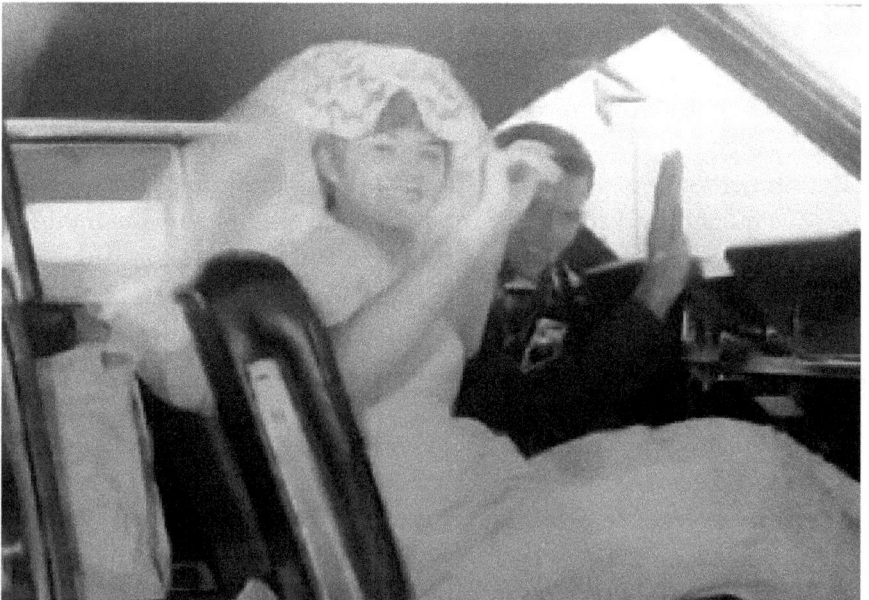

Brown Bag Honeymoon Luggage In Back Seat

Baloney Sandwich Reception

Chapter 57
Chicago, IL, September 10–11, 1966

The Big Life—Our Way

For the first time since I was ten years old, I felt free and totally alive. Luke claimed the same. We were liberated from our families' dominance over our lives. Their problems were now just that: their problems, not our problems. We were safe from their selfish intervening and messing up our lives. This day, we had no problems. We weren't naïve enough to think we'd never have an issue or two along the way, but from that day forward, we'd only be responsible for problems *we* created, not the ones created by everyone else. This was truly our long-awaited life-changing day. And it was; however, our Magnificent, life-changing day continued to present additional unsuspected surprises.

We checked into the hotel using the suite gift certificate from Mr. Parks. The lobby of this hotel wasn't quite how I remembered other fancy Chicago hotel lobbies from my early past. Those were magical with beautiful crystal chandeliers and black shiny floors. This hotel didn't feel magical and looked devoid of any sparkling crystal chandelier. The floor wasn't shiny black either. The disinterested clerk behind the counter brusquely handed Luke our room key, then directed us to the elevator. "Eleventh floor, turn right, last door on the left," he muttered. First impression? So far I wouldn't say I was loving this hotel.

The elevator doors opened, delivering us to the dingy eleventh floor. We took a right turn and stopped at the last door on the left at the end of the dark hall. Luke opened the door and we entered, having no clue what to expect. The good news was we had no expectations, therefore we couldn't be disappointed. Shocked maybe, but not disheartened. It was our wedding day; nothing was going to bring us down.

The room looked tired and smelled like dirty, old, accumulated dust. I rated it a triple-D room: dark, dirty, and dingy. Not quite the romantic little love nest we'd anticipated. I didn't want to put our brown paper bags on the floor or take my shoes off. I refused to think about my skin touching anything in that room. Because it was our wedding night, I decided I'd dwell on that aspect later. On the drive downtown, we decided the first thing we'd do when we got to our suite was open our wedding envelopes. We gathered towels from the bathroom and placed them on the edge of the king-size round bed. I didn't want to directly sit on the icky bedspread in my dressy, new suit. When I glanced up at the ceiling, I was surprised to see my reflection looking back at me. Mounted directly above the bed was a huge, round mirror. I instantly changed the room's rating from a triple-D to a quad-D. The fourth D stood for *disgusting*.

I, ever so carefully, opened each envelope then passed its contents over to Luke to count. When all the envelopes were opened and the money tallied, we had received $686. We whooped and hollered because $686 was the exact amount to the dollar, that we needed for his college tuition, due in five days. Thank you God, again!

Luke put the money in my purse as we headed out to celebrate our first dinner as a married couple: Chateaubriand for two at Chicago's famous Top of the Rock restaurant. Located on the forty-first floor of the Prudential Building, it offered spectacular night views of our beautiful city, the perfect romantic setting for our wedding evening dinner. A night we would remember forever.

The next morning, we were up and out of the hotel, lickety-split. After spending the night there, we concluded it wasn't the type of hotel where honeymooners normally stay. People up and down the hall all through the night, doors slamming, and weird, loud sounds that were disturbing. As we checked out, we noticed several of our hotel mates dressed in skimpy, sexy apparel. High, heels, big hair, and tons of over-applied makeup added to the overall appeal. Luke also noticed a price list for rooms by the hour. We were eager to head back to our clean, new home.

Luke and I never stopped for breakfast as we needed to buy groceries and weren't certain we could afford the food items plus breakfast. There was a Kroger close to our new home. We stopped there to buy the things on our "must have" list. I selected the food while Luke maneuvered the cart and kept a running total of our purchases.

Halfway down the fourth aisle, Luke whispered, "*Stop.*"

I turned around, giving him the "Why?" look. We had eight more aisles to go. He quietly informed me, "We are at the limit of our allotted food budget dollars. We are out of money, so pick and choose what we really need and put the rest back on the shelves. Our shopping spree has to come to an end."

Eggs, butter, a loaf of bread, a large jar of peanut butter, jelly, two cans of tuna, a box of Creamettes, Cheerios, hotdogs, two cans of cream of mushroom soup, potato chips, a small jar of mustard, mayonnaise, and a carton of milk later, we left the store. The good news was, we had new brown paper bags to replace the torn luggage ones from yesterday. Handy, if we had another overnight excursion anytime soon.

From Kroger, we drove across the street to the new Burger King. We were starving. Luke had kept a dollar back from our now-defunct grocery budget money to buy lunch. We split a thirty-nine-cent Whopper burger and a medium coke. The breakfast/lunch bill with tax totaled seventy-seven cents, leaving us twenty-three cents to splurge on something else another day.

With semi-full tummies, we pulled into the apartment parking lot. Big red fire engines surrounded the apartment. Looking up, we noticed black smoke billowing out from the back of our building. Some tenants, still in bathrobes, meandered outside by the pool watching the commotion. No one knew what was on fire or where the smoke was coming from. I was on the brink of tears, thinking everything we hadn't even used would be ruined. Luke was upset for another reason. The parking spot where we had left the green and white Opel station wagon was now empty and the Opel was nowhere to be seen.

The fire in the garbage chute was contained and we were allowed back into our apartment. The smoke was still seeping through our door, so Luke soaked our new towels and placed them on the floor against the door to keep the smoke out as I laid on our new couch crying because he was ruining our only set of towels.

As for Luke's green and white Opel? Luke's parents struck again. We found out shortly after the smoke cleared, that they'd come and taken back Luke's car right after our wedding. They decided they needed his car more than we did.

Later that night, as Luke and I sat together, enjoying our very own home, we looked at each other, smiled, and laughed. We could handle this. We weren't alone; we were married with our whole lives ahead of us and our ever-faithful God by our side.

Life is simply what happens to each of us every day, and together we'll embrace it.

LUKE AND I ARE GONNA LOVE OUR BIG LIFE TOGETHER!

Mr. & Mrs., September 1966

The Who, What, and Where

☙

DAD

Dad was only three years old when his father died suddenly from a raw oyster food poisoning epidemic. At thirteen his mother passed away from a staph infection following a routine surgery. He always believed that he and his younger brother were viewed as poor orphans who were taken in and pitied but not really loved. His mother's family dutifully gave them shelter and food, but it was more out of obligation than love or compassion.

As a result of being dependent on handouts, Dad developed a hero worship for one of his uncles. He absolutely idolized him and knew at an early age that he wanted to grow up and be just like him, extremely wealthy and powerful. In retrospect, I feel that Dad's obsession with achieving that same type of wealth and power was ultimately his downfall. He was gone from home a lot during Sonny's and my childhood concentrating on building his fortunes and whatever else fancied him. In his relentless quest, he compromised his Christian values along with his moral and ethical principles as he strove to attain his unreasonable lofty goals.

Regardless of how successful he became, it was never enough for him. Sadly, he could not fill his inner void through material gains or with the love from his wife and children. His own demons drove him to push harder and further doing whatever it took, including making deals with unsavory people. His decision in 1957 to partner with the man in Chicago resulted in complete disaster. Dad's previous empire suddenly crashed and everything was lost, leaving his family destitute, in debt and in extreme peril. He reconciled this by telling himself and us that everything he had done was for the benefit of our family. After serving six months in prison, Dad continued to work in the car industry until his health forced him to retire. He suffered with ALS (Lou Gehrig disease) and passed away in 1990 at age seventy.

Even today, neither Sonny nor I know much regarding the events behind Dad's catastrophic business problems that caused the demise of his "Shoot to the moon, you're gonna love the big life" story and destroyed our once loving family unit. There are conjectured bits and pieces, personal theories, presumptions and speculations, but we have no real facts or definitive answers. Unfortunately, there is no one alive today, who can set the record straight.

On his deathbed, I asked Dad about the truths versus rumors of what happened through all the years starting in 1957. His reply was, "I've done things that you can't imagine. I am so ashamed and now I will have to answer before God. Just always know how very much I have always loved you and how proud I am of you."

Sonny and I will never have answers to our questions and that's okay with us.

MOM

Mom was the middle child, born to two brave immigrant parents. She was three years younger than her brother, Uncle Gil, and nine years older than her sister, my beloved Aunt Lulu. Mom was raised in a loving, hardworking, old-world strict environment. According to the stories I have heard, Mom was beautiful and very social, not really into academics. She was my grandparent's "wild child," always focusing on her looks, boys, the latest craze, and having fun. Strangely for all her independent "new world" ideas, she was very dependent on her parents and younger sister for shelter and help throughout her life.

Early on Mom was truly a wonderful mother. I idolized her and was very unhappy when I couldn't be right by her side. She was fun and caring, always making our favorite things to eat and rewarding us with special little surprises. Our home was carefully decorated and always immaculate. She was very conscientious about her appearance, exercising daily with Jack LaLanne and applying her makeup prior to leaving her bedroom each morning. As a little girl, I assumed her lips were naturally bright red. I wanted to be just like her when I grew up.

When I was eight, Mom changed in a variety of ways. Not only was she totally fixated on her figure, clothes, hair, and makeup, but now her new friends came first. Cocktail hour soon took precedence over almost everything else, including Sonny and me. Mom thoroughly enjoyed the creature comforts and benefits of having money. "Material things" coupled with the celebrity of wealth in a small town made her feel special, worthy and maybe just a little bit more important than others. I believe this first generation American daughter of brave hardworking immigrant parents, somehow forgot about her roots and came to believe that her self-worth was measured by how good she looked, how much wealth she had and how many people wanted to party with her.

She was devastated by the reactions of her so-called dear friends who completely abandoned her when she needed them the most. Upon hearing the news of my parent's loss of fortune, these "best friends' immediately disappeared from her life, most never making contact with her again. Mom's own perspective of her self-worth was shattered, she'd lost all her precious possessions and felt betrayed by everyone, including her own husband. She was unable to cope with the sudden catastrophic turn of events making it impossible for her to function. She had no idea of who she really was or what was going to happen to her. Mom could not get out of bed each morning, retreating totally into herself and her bottles of bourbon, rendering her unable to care for Sonny, me or anything else. My grandparents and Aunt Lulu moved in with us to support her and her decision to send Sonny and me off to California to live with Uncle Gil and Aunt Sue.

Unfortunately Mom's dependence on alcohol continued throughout the rest of her life. Ovarian and uterine cancer showed up in 1972. She was fortunate to be one of the first Mayo Clinic cancer patients to try chemotherapy. Her cancer was in remission for almost twenty years. The cancer returned in 1990 and she finally succumbed at age seventy in July 1992.

DAD & MOM

In 1973, Dad and Mom divorced their spouses, Linda and Jack, and remarried each other in 1975. Luke's and my relationship with them improved after they got back together. They were good grandparents to our daughters and the girls remember them as sweet, funny, loving and endearing grandparents. That's just as Luke and I had hoped it would be.

Ironically, one day Mom told me she had been reminiscing and realized what great parents Dad and she had been to Sonny and me. When I asked her why she thought that, she explained that all of their friend's kids had caused their parents problems, but Sonny and I had never created any problems or issues, even through our teens.

There were so many retorts I thought about coming back with, but my heart decided that if her delusion gave her comfort or even a bit of joy, I was not going to spoil it for her. I couldn't change our past, so I decided to focus on the present.

Mom and Dad never fully recovered from their past nor loved the sad "big life" they had created for themselves. We supported and cared for them the rest of their lives. Why? Because at the end of the day, they were my parents. Perhaps not the parents I would have chosen or needed, but they were the parents God chose for me and in spite of everything that had happened, I still loved them.

JOHNNY

My relationship with my mother grew closer once I married Luke, especially after we had our first child. I wanted to remain close to her so I could watch out for Johnny. In my heart, I felt that Johnny was an innocent victim in the whole messy story with no one else to be his true advocate. I needed to monitor how Johnny was doing because I never thought Mom acknowledged his true potential. On one hand she denied that there was anything actually wrong with him, yet she sheltered him to the point of smothering him and not letting him out of her sight. I think she felt enormous guilt and shame about Johnny being handicapped. I challenged her on her overprotectiveness for years. Finally out of total frustration, I reminded her that giving him birth was one thing, but when was she going to give him a chance at life. Sadly, she never grasped the concept, refusing to let him attend any workshops or programs suited to teach the skills and enhance Johnny's abilities that he needed to become a self-sufficient-productive member of a group home.

Unbeknown to Sonny and me, neither Dad nor Mom had made any type of arrangements for Johnny's future care or well-being. Therefore, immediately after Mom's death, Sonny and I were forced to place him in a state home that was less than appropriate for him. However, a few months later, he was enrolled in workshop programs that proved he was a quick learner, enabling him to move into a group home where he flourished and was able to take a bus to and from his job at Goodwill. He passed away suddenly from a seizure in December 2003 at the age of forty-three.

AUNT LULU

Aunt Lulu is alive and well today! She remains to be the same beautiful, loving, and smart role model that I have always admired and adored. She has blessed me with so many cherished memories. She supported me, saved me, and laughed with me throughout my entire life. I am thrilled and thankful that she is in great health, both mentally and physically. Full of energy at almost ninety, Aunt Lulu keeps us all laughing and on our toes as she shows off her computer and technology expertise. She will always be one of my most admired, favorite and beloved persons in my life.

SONNY

Happily married to Ella for fifty-four plus years. They have three great sons and daughters-in-law, plus seven cherished grandchildren. The Air Force was Sonny's major career. After leaving the service, he enjoyed a second career with an international manufacturing Fortune 500 company. In great health, now retired, he and Ella spend much of their time enjoying their family along with volunteering and supporting local charities.

Oddly enough, throughout all of Sonny's and my adult years, we had never discussed any of our "Big Life" past until I called him to ask how he felt about me sharing our childhood secrets with the world. His immediate response was, "Great, how can I help?" Then he cheekily inquired, "Am I in the book?" The early child in me responded, "No, silly, it's about me—not you!" Once I began to write I realized it was his story as well. I had to call him back and tell him, "You are in my book—and you're a major character!" I can still hear him cackling!

Our shared memories rekindled our closeness and amazingly we found that independently, we both had come to the same conclusion; as dysfunctional as those years were, we were okay and in an odd way, happy, because we always had each other. Our desire is that our story will offer hope to others who feel powerless and trapped in their circumstances. Sonny will always be my hero.

LUKE (US)

Luke and I have known each other and been best friends for more than fifty-eight years. We recently celebrated our fifty-fourth wedding anniversary. Through the years we have been blessed with two amazing and loving daughters, Kim and Kathy, two wonderful sons-in-law, Jeff and Paul, and three precious grandchildren, Nicolas, Abbie, and Bennett. Luke enjoyed a very successful career in business publishing, resulting in us forming our own company in 1990. We are now retired—sort of! Our life adventures have taken us all over the globe.

"Our Big Life", that we imagined on our wedding day, all those years ago, has definitely superseded our wildest hopes, wishes and dreams. He is the love of my life and continues to make my little girl dreams come true. Together, we are eternally grateful to God for his abundant blessings. He is truly forever faithful!

For more information regarding
Diana Lynn, please visit:
www.dianalynnlife.com.

ONE MORE NOTE FROM DIANA

Why Did I Write My Story?

&

I am a woman in my seventies, happily traveling through my life's unique journey. Never in my wildest dreams, could I have imagined I would tell, much less write, my life story. Frankly, I feel I've fallen off the edge of my comfort zone, dangling uncomfortably somewhere beyond.

So *why* am I putting my life out there now?

Looking back at the stepping stones of my journey, I clearly know they have been divinely linked together to perfectly craft the jigsaw puzzle called my life, one unique crazy shaped piece at a time. I call it God's master plan for Diana Lynn.

I also think God sometimes chooses the least likely people to do his work. Why? Because I am certainly one of them. He sent me to work with the elderly, the homeless, then with young women who had recently been released from jail. Women who had been convicted of drug offenses, prostitution, and some women, brave victims, just rescued from the bondage of human sex trafficking. God also encouraged me to share my story as a message of hope to these broken and demoralized ladies. He changed my outlook from one of disdain to one of compassion and love for the beautiful women he placed in my life. A very insightful man once wrote, "If you change the way you look at things, the things you look at change."

No one person, including Sonny and my husband, ever fully knew my story until I wrote this book. I assume the reason was because I had compartmentalized those bad times and decided to leave them behind. It may have been that I was frightened for anyone to know the whole story, fearing it could have a negative effect on my family or me. Consequently, I shared very little with my children, less with my grandchildren and pretty much nothing with anyone else. Even my beloved Aunt Lulu was unaware of most of my story until she read it.

To me, it all happened in a flash. One night Sonny and I fell asleep in our loving, secure, happy life as privileged rich kids and a few hours later, woke up to our new life as insecure, frightened, homeless orphans. Our dad's promise of "You're Gonna Love the BIG LIFE" turned out to be the exact opposite.

Throughout my most challenging childhood years, I would fantasize about living in a loving, happy, secure home. Amazingly, my fantasy did come true. It didn't happen in the home of my childhood, instead it was in the home Luke and I created for our family. I believe I experienced greater joy being the mom than I would have felt being the child. It made me realize that you can have what you want, it just may not look the same as you first envisioned it. The funny thing is, I believe God always knew what I would do with my story when the timing was right. I have always sensed Him by my side. His love instilling me with the hope, strength, and courage to face every challenge and keep my eyes fixed forward, never to dwell on the past. The difficult circumstances in my life were designed to teach and prepare me for the future responsibilities God had for me.

Life is definitely a journey. I liken it to a cross country road trip. The life route you choose to travel can take you in several diverse directions. What's your ultimate destination? Who do you want to be? What do you want for and out of your life? Don't worry about how old you are or whatever you have done. Life is what happens to us on a day to day basis. Regardless of where you are, you have the opportunity to change the course of your life at any time.

IT'S YOUR CHOICE!

The journey will be packed with surprises, numerous bumps in the road and times when you find yourself at a dead end. The entire trip may not be as you dreamed or hoped for, but the bottom line is that the final destination will most always reflect your choices, regardless of the journey's twists and turns along the route. There is more for each of us than being a victim. Victims give up their power because they think they don't have any! It's all up to you, you have the power to choose.

IT'S YOUR LIFE!

Allow yourself to go ahead and dream what you dare to dream. In your mind, go where you want to go. Imagine you can be what you want to be. Did you know that imagination is the start of innovation for your plan, and your goals for your future? Imagination creates HOPE! Just because something is hard doesn't mean it's impossible. Eleanor Roosevelt once said: "The future belongs to those who believe in the beauty of their dreams!"

All my childhood, nightmare-filled years were God's life lessons preparing me to someday serve those who are battered, bruised, gone astray, homeless, enslaved, or hopeless with compassion, love, and hope. My passion and love for those who are invisible and hurting is a gift from Him. He used my pain when the barrage of harsh words and exploding arguments sounded from the other side of the thin wall to show me how to pass his gift of love on to others. Even when lying in bed, frozen by fear, I felt Jesus encouraging me to love my difficult parents as he patiently loved me.

How many of us want to know, "Why?" Why did this happen to me?

CS Lewis tells us: "Hardships often prepare an ordinary person for a greater destiny."

My wish for each of you is that you find courage, strength, love, joy, and hope in each day. May you feel God's loving caresses and awesome blessings as he walks alongside guiding you on your life's amazing journey — You're Gonna Love that Big Life!

With love and hope,

— Diana Lynn

Acknowledgments

I never knew I had a story to tell until my dearest friend and handpicked, non-related "sister", Gale Hillenmeyer, called informing me she had just finished reading a remarkable memoir. She insisted I read it right away and that I absolutely must write my own story. I thought she was crazy! (Well, she sort of is crazy, in a very good, fun way!) Frankly, I ignored her second suggestion, but did read and relate to the beautiful memoir. Thank you Gale for your loving friendship, critiques, and wordsmithing skills and for challenging me to go down this uncomfortable road.

A second strong nudge, came from the amazing, courageous women in the HAT—Healing and Transition—program who I, as a volunteer, mentored and life coached. We connected best through the bits and pieces of my story that I shared with them. They encouraged me to share my journey and message of HOPE to as many people as possible. To all of you lovely ladies, thank you for your inspiration.

My special friends, Maria Penzes and Penny Rizzo, also my spiritual mentors and sisters in Christ. Thank you for your belief, support, and constant encouragement. You both had the patience of Job in reading draft after draft of this book. I love you and am very grateful to you for reminding me that Jesus was always next to me guiding my pen.

Bev, thank you for taking the time to proofread the entire manuscript in record time and to dear sweet Rachel, who from the beginning spent hours listening to my thoughts and ideas and never acted bored.

Many months ago, my two daughters organized a focus group study for me. The following wonderful women slogged through an early manuscript draft and on a rainy, humid, Sunday afternoon in May 2018, we all met to discuss the likes, dislikes, questions, etc., of all those pages of type.

I sincerely appreciated the clarity that evolved from their input. Thank you again, Jamie, Gena, Melissa, Karen, Shirley, Gale, Liza, Rachel, Penny, Anne, and Donna.

Sorry I forgot your Hershey bars!

A huge shout out to Taylor Graham, my awesome editor and coordinator. Her time and advice, the long phone calls and her willingness to listen to every question and thought gave me the confidence and excitement to keep on writing. You have been amazing! Every aspiring author should have a Taylor Graham, or better yet, the real Taylor Graham!

My precious family! Without them, past and present, there would be no book and definitely I would not be the same me who just relived and wrote my journey. Thank you!

Aunt Lulu, you are my glue and role model throughout my life. The one adult in my young life that saw me and heard me even when I kept silent. Just thinking of her, anchored me and I felt loved.

My cousin, Marie, who let me pretend for those few months in seventh grade, that she was my little sister and happily shared her bed with me. She thought I was cuddling her, but in reality, she was cuddling me.

To my big brother and hero, Sonny! My childhood rock! No one else knows or understands those scary years better than him. We lived that awful "Big Life" together, hand in hand, each day. Together we were strong and courageous. We overcame the insanity of our parents and somehow ended up okay. Apart I would not have fared as well. Thanks Sonny for then and for being so supportive of me sharing our story.

My grandchildren, Nic, Abbie, and Bennett: I love being your MIMI! You all make me so proud.

Nic: thanks for rooting me on and standing next to me as I placed the period after the final word in Chapter 57! You are a man of high integrity and strong values. I admire your courage and hard work ethic.

Abbie: I am so honored you chose to use my story for a college English assignment. Your outstanding, high, academic success, your big sweet heart and your good choices make my heart sing.

Bennett: You have the inner strength and commitment to making your goals come true. You may be the youngest, but you are an inspiration to us all. Keep on reaching!

My beautiful daughters, Kim and Kathy: You girls have always been my biggest blessings! I was able to be the mom for the loving family I had always yearned for. Thank you for the love and laughter through all these years. The empathy and caring you showed as you read my story—the unabridged version you had never known. Your solid support and belief that my journey needed to be told and would be of help to more women than just those beautiful women I had mentored. You encouraged me and made me believe that my life was worth revealing. You emboldened me to write it. I love you and thank you.

Luke: Just thinking of you and typing your name makes my throat tighten and my eyes tear up. My heart still skips a beat when you walk into a room. You scared the boogie man away. You made my little girl dreams become reality. Together we created our family and provided the loving home life that I always dreamed of having. Your love, encouragement, and support allowed me to unlock all those difficult memories and tell my journey's message of hope, choices, and life! Thanks for sharing your fried clams and pestering me to go to the prom with you, every morning for at least three weeks! I love you!

Jesus, first and last I am forever grateful. You have protected me and held my hand through every fearful and joyful moment of my life. All my strength, courage and fortitude during those difficult earlier years came from knowing that you were right there with me. Every day of my life's journey I have felt your presence, love, and faithfulness. You gave me the hope, guidance and courage to choose to become a victor and not a victim.

www.ingramcontent.com/pod-product-compliance
Lightning Source LLC
Chambersburg PA
CBHW071855090426
42811CB00004B/617